Have Fun With Math

D1518958

Louis Grant Brandes

J. WESTON
WALCH
PUBLISHER

PORTLAND, MAINE

2   3   4   5   6   7   8   9   10

ISBN 0-8251-1309-1

Copyright © 1988
J. Weston Walch, Publisher
P.O. Box 658 • Portland, Maine 04104-0658

Printed in the United States of America

TABLE OF CONTENTS

Preface

While doing math book exhibits at teacher conferences, I asked secondary school teachers what kind of supplementary math book they would like most. *Have Fun with Math* is the kind of book they said they wanted.

The book is a collection of math oddities, fun tests, puzzles, problem sets, and picture graphs, dovetailed with the basic math curriculum as usually used in the junior- and senior-high-school grades. Its purpose is to provide enrichment materials for math students in these grades.

Many of the materials in the book are entirely new and unique. Other pages are revisions of materials from my previous books. The materials are complete on each page, and are sufficient in number to provide an enrichment page for a class during every day of a school year. They provide enrichment not currently available for students, they are useful in math courses other than general mathematics, and the sheets can be reproduced by teachers for use with their classes. There is no known book with all these qualities.

Ways in which the materials in the book can be used with students are as follows: as a regular part of class work (a daily, semi-weekly, or weekly enrichment lesson); as a source of review materials, unlike the usual "bill of fare"; as a means of gaining student interest and attention; as a class reward for work well done;

and as useful materials for substitute teachers. These materials can also be used to fill odd times (before and after vacations, rainy days, etc.), for extra-credit assignments, and for ways otherwise to arouse student interest in mathematics.

It is expected that only a portion of a classroom math period will be spent on any page of the book. Some of the pages can be completed by most students in ten to twenty minutes; other pages will take much longer, depending upon the abilities of the students. Pages can be assigned, or otherwise retained by students to work on outside of class, in which case answers can be reviewed at a later scheduled time.

The time limits that have been set on a number of the pages, along with the humorous scorings, are to serve for motivational purposes rather than as established criteria for measuring student abilities. It is expected that the time limits provided will give all students time to answer some items on respective pages, and, for some students, time to answer all of the items. The idea is to get all students involved; most of the student learning will take place as the teacher reviews the items with a class.

Should the book serve to help teachers stimulate interest in mathematics on the part of young people, it will have served its purpose well.

Louis Grant Brandes

Acknowledgments

Many of the materials in this book are original ideas that have been developed by the writer with the help of teachers who have made use of the materials in their classrooms. Other materials are ideas that have been drawn from the literature related to mathematics, then further revised and developed over the years for classroom use.

The book is different from other enrichment books on mathematics in the following ways: the contents are in curriculum sequence for general mathematics as taught in the secondary school grades, there are sufficient materials for a class during every day of a school year, the materials are complete on each page, the pages can be reproduced for classroom use, and there are many cartoon illustrations to enliven the pages. These differences came about as the result of the responses of many general mathematics teachers to the question, "What kind of enrichment book would you like for classroom use?"

Special thanks are due the following people associated with the schools of the Alameda, California, Unified School District: Dr. Walter Klas, Assistant Superintendent in Charge of Educational Services, for his guidance and direction in working with school district personnel, and Mrs. Julie Cowell, Mathematics Supervisor, for referring the materials of the book to teachers of the junior-senior high school grades for trial use and evaluation, namely; Mr. Vern Lowery, Encinal High School; Mr. Earl Nethercutt, Alameda High School; Miss Judy Quan and Mr. Don Sharp, Chipman Middle School; Mrs. Nancy Phillipsen and Miss Pam Curtis, Lincoln Middle School; Mrs. Diane Richmond, Haight Middle School; and Mrs. Joy Signor, Wood Middle School. Especially appreciated are the contributions of Mr. John Cotter and Mr. Jack Fink for their able assistance in proofreading the book and otherwise making suggestions.

A bibliography of recreational mathematics publications, thought to be of interest to secondary school mathematics teachers and their students, is included in the appendix. The interest and cooperation of the book publishers who provided review materials made it possible to include this bibliography.

If the book serves to create an interest in mathematics on the part of young people, and otherwise serves to assist mathematics teachers in motivating their classes, it will be because of all those persons mentioned herein who have collectively provided help by their assistance, suggestions, and contributions.

Louis Grant Brandes

I thought zero was a nothing!

Zero the Hero

Part I
Whole Numbers

Making Numbers with Four Different Digits

How many different whole numbers can you make using only four different digits? Here is a chance to find out. Starting with the smallest number, list all the numbers possible using these four digits: 1, 3, 6, and 9. Insert the numbers in the spaces provided below.

1. **1369**
2.
3.
4.
5.
6.
7.
8.
9.
10.
11.
12.

13.
14.
15.
16.
17.
18.
19.
20.
21.
22.
23.
24.

Have Fun with Math

Weight Puzzle

The object of this puzzle is to find which is heavier, the elephant or the rhinoceros. The respective weights are the sums of the digits making up each animal. The final answer should tell how much heavier one is than the other. The digits range from 1 to 9. There are no 0's. Note that the 9's have straight legs (9); the tops of the 6's are curved (6). Try to be patient and accurate in your efforts.

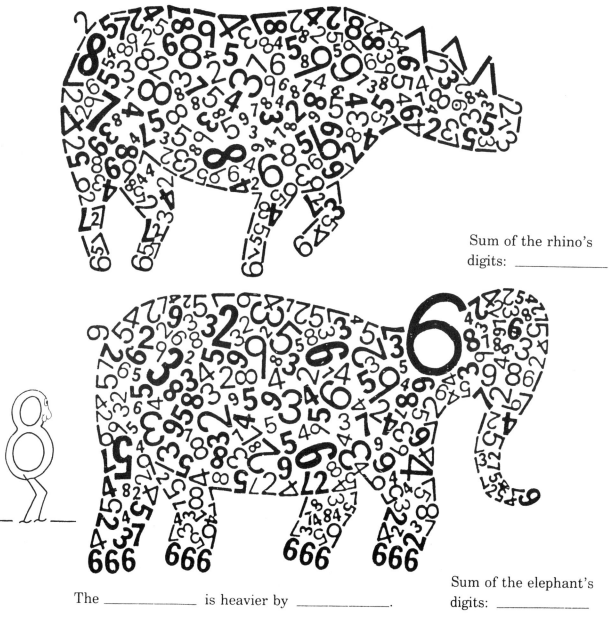

Sum of the rhino's digits: _____

The _____ is heavier by _____.

Sum of the elephant's digits: _____

Have Fun with Math

Fun Test on Addition Facts

See how quickly you can complete these 100 basic addition combinations. Write your answers to the addition problems in the respective cells; continue working until you have completed all of the problems. Your teacher will tell you when to start and will time your effort. After you have corrected your answers, add 5 for each mistake to your elapsed time in seconds to figure your score. It's all in fun!

7 7	3 9	2 6	3 2	4 5	1 2	8 8	9 2	5 1	0 9	8 6	9 6	0 7
3 1	0 8	2 5	1 1	3 6	1 8	6 3	2 0	7 4	9 8	5 6	2 3	7 0
4 9	0 3	5 8	1 6	4 7	1 3	4 0	5 2	1 0	3 3	5 9	7 6	8 0
7 1	2 9	4 6	7 8	4 4	0 1	7 2	3 7	3 4	7 5	0 2	4 3	9 0
2 1	8 4	9 5	9 4	0 4	8 9	5 4	3 0	6 2	0 5	6 5	9 3	4 1
6 1	9 7	6 8	2 4	5 3	8 1	6 6	7 9	5 5	9 1	6 9	8 7	9 9
3 5	2 8	4 8	3 8	7 3	1 7	6 4	6 0	2 7	0 0	1 4	8 2	4 2
		6 7	8 5	2 2	0 6	1 9	1 5	5 7	8 3	5 0		

Scores: Less than 75, Volcanic   76–90, Hot   91–105, Warm
106–120, Cool   121–135, Cold   136 or more, Frigid

Your Score: Elapsed time (_____) plus number of mistakes × 5 (_____) = _____.

Have Fun with Math

Number Combination Puzzles

The object of these puzzles is to circle every combination of numbers that adds up to the specified common sum. The following rules apply:

1. The numbers in each combination must be next to each other in the puzzle grid.
2. No number may be used more than once in a combination.
3. As many numbers as necessary may be used in a single combination.
4. Combinations may not overlap.
5. A combination may not be split between two lines.
6. The solution time for a puzzle is limited to 15 minutes.

The two puzzles on this sheet each contain fifty correct number combinations. The common sums for the puzzles are 14 and 19, respectively. Six number combinations of 14 have been circled in the first puzzle. See how many more combinations of 14 you can find in this puzzle. Then try to find the fifty combinations of 19 in the remaining puzzle.

Common Sum: 14

```
7 (8 2 4) 5 6 (3 6 5) 3 7 (6 3 1 4) 5 8 (3 5 2 4) 7 0 8 (3 5 6) 0 1 9 7 (6 7 1) 8 0
1 3 0 4 6 5 8 9 5 6 6 3 1 4 2 1 5 6 4 1 3 7 6 2 4 1 0 7 9 7 6 4 5 2 3 5
7 1 5 8 4 3 2 9 6 5 1 3 6 4 8 3 1 2 1 6 2 4 0 3 5 8 8 7 2 5 1 5 6 1 7 3
3 2 4 5 7 3 3 2 0 5 4 7 0 4 4 3 5 2 1 2 5 8 1 8 6 3 3 1 0 4 6 5 6 5 7 2
0 7 2 4 3 5 3 6 3 6 0 4 1 7 8 2 5 4 3 6 2 2 3 5 4 0 3 8 1 6 7 5 7 1 6 5
1 3 4 0 6 2 7 3 5 4 2 7 2 8 1 3 4 5 3 4 7 9 1 5 4 2 3 7 3 3 5 4 2 0 4 0
2 7 9 4 1 4 2 8 3 7 3 2 4 5 6 8 3 1 4 6 7 9 3 4 2 5 5 6 1 2 2 4 1 3 6 1
3 5 6 7 5 1 4 3 6 6 6 7 4 2 3 5 8 4 1 6 7 4 9 2 5 0 3 4 5 7 8 2 1 3 5 8
```

Common Sum: 19

```
9 7 4 8 9 5 2 4 8 6 7 8 6 2 3 2 4 7 5 4 2 8 6 4 6 1 5 3 6 9 5 2 8 5 0 4
9 8 2 8 4 2 8 5 9 6 8 9 2 2 9 7 2 5 3 1 8 9 5 2 1 3 8 4 2 8 7 4 7 9 7 3
9 0 8 3 7 9 5 6 6 8 2 3 5 6 2 8 4 5 7 2 3 8 5 1 8 6 1 7 2 4 5 7 4 7 3 5
3 7 3 9 6 7 9 5 4 1 5 8 7 1 2 3 6 3 0 8 5 4 7 2 1 3 8 9 2 1 1 5 4 2 7 5
9 4 6 4 8 5 8 4 2 7 0 2 2 9 8 6 2 0 3 8 9 3 2 1 6 7 7 6 9 3 7 4 6 8 2 9
0 6 8 7 2 5 3 2 8 2 3 5 3 1 8 2 3 0 3 6 4 2 7 3 5 6 2 8 6 3 8 0 5 5 8 6
2 7 9 3 8 3 4 5 8 2 6 8 7 5 4 3 1 5 2 3 6 8 6 8 2 8 9 8 3 7 9 6 7 4 7 8
3 7 4 5 4 9 5 7 1 4 2 6 8 6 7 2 1 3 8 2 2 5 1 8 3 9 1 4 8 7 2 6 7 3 4 5
```

Have Fun with Math

Shooting Gallery with Whole Numbers

Below is a shooting gallery of whole numbers. There are six targets filled with different whole numbers. You will be taking "shots" at the targets. A shot consists of circling a number in the target. A number is considered "hit" when you circle it. The object for each target is to provide six "hits" with a sum equal to the target number. The rules are as follows:

1. You get six shots at a target.
2. Each shot must hit a number.
3. All six shots must be totaled.
4. A number can be hit only once.

See if you can score winners on all the targets. You must plan your "shots" carefully.

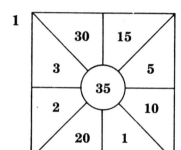

Target Number: 100

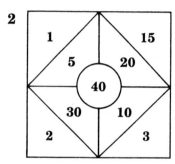

Target Number: 100

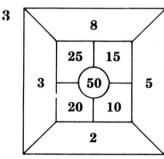

Target Number: 100

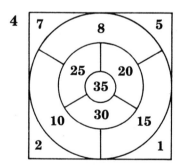

Target Number: 100

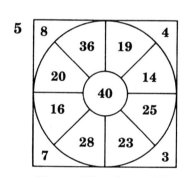

Target Number: 100

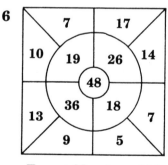

Target Number: 100

Have Fun with Math

Circular Maze Puzzle with Whole Numbers

Below is a circular maze puzzle—a diagram with six concentric circles. Each circle has six number gates. The object of this puzzle is to pass through one gate of each circle in an effort to reach the center with a gate number total of 159.

See if you can find a route through the gates to the center that provides the desired gate number total of 159. Remember, only six gates may be traversed; one gate in each circle.

If you are able to find a route with the correct number combination, see if you can find another such route using different gates.

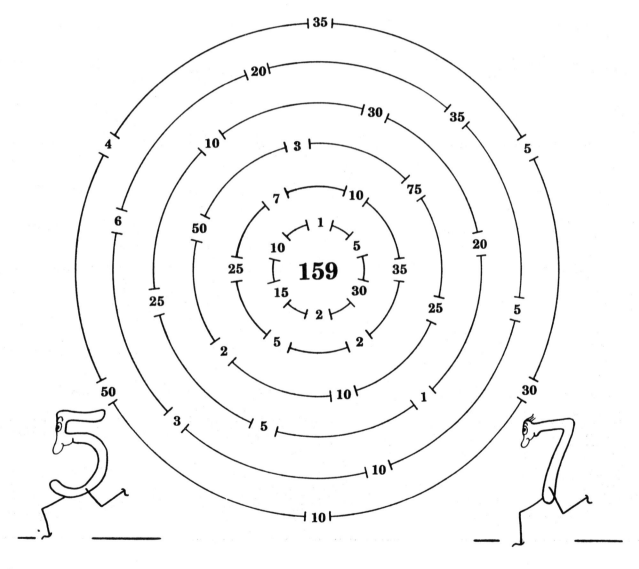

Have Fun with Math

Magic Triangles with Whole Numbers

A magic triangle is a triangular arrangement of numbers in which the sums of the numbers on each of the sides are the same. The arrangements below are magic triangles. Check the totals for each of the sides of these triangles to verify their magic quality.

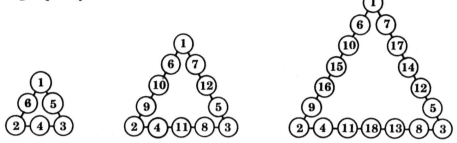

If you study the examples above, you will note a pattern for arranging the numbers to form the magic triangles. Try to follow the patterns above and make magic triangles from group arrangements A, B, and C below.

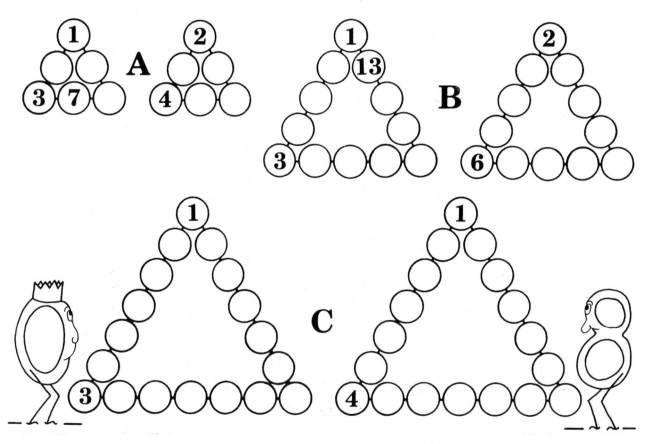

Have Fun with Math

Magic Squares with Whole Numbers

A magic square is an arrangement of numbers in the shape of a square with the sums of each vertical column, each horizontal column, and each diagonal all equal. Here is an example of a magic square:

47	5	8	38	—98
14	32	29	23	—98
26	20	17	35	—98
11	41	44	2	—98

98 (top corner), 98 98 98 98 (bottom)

It is easy to make a magic square of 16 numbers. Any 16 consecutive numbers will do. Place these numbers, in order of their size, in a square divided into 16 smaller squares. The small squares are called cells. Interchange the numbers in the opposite corner cells; then interchange the numbers in the opposite middle cells. The diagrams below show how this interchange was made. Check the sums of the numbers in the columns of vertical cells, horizontal cells, and diagonal cells in the square on the right to verify that it is a magic square.

1	2	3	4
5	6	7	8
9	10	11	12
13	14	15	16

Before Interchange

16	2	3	13
5	11	10	8
9	7	6	12
4	14	15	1

After Interchange

Try completing the magic squares below, using 16 consecutive numbers (A), then 16 consecutive odd numbers (B), and then 16 consecutive even numbers (C). Next, construct magic squares with 16 consecutive numbers counting by 3's (D), 4's (E), and 5's (F), and starting with 3 (D), 4 (E), and 5 (F).

A

11	12	13	14
15	16	17	18
19	20	21	22
23	24	25	26

Before Interchange

26			
			11

After Interchange

B

1	3	5	7
9	11	13	15
17	19	21	23
25	27	29	31

Before Interchange

	13		

After Interchange

C

	4	6	
		2	

D

	6		
12			

E

	44		
		60	

F

		30	
20			

Have Fun with Math

More Magic Squares with Whole Numbers

			15
8	1	6	-15
3	5	7	-15
4	9	2	-15
15	15	15	15

					65
23	12	1	20	9	-65
4	18	7	21	15	-65
10	24	13	2	16	-65
11	5	19	8	22	-65
17	6	25	14	3	-65
65	65	65	65	65	65

							175
46	31	16	1	42	27	12	-175
5	39	24	9	43	35	20	-175
13	47	32	17	2	36	28	-175
21	6	40	25	10	44	29	-175
22	14	48	33	18	3	37	-175
30	15	7	41	26	11	45	-175
38	23	8	49	34	19	4	-175
175	175	175	175	175	175	175	175

Directly above are examples of magic squares with an odd number of cells on each side. Directions for making a magic square with an odd number of cells on each side are as follows:

1. Place the starting number in the middle cell of the top row.
2. Each consecutive number is placed two cells down and one cell to the right.
3. In counting down, when you run out of cells at the bottom of the square, return to the top of the column and start or keep on counting from there.
4. If moving to the right would place a number outside the square, place the number at the opposite end of the row instead.
5. If a number would fall in a cell already occupied, place that number in the cell directly below the previous entry.

Starting with a number other than 1, and using consecutive whole numbers, make some magic squares of your own in the diagrams provided below. Check the sums of the numbers in the columns, rows, and diagonals of each square to verify that you have produced a "magic" arrangement of numbers.

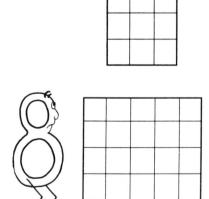

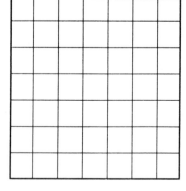

Have Fun with Math

Palindromic Numbers

Words, sentences, or numbers that can be written the same forward and backward are called "palindromes." A sentence example is "Able was I ere I saw Elba." Numerical examples are 343, 2332, and 234432.

An interesting pattern occurs in the addition of numbers when their digits are reversed. If we start with any whole number and add the number formed by reversing the digits, and continue to repeat this process, a number is eventually reached which is palindromic. It reads the same from either end.

The examples at the right take three, four, and seven reversing and addition steps, respectively, to reach a palindromic sum. Study these examples carefully. Then apply the reversing and addition process to the numbers below until they become palindromic.

```
   455        570        584
   554        075        485
  ─────      ─────      ─────
  1009        645       1069
  9001        546       9601
 ─────      ─────      ─────
 10010       1191      10670
 01001       1911      07601
 ─────      ─────      ─────
 11011       3102      18271
             2013      17281
            ─────      ─────
             5115      35552
                       25553
                      ─────
                       61105
                       50116
                      ──────
                      111221
                      122111
                     ───────
                      233332
```

(1) 158	(2) 653	(3) 174	(4) 372

(5) 782	(6) 998

Have Fun with Math

Magic Square Puzzles with Whole Numbers

Magic square puzzles are magic square arrangements in which one or more of the numbers forming the magic square are missing. For example, in the first puzzle below, which has been solved, four of the numbers were missing. Each of the missing numbers could be found, since it was known that the sums of the numbers in each column, row, and diagonal were the same.

The first puzzle was solved by noting that the sum of the numbers in one diagonal was 33 (9 + 11 + 13). The number in the left top cell was found by subtracting the sum of the other two numbers in the top horizontal row from the "magic sum" (33 minus the sum of 3 and 13). The missing numbers in other cells were found in the same way.

Try solving the other puzzles on this sheet.

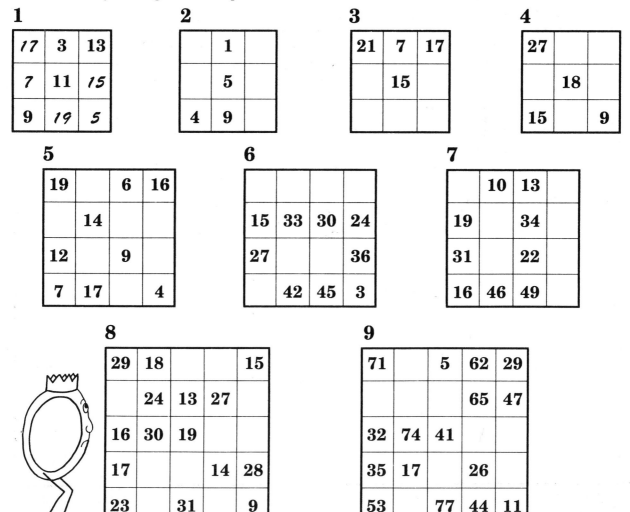

Have Fun with Math

Fun Test on Multiplication Facts

If you are to have success in mathematics, you must know the multiplication facts. See how much of the following table you can complete without errors in the time allotted. You are to find the product of the two digits that locate each cell. The first two products have been done for you ($3 \times 5 = 15$ and $3 \times 8 = 24$). Subtract 5 points for each error from the number correct to obtain your score. Time is limited to 3 minutes.

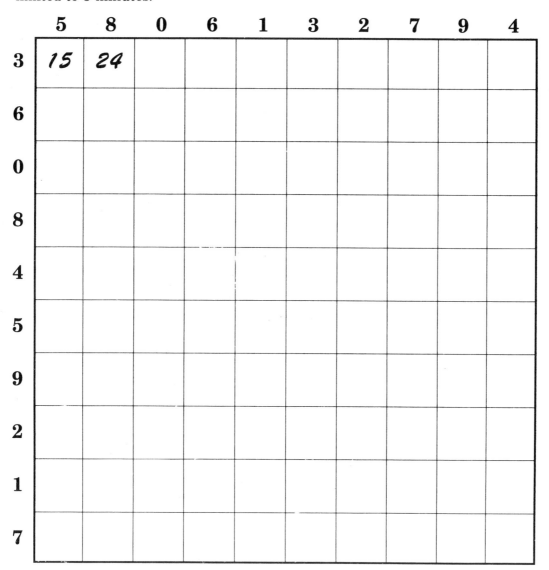

	5	8	0	6	1	3	2	7	9	4
3	15	24								
6										
0										
8										
4										
5										
9										
2										
1										
7										

Scores: 0–50, Bankrupt   51–70, Going Broke   71–80, Needs a Loan
            81–90, Getting Along   90–95, Rich   96–100, Wealthy

Have Fun with Math

Multiplication Puzzle

This puzzle consists of an arrangement of numbers in the cells of a number block. You are challenged to make multiplication statements in any of the rows, columns, or diagonals of the block, using the numbers as arranged in the block. The puzzle contains 25 of these multiplication combinations. As a sample, 2 have been marked. Try to complete the puzzle by seeing how many of the other multiplication statements you can find.

3 X 8 = 24	11	64	13	7	10	70	43
23	4	58	8	6	9	54	7	55	60
1	31	8	47	5	17	8	46	63	72
49	8	59	32	30	56	33	5	9	45
4	2	8	44	9	2	18	8	34	50
35	44	53	6	37	6	39	28	5	35
5	57	6	16	3	38	4	3	12	40
7	36	6	7	41	7	38	24	2	51
54	65	3	45	42	61	21	15	10	26
1	2	2	29	64	27	3	9	20	14

Multiple Number Puzzle

You solve this puzzle by shading the cells of the multiples in the number blocks as directed below. Don't stop until you have finished the shading in all the blocks. Any errors will be obvious.

Shade all multiples of 2.

76	28	32	16	98
86	49	87	99	36
40	52	12	64	82
22	61	17	37	19
48	53	75	23	41

Shade all multiples of 3.

51	91	68	37	33
48	29	85	53	69
87	82	22	19	63
72	49	76	44	96
42	27	78	45	18

Shade all multiples of 4.

16	52	84	32	96
62	47	67	92	50
13	49	40	75	29
67	24	39	98	33
56	92	36	76	12

Shade all multiples of 5.

15	50	95	45	75
73	97	41	70	56
82	54	35	53	79
91	85	83	46	58
55	90	65	30	25

Shade all multiples of 6.

36	27	82	19	74
54	38	98	71	57
72	32	45	83	39
18	49	56	15	69
30	84	42	96	24

Shade all multiples of 7.

63	14	56	91	35
77	83	39	46	48
28	42	98	21	55
56	65	85	71	67
49	84	63	84	70

Shade all multiples of 8.

72	96	80	48	64
32	95	67	33	65
88	40	56	16	38
24	68	18	65	57
56	53	82	47	98

Shade all multiples of 9.

36	43	39	49	90
72	69	15	96	45
99	48	34	79	54
27	67	87	94	81
63	18	45	72	27

Shade all multiples of 10.

20	95	55	15	40
10	40	74	65	90
70	66	50	77	30
30	33	45	60	80
50	75	88	25	10

Have Fun with Math

Unusual Number Patterns with Whole Numbers

The results of certain multiplications with whole numbers may surprise you. Multiply the following sets of numbers and write your answers in the spaces provided to satisfy yourself that there is something unusual about the results.

1. $2 \times 91 =$ _____
   $3 \times 91 =$ _____
   $4 \times 91 =$ _____
   $5 \times 91 =$ _____
   $6 \times 91 =$ _____
   $7 \times 91 =$ _____
   $8 \times 91 =$ _____
   $9 \times 91 =$ _____

2. $999999 \times 2 =$ _____
   $999999 \times 3 =$ _____
   $999999 \times 4 =$ _____
   $999999 \times 5 =$ _____
   $999999 \times 6 =$ _____
   $999999 \times 7 =$ _____
   $999999 \times 8 =$ _____
   $999999 \times 9 =$ _____

3. $15873 \times 7 =$ _____
   $31746 \times 7 =$ _____
   $47619 \times 7 =$ _____
   $63492 \times 7 =$ _____
   $79365 \times 7 =$ _____
   $95238 \times 7 =$ _____
   $111111 \times 7 =$ _____
   $126984 \times 7 =$ _____
   $142857 \times 7 =$ _____

4. $12345679 \times 9 =$ _____
   $12345679 \times 18 =$ _____
   $12345679 \times 27 =$ _____
   $12345679 \times 36 =$ _____
   $12345679 \times 45 =$ _____
   $12345679 \times 54 =$ _____
   $12345679 \times 63 =$ _____
   $12345679 \times 72 =$ _____
   $12345679 \times 81 =$ _____

5. $987654321 \times 9 =$ _____
   $987654321 \times 18 =$ _____
   $987654321 \times 27 =$ _____
   $987654321 \times 36 =$ _____
   $987654321 \times 45 =$ _____
   $987654321 \times 54 =$ _____
   $987654321 \times 63 =$ _____
   $987654321 \times 72 =$ _____
   $987654321 \times 81 =$ _____

Have Fun with Math

More Unusual Number Patterns
with Whole Numbers

The results of certain arithmetical operations with selected numbers may surprise you. Record your answers to the following problems and observe the unusual number patterns.

1.
$1 \times 8 + 1 =$ ___
$12 \times 8 + 2 =$ ___
$123 \times 8 + 3 =$ ___
$1234 \times 8 + 4 =$ ___
$12345 \times 8 + 5 =$ ___
$123456 \times 8 + 6 =$ ___
$1234567 \times 8 + 7 =$ ___
$12345678 \times 8 + 8 =$ ___
$123456789 \times 8 + 9 =$ ___

2.
$9 \times 1 + 2 =$ ___
$9 \times 12 + 3 =$ ___
$9 \times 123 + 4 =$ ___
$9 \times 1234 + 5 =$ ___
$9 \times 12345 + 6 =$ ___
$9 \times 123456 + 7 =$ ___
$9 \times 1234567 + 8 =$ ___
$9 \times 12345678 + 9 =$ ___
$9 \times 123456789 + 10 =$ ___

3.
$9 \times 1 - 1 =$ ___
$9 \times 12 - 1 =$ ___
$9 \times 123 - 1 =$ ___
$9 \times 1234 - 1 =$ ___
$9 \times 12345 - 1 =$ ___
$9 \times 123456 - 1 =$ ___
$9 \times 1234567 - 1 =$ ___
$9 \times 12345678 - 1 =$ ___
$9 \times 123456789 - 1 =$ ___

4.
$(3-1) \times (3+1) = 3 \times 3 - 1 =$ ___
$(4-1) \times (4+1) = 4 \times 4 - 1 =$ ___
$(5-1) \times (5+1) = 5 \times 5 - 1 =$ ___
$(6-1) \times (6+1) =$ ___ $=$ ___
$(7-1) \times (7+1) =$ ___ $=$ ___
$(8-1) \times (8+1) =$ ___ $=$ ___
$(9-1) \times (9+1) =$ ___ $=$ ___
$(15-1) \times (15+1) =$ ___ $=$ ___
$(50-1) \times (50+1) =$ ___ $=$ ___

5. $1 + 1 + 1 = 3$ and $3 \times 37 =$ ___
$2 + 2 + 2 = 6$ and $6 \times 37 =$ ___
$3 + 3 + 3 = 9$ and $9 \times 37 =$ ___
$4 + 4 + 4 = 12$ and $12 \times 37 =$ ___
___ $= 15$ and $15 \times 37 =$ ___
___ $= 18$ and $18 \times 37 =$ ___
___ $= 21$ and $21 \times 37 =$ ___
___ $= 24$ and $24 \times 37 =$ ___
___ $= 27$ and ___ $= 999$

Have Fun with Math

Ancient Method of Multiplication

An ancient method of multiplication, sometimes called the doubling and halving method, is still used in some sections of the world. It is illustrated by the examples below.

To find the product in the first example (95 × 72), write the multiplier (72) to the left and the multiplicand (95) to the right (or whichever is more convenient). Double one of these numbers and halve the other, continuing until the number 1 is reached in the halving column. Drop any remainders. Cross out each number in the doubling column that is opposite an even number in the halving column; add the remaining numbers in the doubling column. The sum of these numbers is the desired product.

(1) *Halve*	*Double*	95 × 72		(2) *Halve*	*Double*	268 × 53
72	~~95~~			53	268	268
36	~~190~~			26	~~536~~	
18	~~380~~			13	1,072	1,072
9	760	760		6	~~2,144~~	
4	~~1,520~~			3	4,288	4,288
2	~~3,040~~			1	8,576	8,576
1	6,080	6,080				
	(product)	6,840			(product)	14,204

(1) 76 × 47	(2) 68 × 34
(3) 379 × 75	(4) 458 × 86

Have Fun with Math

The Grating Method of Multiplication

The grating method of multiplication, also known as the lattice method, was used until the invention of the printing press. Since the grating was difficult to produce with the press, the method gradually fell into disuse. However, it still remains a very satisfactory method for multiplying whole numbers. After you have studied the procedure and example below, try using the grating method to solve the problems at the bottom of this page.

1. Construct a grating for each multiplication. Place the multiplicand above the grating and the multiplier to its right. Note that cells are immediately below and immediately to the left of the digits of the multiplicand and multiplier, respectively. Each cell is divided by a diagonal line from the upper right to lower left corner.

2. Write the partial product for each pair of digits (one digit from the multiplicand and one digit from the multiplier) in the respective cells, placing the tens digit in the top portion of the cell and the units digit in the lower portion of the cell; if one of the pair of digits is 0, put 0 in each portion of the cell.

Example

356×78

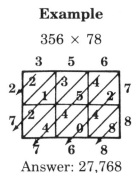

Answer: 27,768

3. Find the desired product by adding the digits in the oblique columns (follow the arrows in the example above). Start at the lower right and continue around the bottom and up the left side of the grating. When a sum of the numbers in an oblique column is 10 or greater, the tens digit is "carried" to the next column. The answer reads from the top left of the grating down to the lower right, as in the example.

---

(1) 76×47

      7   6

             4

             7

Answer: _____

(2) 87×59

      8   7

             5

             9

Answer: _____

(3) 638×47

     6   3   8

               4

               7

Answer: _____

(4) 807×64

Answer: _____

(5) $3,864 \times 37$

Answer: _____

Magic Multiplication Square Puzzles with Whole Numbers

In a multiplication magic square the products of the numbers in each row, column, and diagonal are the same. The squares below are all multiplication magic squares. The first magic square has been completed for you. Study the completed number square carefully. Then try to find the numbers that complete the five other magic multiplication squares.

1

2	25	20
100	10	1
5	4	50

2

		32
		64
8		2

3

150		
3		
60		6

4

10		25
	50	
		250

5

96	3	
	48	
		24

6

729	81	9
3		

Have Fun with Math

Fun Test on Division Facts

See if you can complete the ninety division items below correctly in the time allotted. Write your answers to the items in the respective cells. The first two are done for you. Time is limited to 3 minutes. To figure your score, subtract 5 points for each error from the number correct.

$\frac{6}{4)24}$	$\frac{8}{7)56}$	5)25	5)5	9)72	1)1	9)27	8)0	7)21
5)45	9)63	3)6	1)0	6)12	8)48	7)28	4)4	1)6
8)16	6)48	2)10	7)7	4)28	6)24	9)36	6)0	2)14
3)9	8)40	7)49	1)2	5)10	7)14	5)20	9)9	5)30
8)32	6)6	2)12	7)0	4)8	3)12	2)6	7)63	3)15
8)56	4)32	5)40	8)24	5)35	9)81	4)16	4)12	5)15
6)18	7)42	3)24	3)3	3)27	6)36	2)18	4)0	1)5
2)16	8)8	1)9	2)4	3)0	7)35	2)6	8)72	1)8
9)18	9)45	6)30	1)4	9)54	1)7	2)8	5)0	6)54
4)36	2)2	2)0	3)21	8)64	1)3	4)20	6)42	3)18

Scores: 0–45, Got Lost 46–60, Way Behind 61–75, Also-Ran
76–80, Show 81–85, Place 86–90, Winner

Have Fun with Math

Divisible Numbers

It's easy to tell when a number is divisible by 2, 3, 4, 5, 6, 8, 9, 10 and/or 12. You apply the following rules:

A number is divisible by 2 when it is even. For example, these numbers are divisible by 2: 4; 8; 12; 38; 736; and 5,362.

A number is divisible by 3 when the sum of its digits is divisible by 3. For example, these numbers are divisible by 3: 24; 72; 321; 3,162; and 8,217,516.

A number is divisible by 4 when the last two digits of the number are 00 or, expressed as a separate number, are divisible by 4. For example, these numbers are divisible by 4: 200; 324; 516; 744; 6,148; 52,524; and 7,263,532.

A number is divisible by 5 when it ends in 5 or 0. For example, these numbers are divisible by 5: 75; 325; 540; 8,150; 67,300; and 283,815.

A number is divisible by 6 when it is divisible by both 3 and 2. For example, these numbers are divisible by 6: 36; 78; 234; 3,162; 91,032; and 8,517,324.

A number is divisible by 8 when the last three digits are 000 or, expressed as a separate number, are divisible by 8. For example, these numbers are divisible by 8: 3,248; 5,072; 71,912; 73,000; 75,424; 153,488; and 4,327,256.

A number is divisible by 9 when the sum of its digits is divisible by 9. For example, these numbers are divisible by 9: 279; 1,737; 8,676; 56,871, and 5,283,927.

A number is divisible by 10 when the last digit of the number ends in 0. For example, these numbers are divisible by 10: 80; 160; 3,180; 33,870; and 7,653,340.

A number is divisible by 12 when it is divisible by both 3 and 4. For example, these numbers are divisible by 12: 648; 4,728; 63,624; 573,408; and 3,847,212.

Most numbers are divisible by the numbers for which one or more of the above rules apply. Using the rules to test each of the numbers listed below, circle each number *not* divisible by 2, 3, 4, 5, 6, 8, 9, 10, or 12. Then draw a line under the numbers in each column that are divisible by the number in parentheses at the top of the column—for example, underline all numbers in Column I that are divisible by 3.

Col. I(3)	Col. II(4)	Col. III(5)	Col. IV(6)	Col. V(8)	Col. VI(9)	Col. VII(12)
5,234	7,912	7,024	2,388	875	657	12,308
9,108	52,168	40,355	6,083	5,716	1,971	312
783	247,686	25,284	8,564	15,036	514,865	4,137
7,345	8,643	5,552	297	25,127	5,781	7,128
47,881	211	350	2,795	14,223	42,569	928
812	114	927	40,812	453	384	84
74,842	14,892	3,125	63,624	7,216	7,295	2,132
7,356	7,546	84,262	522	92,576	27,633	62,736
1,257	723	1,487	2,375	1,492	1,548	17,216
382	5,628	600	724	1,152	837	719

Have Fun with Math

Ancient Method of Division

This ancient method of division, which does not make use of multiplication tables, was used thousands of years ago. After you have studied the procedure and example below, try using this method to solve the problems at the bottom of the page.

1. Draw two intersecting straight lines, one horizontal and the other vertical.
2. On the right side of the vertical line, directly below the intersection, write the divisor.
3. In a neat column, progressively double the divisor until a result is reached that is as large as or larger than the dividend.
4. On the left side of the vertical line, directly opposite the progressively doubled figures, indicate the number of times the divisor is contained in the respective numbers to the right (1, 2, 4, 8, 16, 32, etc.).
5. Select the numbers in the right-hand column whose sum is equal or closest to the dividend. If the sum is less than the dividend, indicate the number (it must be less than the divisor) that must be added to make the sum equal to the dividend. Place this number in parentheses; it will be the remainder portion of the answer.
6. Now add together the numbers on the left side of the vertical line that correspond to the selected numbers on the right side whose sum is nearest the dividend, plus any remainder. This gives you the desired answer.

Example: $187 \div 12$

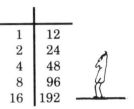

1	12
2	24
4	48
8	96
16	192

$187 = 96 + 48 + 24 + 12 + (7)$
$ = 8 + 4 + 2 + 1 + (7)$
Ans. $= 15\ R7$

(1) $126 \div 7$	(2) $228 \div 12$	(3) $349 \div 15$
Answer: _____	Answer: _____	Answer: _____
(4) $457 \div 36$	(5) $518 \div 19$	(6) $629 \div 24$
Answer: _____	Answer: _____	Answer: _____

Have Fun with Math

Cross-Number Puzzles with Digits

Here are some challenging cross-number puzzles. You are given some of the numbers and all of the necessary arithmetical signs that lead to the correct horizontal and vertical totals. See if you can insert numbers in the empty spaces that will give you the desired totals. There are no zeros. Make sure your solution checks out both horizontally and vertically. The first puzzle has been solved as an example.

1

3	×	2	÷	2	=	3
×	■	×	■	×	■	+
3	+	4	−	2	=	5
−	■	÷	■	×	■	−
5	+	1	−	2	=	4
=	■	=	■	=	■	=
4	+	8	−	8	=	4

2

	×	6	÷		=	
+	■	÷	■	+	■	×
9	+		−		=	3
−	■	+	■	−	■	−
	+		−	2	=	
=	■	=	■	=	■	=
5	+		−		=	3

3

4	×		−		=	5
+	■	+	■	−	■	+
	÷		−		=	
−	■	+	■	−	■	−
	×	4	−		=	7
=	■	=	■	=	■	=
9	−		+		=	1

4

	÷		+		=	5
÷	■	×	■	×	■	+
	×		−	4	=	
−	■	−	■	−	■	−
	×		−	7	=	5
=	■	=	■	=	■	=
1	+		+		=	8

Cross-Number Puzzles with Signs of Operation

Here are some cross-number puzzles with numbers arranged to provide a given result, but the arithmetical signs of operation are missing. You are challenged to insert the signs of operation in the empty spaces to provide the results shown. Remember, a correct solution must check out both horizontally and vertically. The first puzzle has been solved as an example.

1

3	×	3	−	2	=	7
×	■	×	■	×	■	−
3	×	2	−	3	=	3
−	■	−	■	÷	■	+
2	×	3	÷	6	=	1
=	■	=	■	=	■	=
7	−	3	+	1	=	5

2

9		3		2	=	1
	■		■		■	
3		6		9	=	9
	■		■		■	
2		7		6	=	3
=	■	=	■	=	■	=
5		2		3	=	6

3

6		2		4	=	3
	■		■		■	
6		3		2	=	9
	■		■		■	
8		2		1	=	5
=	■	=	■	=	■	=
8		4		5	=	7

4

4		6		3	=	8
	■		■		■	
4		2		1	=	3
	■		■		■	
8		4		2	=	4
=	■	=	■	=	■	=
8		3		4	=	1

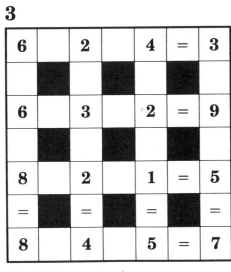

Have Fun with Math

Fun Test on Whole Numbers

Here's a chance 4 U 2 C how much you have learned about whole numbers. Write your answers in the spaces provided below the problems. Be sure to read the problems very carefully. Test time is limited to 15 minutes.

1. Write the following number with five digits: Thirteen thousand, thirteen hundred, thirteen.

   Answer: _____

2. How much more than 2 less than 3 is 1 less than 4?

   Answer: _____

3. If I multiply a number by 7, I obtain 56 for a product. What would have been the difference if I had subtracted by 7?

   Answer: _____

4. A student divided a number by 6 instead of multiplying. He obtained 16 as a quotient. What would his answer have been if he had multiplied?

   Answer: _____

5. How much is $1 \times 2 \times 3 \times 4 \times 5 \times 6 \times 7 \times 8 \times 9 \times 0$?

   Answer: _____

6. What is the quotient of any number divided by itself?

   Answer: _____

7. What is the difference between twice 30 plus 3 and twice 3 plus 30?

   Answer: _____

8. What is the sum of all the consecutive numbers between 1 and 10?

   Answer: _____

9. A farmer had 35 head of cattle. During a severe winter all but 11 died. How many live cattle remained?

   Answer: _____

10. A bottle and a stopper cost $1.10. If the bottle cost $1.00 more than the stopper, how much does the stopper cost?

    Answer: _____

Scores:
0–1, Frigid   2–3, Cold   4–5, Moderate
6–7, Warm   8–9, Hot   10, Super Hot

Have Fun with Math

Cross-Number Puzzle on Whole Numbers*

Across

1. Five thousand five hundred fifty in digits.
5. The nearest number of thousands in 76,499.
7. Add 203, 371, 96, and 289.
8. Multiply 32 by 23.
9. Subtract 198 from 207.
10. Divide 70,295 by 827.
11. The minuend is 15 and the subtrahend is 8. Find the difference.
12. What is the sum of 19 and 49?
13. The dividend is 632 and the divisor is 79. Find the quotient.
14. Find the product of 14 and 3.
15. $\dfrac{24 \times 35 \times 36}{5 \times 63 \times 32}$
16. The product of 19 and 91 is how much larger than 1,681?
17. Quotient when a number other than 0 is divided by itself.
18. Find the average of 97; 316; 1,459; 25; and 783.
20. Which number is divisible by 9: 366, 187, 207, 721, or 529?
22. Divide the sum of 789 and 4,755 by 72.
23. The product of the next three consecutive numbers after 15.

Down

1. Find the quotient when the dividend is 5,605 and the divisor is 95.
2. Multiply 311 by 18.
3. Quotient when the dividend is 413 and the divisor is 7.
4. $17 \times 13 \times 7 \times 3 \times 0$.
5. Divide 7,081 by 97.
6. The sum of 4,851; 8; 525; 987; 65; and 236.
8. The sum of the next three consecutive odd numbers after 21.
10. The multiplicand is 37 and the multiplier is 24. Find the product.
12. Using number symbols, write six thousand three hundred fifty-seven.
14. $742 + 39 + 435 + 6 + 2,887$
16. Nearest number of hundreds in 4,561.
19. From the product of 67 and 76, subtract 5,055.
20. $\dfrac{63 \times 96 \times 30}{15 \times 36 \times 12}$
21. Find the average of 167, 7, 41, and 89.
23. Difference when 4,369 is subtracted from the sum of 917 and 3,456.

*Cross-number puzzles are solved in the same manner as crossword puzzles.

Have Fun with Math

Mystic Square with Whole Numbers

Solve each of the 16 problems below. Then place the answers in the respective cells of the mystic square. When all the answers are in their cells, find the sums of the rows, columns, and diagonal of answers. If the answers are all correct, all the sums will be the same.

Sum

1.	2.	3.	4.	
5.	6.	7.	8.	
9.	10.	11.	12.	
13.	14.	15.	16.	

Sum

1. Write three hundred eighty-seven using digits.
2. Round off 51,498 to the nearest number of thousands.
3. What is the sum of 59 and 16?
4. Find the difference of 1,213 and 898.
5. State the product of 3 and 41.
6. If the dividend is 7,743 and the divisor is 29, find the quotient.
7. Determine the sum of 66 and 177.
8. Add the following: 23, 15, 46, 18, and 93.
9. Multiply the difference of 72 and 69 by 73.
10. Divide 16,587 by 97.
11. Find the average of 327, 69, 86, and 106.
12. Solve: $\dfrac{194 \times 32 \times 162}{96 \times 36}$
13. From the sum of 357 and 269 subtract 527.
14. Dorothy scored 109 field goals (2 points each) and 121 foul tosses during the basketball season. How many points did she score?
15. The sum of the next three consecutive numbers after 119.
16. A ship sailed from Panama City to Jacksonville, Florida, a distance of 1,512 nautical miles, in 56 hours. What was the average speed of the ship in number of knots (nautical miles per hour)?

Have Fun with Math

I'm larger than the two of you!

Part II
Fractions

Changing Fractions

See if you can correctly complete the following 50 fraction changes. The changes include expressing fractions in lowest terms and changing improper fractions to a whole number or mixed number in lowest terms. You are to write in the top portion of each cell the number that replaces the question mark of an item. The first two have been solved for you. Time is limited to 15 minutes. To figure your score, subtract the total number wrong from the total number correct (untried items are not counted).

1	*2*			
$\frac{2}{4} = \frac{?}{2}$	$\frac{4}{8} = \frac{1}{?}$	$\frac{7}{21} = \frac{?}{3}$	$\frac{12}{4} = ?$	$\frac{7}{35} = \frac{?}{5}$
$\frac{5}{5} = ?$	$\frac{2}{12} = \frac{1}{?}$	$\frac{6}{2} = ?$	$\frac{23}{46} = \frac{1}{?}$	$\frac{16}{2} = ?$
$\frac{4}{20} = \frac{1}{?}$	$\frac{7}{5} = 1\frac{?}{5}$	$\frac{6}{42} = \frac{1}{?}$	$\frac{13}{8} = ?\frac{5}{8}$	$\frac{32}{96} = \frac{?}{3}$
$\frac{25}{16} = 1\frac{?}{16}$	$\frac{27}{81} = \frac{1}{?}$	$\frac{19}{12} = ?\frac{7}{12}$	$\frac{8}{10} = \frac{?}{5}$	$\frac{13}{10} = 1\frac{3}{?}$
$\frac{9}{12} = \frac{3}{?}$	$\frac{6}{4} = 1\frac{?}{2}$	$\frac{10}{12} = \frac{?}{6}$	$\frac{12}{9} = 1\frac{?}{3}$	$\frac{21}{28} = \frac{?}{4}$
$\frac{28}{16} = 1\frac{3}{?}$	$\frac{12}{16} = \frac{?}{4}$	$\frac{18}{12} = 1\frac{?}{2}$	$\frac{18}{24} = \frac{3}{?}$	$\frac{52}{32} = 1\frac{?}{8}$
$\frac{20}{36} = \frac{5}{?}$	$\frac{7}{3} = ?\frac{1}{3}$	$\frac{56}{64} = \frac{7}{?}$	$\frac{13}{4} = 3\frac{?}{4}$	$\frac{58}{87} = \frac{?}{3}$
$\frac{22}{7} = ?\frac{1}{7}$	$\frac{52}{91} = \frac{4}{?}$	$\frac{32}{9} = 3\frac{?}{9}$	$\frac{91}{104} = \frac{?}{8}$	$\frac{67}{12} = ?\frac{?}{12}$
$\frac{135}{144} = \frac{15}{?}$	$\frac{115}{16} = ?\frac{3}{16}$	$\frac{80}{100} = \frac{?}{5}$	$\frac{10}{4} = 2\frac{1}{?}$	$\frac{360}{456} = \frac{15}{?}$
$\frac{34}{6} = ?\frac{2}{3}$	$\frac{405}{567} = \frac{?}{7}$	$\frac{45}{20} = 2\frac{1}{?}$	$\frac{256}{352} = \frac{8}{?}$	$\frac{50}{12} = 4\frac{?}{6}$

Scores:

0–10, Brr!!	11–20, Very Cold	20–30, Warming Up
31–40, Going Great	41–46, Lots of Power	47–50, Super Power

Have Fun with Math

More Changing Fractions

See if you can correctly complete the following 50 fraction changes. The changes include changing mixed numbers to simplest form and changing fractions to higher terms. You are to write in the top portion of each cell the number that replaces the question mark of an item. The first two have been solved for you. Time is limited to 15 minutes. To figure your score, subtract the total number wrong from the total number correct (untried items are not counted).

3	**5**			
$2^3/_3 = ?$	$^1/_3 = ^?/_{15}$	$6^7/_7 = ?$	$^1/_4 = ^?/_{28}$	$6^{16}/_{16} = ?$
$^1/_8 = ^?/_{48}$	$8^6/_3 = ?$	$^1/_{12} = ^?/_{72}$	$8^{18}/_9 = ?$	$^1/_6 = ^?/_{42}$
$6^{30}/_5 = ?$	$^1/_{10} = ^?/_{70}$	$5^6/_9 = 5^?/_3$	$^5/_6 = ^?/_{12}$	$4^5/_{20} = 4^1/_?$
$^2/_3 = ^?/_{12}$	$6^{35}/_{42} = 6^5/_?$	$^7/_8 = ^?/_{32}$	$7^8/_{12} = 7^?/_3$	$^3/_{16} = ^?/_{48}$
$2^{16}/_{30} = 2^8/_?$	$^{17}/_{32} = ^?/_{64}$	$5^{25}/_{40} = 5^5/_?$	$^5/_9 = ^?/_{72}$	$6^9/_5 = 7^?/_5$
$^5/_7 = ^{15}/_?$	$8^5/_2 = ?^1/_2$	$^3/_8 = ^9/_?$	$3^{13}/_8 = 4^?/_8$	$^5/_9 = ^?/_{45}$
$5^7/_6 = ?^1/_6$	$^7/_{12} = 2^1/_?$	$2^{19}/_{10} = 3^?/_{10}$	$^3/_4 = ^{18}/_?$	$6^{29}/_{12} = ?^5/_{12}$
$^9/_{16} = ^?/_{96}$	$5^{10}/_4 = ?^1/_2$	$^{11}/_{16} = ^{44}/_?$	$6^8/_6 = 7^1/_?$	$^{15}/_{16} = ^?/_{80}$
$7^{32}/_{12} = 9^2/_?$	$^9/_{10} = ^{90}/_?$	$5^{15}/_{10} = 6^1/_?$	$^3/_5 = ^?/_{100}$	$1^{10}/_8 = 2^?/_4$
$^4/_{25} = ^{16}/_?$	$4^{15}/_6 = 6^1/_?$	$^{17}/_{20} = ^?/_{100}$	$2^{26}/_{16} = 3^?/_8$	$^{17}/_{50} = ^?/_{100}$

Scores: 0–10, Dead Battery 11–20, Slow to Start 21–30, Tune-Up Needed
31–40, Will Get There 41–46, Good Mileage 47–50, Running Great

Have Fun with Math

Lineup with Fractions

Draw a straight line through any three numbers in a block that are in order of their values (smaller to larger or larger to smaller). It may be possible to draw more than one straight line in a block. The straight lines may be horizontal, vertical, or diagonal. A lineup in the first block has been marked as an example. Try to find the lineups in the other blocks.

1

$1/8$	$1/2$	$1/4$
$1/4$	$1/6$	$1/2$
$1/12$	$1/4$	$1/8$

2

$5/8$	$3/8$	$7/8$
$3/4$	$1/8$	$1/4$
$3/8$	$1/2$	$3/4$

3

$7/10$	$1/2$	$3/10$
$9/10$	$1/5$	$3/5$
$4/5$	$9/10$	$2/5$

4

$3/4$	$1/4$	$7/12$
$1/12$	$1/2$	$1/3$
$1/6$	$2/3$	$5/12$

5

$1/4$	$5/6$	$1/2$
$5/12$	$7/12$	$1/6$
$11/12$	$2/3$	$3/4$

6

$9/16$	$3/8$	$1/2$
$1/8$	$7/16$	$3/4$
$7/8$	$1/4$	$5/8$

7

$5/8$	$3/16$	$3/8$
$1/2$	$7/8$	$5/16$
$3/4$	$1/8$	$1/4$

8

$5/8$	$5/24$	$1/4$
$11/12$	$2/3$	$5/6$
$1/8$	$1/12$	$3/4$

9

$1/3$	$3/8$	$5/12$
$7/12$	$7/8$	$1/2$
$7/24$	$1/12$	$1/6$

10

$5/24$	$3/8$	$1/6$
$1/2$	$7/12$	$5/12$
$1/10$	$3/4$	$1/5$

11

$5/6$	$3/10$	$2/3$
$2/5$	$5/8$	$1/4$
$3/5$	$7/24$	$4/5$

12

$7/24$	$1/8$	$9/10$
$7/10$	$1/2$	$1/4$
$7/12$	$11/12$	$1/3$

Have Fun with Math

Addition Block with Basic Fractions

This is a chance for you to see how well you can add some of the basic fractions. See if you can complete the additions in the following table correctly in the allotted time. You are to find the sums of the two fractions that locate each cell in the block, placing your answers in the respective cells. The first two are done for you. (Examples: ¾ + ⅙ = ¹¹/₁₂ and ¾ + ¾ = 1½.) To figure your score, subtract the total number wrong from the total number correct. Time is limited to 30 minutes.

	$\frac{1}{6}$	$\frac{3}{4}$	$\frac{1}{3}$	$\frac{2}{3}$	$\frac{1}{2}$	$\frac{5}{6}$	$\frac{1}{4}$	$\frac{5}{12}$	$\frac{1}{12}$	$\frac{7}{12}$
$\frac{3}{4}$	$\frac{11}{12}$	$1\frac{1}{2}$								
$\frac{1}{3}$										
$\frac{7}{12}$										
$\frac{1}{4}$										
$\frac{1}{12}$										
$\frac{1}{6}$										
$\frac{2}{3}$										
$\frac{5}{6}$										
$\frac{1}{2}$										
$\frac{11}{12}$										

Scores: 0–20, Try Harder 21–40, Fair 41–60, OK
61–80, Good 81–95, Great 96–100, Wow!

Have Fun with Math

Shooting Gallery with Fractions

Here is a shooting gallery with fractions. There are six targets filled with different fractions. You will be taking "shots" at the targets. A shot consists of circling a number in the target. A number is considered "hit" when you circle it. The object for each target is to provide six "hits" with a sum equal to the target number. The rules are as follows:

1. You get six shots at a target.
2. Each shot must hit a number.
3. All six shots must be totaled.
4. A number can be hit only once.

See if you can score winners on all the targets. Be sure to plan your "shots" carefully.

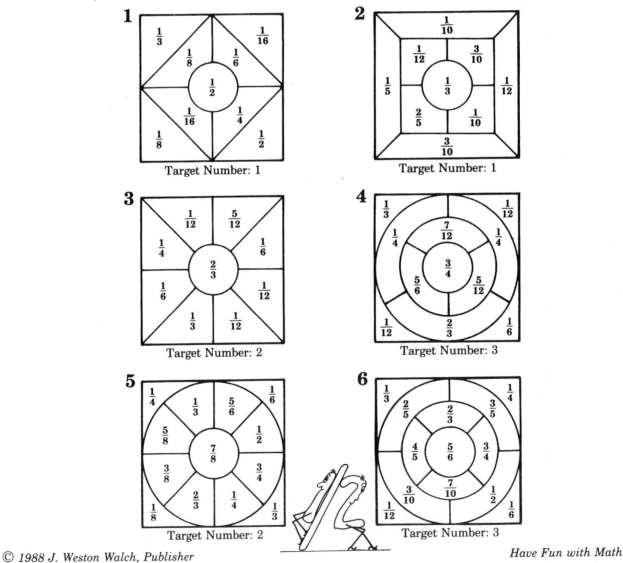

Target Number: 1 (Target 1)

Target Number: 1 (Target 2)

Target Number: 2 (Target 3)

Target Number: 3 (Target 4)

Target Number: 2 (Target 5)

Target Number: 3 (Target 6)

Have Fun with Math

Circular Maze Puzzle with Fractions

Below is a circular maze puzzle with fractions — a diagram with six concentric circles. Each circle has a number of gates containing a fraction or mixed number. The object of the puzzle is to pass through one gate of each circle in an effort to reach the center with a gate number total of 10.

See if you can find the route through the gates to the center that provides the desired gate number total of 10. Remember, only six gates may be traversed; one gate in each circle.

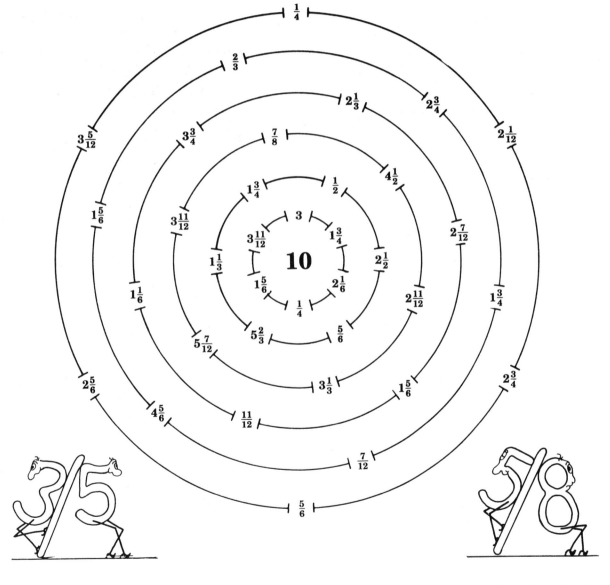

Have Fun with Math

Cross-Number Addition and Subtraction Blocks with Fractions

Fill in the empty cells in the blocks below with fractions or mixed numbers that will make the additions and subtractions work. The number in the lower right cell of each block should "check out" both vertically and horizontally.

1

$4\frac{1}{3}$	+	$1\frac{3}{5}$	=	
+	■	+	■	+
$2\frac{4}{5}$	+	$3\frac{2}{3}$	=	
=	■	=	■	=
	+		=	

2

$9\frac{1}{2}$	−	$6\frac{2}{3}$	=	
−	■	−	■	−
$6\frac{3}{4}$	−	$4\frac{5}{6}$	=	
=	■	=	■	=
	−		=	

3

$5\frac{5}{6}$	−	$3\frac{1}{2}$	=	
+	■	+	■	+
$4\frac{3}{4}$	−	$2\frac{2}{3}$	=	
=	■	=	■	=
	−		=	

4

	+	$\frac{3}{4}$	=	$1\frac{1}{4}$
+	■	+	■	+
$\frac{2}{3}$	+		=	
=	■	=	■	=
	+		=	$2\frac{3}{4}$

5

$2\frac{5}{6}$	−		=	
−	■	−	■	−
	−	$1\frac{1}{4}$	=	
=	■	=	■	=
	−	$\frac{1}{4}$	=	$\frac{11}{12}$

6

$5\frac{3}{4}$	+		=	
−	■	−	■	−
	+	$1\frac{1}{2}$	=	$5\frac{1}{6}$
=	■	=	■	=
	+	$1\frac{2}{3}$	=	

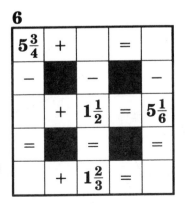

Have Fun with Math

Magic Squares with Fractions

Using $\frac{2}{5}$ ⟋70

$18\frac{2}{5}$	$12\frac{2}{5}$	$6\frac{2}{5}$	$\frac{2}{5}$	$16\frac{4}{5}$	$10\frac{4}{5}$	$4\frac{4}{5}$	−70
2	$15\frac{3}{5}$	$9\frac{3}{5}$	$3\frac{3}{5}$	$17\frac{1}{5}$	14	8	−70
$5\frac{1}{5}$	$18\frac{4}{5}$	$12\frac{4}{5}$	$6\frac{4}{5}$	$\frac{4}{5}$	$14\frac{2}{5}$	$11\frac{1}{5}$	−70
$8\frac{2}{5}$	$2\frac{2}{5}$	16	10	4	$17\frac{3}{5}$	$11\frac{3}{5}$	−70
$8\frac{4}{5}$	$5\frac{3}{5}$	$19\frac{1}{5}$	$13\frac{1}{5}$	$7\frac{1}{5}$	$1\frac{1}{5}$	$14\frac{4}{5}$	−70
12	6	$2\frac{4}{5}$	$16\frac{2}{5}$	$10\frac{2}{5}$	$4\frac{2}{5}$	18	−70
$15\frac{1}{5}$	$9\frac{1}{5}$	$3\frac{1}{5}$	$19\frac{3}{5}$	$13\frac{3}{5}$	$7\frac{3}{5}$	$1\frac{3}{5}$	−70

70 70 70 70 70 70 70 ⟍70

Using $\frac{1}{4}$ ⟋$3\frac{3}{4}$

2	$\frac{1}{4}$	$1\frac{1}{2}$	−$3\frac{3}{4}$
$\frac{3}{4}$	$1\frac{1}{4}$	$1\frac{3}{4}$	−$3\frac{3}{4}$
1	$2\frac{1}{4}$	$\frac{1}{2}$	−$3\frac{3}{4}$

$3\frac{3}{4}$ $3\frac{3}{4}$ $3\frac{3}{4}$ ⟍$3\frac{3}{4}$

Using $\frac{1}{6}$ ⟋$10\frac{5}{6}$

$3\frac{5}{6}$	2	$\frac{1}{6}$	$3\frac{1}{3}$	$1\frac{1}{2}$	−$10\frac{5}{6}$
$\frac{2}{3}$	3	$1\frac{1}{6}$	$3\frac{1}{2}$	$2\frac{1}{2}$	−$10\frac{5}{6}$
$1\frac{2}{3}$	4	$2\frac{1}{6}$	$\frac{1}{3}$	$2\frac{2}{3}$	−$10\frac{5}{6}$
$1\frac{5}{6}$	$\frac{5}{6}$	$3\frac{1}{6}$	$1\frac{1}{3}$	$3\frac{2}{3}$	−$10\frac{5}{6}$
$2\frac{5}{6}$	1	$4\frac{1}{6}$	$2\frac{1}{3}$	$\frac{1}{2}$	−$10\frac{5}{6}$

$10\frac{5}{6}$ $10\frac{5}{6}$ $10\frac{5}{6}$ $10\frac{5}{6}$ $10\frac{5}{6}$ ⟍$10\frac{5}{6}$

Magic squares with fractional numbers can be constructed in the same way as magic squares with whole numbers. The difference is that consecutive fractions (¼, ½, ¾, 1, 1¼, etc. or ⅔, 1⅓, 2, 2⅔, 3⅓, etc.) are used to build a number square instead of whole numbers. The rules are as follows:

1. Place the starting fraction in the middle cell of the top row.
2. Each consecutive fraction is placed two cells down and one cell to the right.
3. In counting down, when you run out of cells at the bottom of the square, return to the top of the column and start or keep on counting from there.
4. If moving to the right would place a fraction outside the square, place the fraction at the opposite end of the row instead.
5. If the fraction would fall in a cell already occupied, place that number in the cell directly below the previous entry.

Using consecutive fractions other than those above, make some magic squares of your own in the diagrams provided below. Check the sums in the columns, rows, and diagonals of each square to verify that you have produced a "magic" arrangement of fractions.

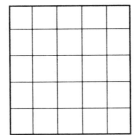

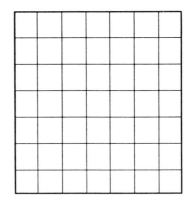

Have Fun with Math

Magic Square Puzzles with Fractions

Magic square puzzles with fractions are like magic square puzzles with whole numbers. In these puzzles some of the numbers are missing. Each of the missing numbers of the puzzle can be found, since the sums of the numbers in each column, row, and diagonal are the same.

Puzzle 1 can be solved by noting that the sum of the numbers in one diagonal is 3¾ ($2 + 1\frac{1}{4} + \frac{1}{2}$). The number in the middle cell of the top horizontal row can be found by subtracting the sum of the two numbers in this row from the "magic sum" (3¾ minus the sum of 1½ and 2). The missing numbers in the other cells can be found the same way.

Try solving the other puzzles on this sheet.

1

2	$\frac{1}{4}$	$1\frac{1}{2}$
$\frac{3}{4}$	$1\frac{1}{4}$	$1\frac{3}{4}$
1	$2\frac{1}{4}$	$\frac{1}{2}$

2

$5\frac{2}{3}$		
$2\frac{1}{3}$	$3\frac{2}{3}$	
3		

3

	$1\frac{1}{6}$	
	$2\frac{1}{2}$	
$2\frac{1}{6}$	$3\frac{5}{6}$	

4

	$1\frac{1}{5}$	$4\frac{1}{5}$
	$3\frac{3}{5}$	
3		

5

$6\frac{1}{3}$	$1\frac{2}{3}$	2	
		$4\frac{1}{3}$	
4		3	
$2\frac{1}{3}$	$5\frac{2}{3}$	6	

6

12		$2\frac{1}{4}$	$9\frac{3}{4}$
	$8\frac{1}{4}$		
$6\frac{3}{4}$		$4\frac{1}{2}$	
3	$10\frac{1}{2}$		$\frac{3}{4}$

7

$3\frac{4}{5}$	$7\frac{2}{5}$	$6\frac{4}{5}$	$5\frac{3}{5}$
$6\frac{1}{5}$			8
	$9\frac{1}{5}$	$9\frac{4}{5}$	$1\frac{2}{5}$

8

3			$2\frac{5}{8}$	$1\frac{1}{4}$
	$2\frac{3}{8}$		$2\frac{3}{4}$	
	$3\frac{1}{8}$	$1\frac{3}{4}$		$2\frac{1}{8}$
$1\frac{1}{2}$	$\frac{3}{4}$	$2\frac{1}{2}$		
$2\frac{1}{4}$		$3\frac{1}{4}$	$1\frac{7}{8}$	$\frac{1}{2}$

9

$14\frac{2}{5}$	$7\frac{4}{5}$			6
3	$11\frac{2}{5}$		$13\frac{1}{5}$	
$6\frac{3}{5}$		$8\frac{2}{5}$		$10\frac{1}{5}$
		12	$5\frac{2}{5}$	
$10\frac{4}{5}$		$15\frac{3}{5}$	9	$2\frac{2}{5}$

Have Fun with Math

Six-Pointed Magic Star Puzzle with Fractions

The characteristics of the magic star, as diagrammed below, are as follows:

1. Six rows with four numbers in a row; the six sums of the numbers in each of the six rows are equal.
2. Three rows with three numbers in a row; the three sums of the numbers in each of the three rows are equal.
3. Six triangles that form the points of the star, with three numbers in a triangle; the six sums of the three numbers in each of the six triangles are the same.
4. The three sums of the three numbers in each of the three rows and the sums of the three numbers in each of the six triangles are the same.

Five of the thirteen fractions that make up the star are given. From these five given numbers, and using the characteristics of the six-pointed magic star, you can find the other eight numbers. See if you can complete the numbers that make up the magic star. Check your results carefully to make sure that all the requirements for the six-pointed magic star are met.

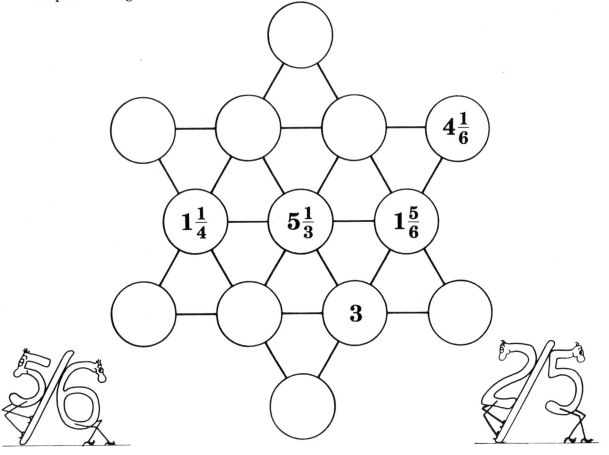

Have Fun with Math

Multiplication Block with Basic Fractions

This is a chance 4 U 2 C how well you can multiply with some of the basic fractions. See if you can complete the multiplications in the following table correctly in the allotted time. You are to find the product of the two fractions that locate each cell in the block, placing your answers in the respective cells. The first two are done for you. (Examples: ¾ × ⅖ = ³⁄₁₀ and ¾ × ¼ = ³⁄₁₆.) To figure your score, subtract the total number wrong from the total number correct. Time is limited to 30 minutes.

	$\frac{2}{5}$	$\frac{1}{4}$	$\frac{2}{3}$	$\frac{5}{6}$	$\frac{1}{5}$	$\frac{3}{4}$	$\frac{1}{3}$	$\frac{4}{5}$	$\frac{1}{2}$	$\frac{5}{12}$
$\frac{3}{4}$	$\frac{3}{10}$	$\frac{3}{16}$								
$\frac{1}{5}$										
$\frac{1}{6}$										
$\frac{11}{12}$										
$\frac{1}{2}$										
$\frac{7}{12}$										
$\frac{4}{5}$										
$\frac{1}{12}$										
$\frac{2}{3}$										
$\frac{1}{4}$										

Scores: 0–20, Safety   21–40, Lost the Ball
41–60, Tackled for Loss   61–80, First Down
81–95, Field Goal   96–100, Touchdown!

Have Fun with Math

Unusual Number Patterns with Fractions

Below are some unusual number patterns involving fractions. Study the patterns carefully; then see if you can fill in the blank spaces.

(1)

$$\frac{1}{2} + \frac{1}{3} = \frac{3+2}{2\times 3} = \frac{5}{6}$$

$$\frac{1}{3} + \frac{1}{4} = \frac{4+3}{3\times 4} = \frac{7}{12}$$

$$\frac{1}{4} + \frac{1}{5} = \frac{5+4}{4\times 5} = \frac{9}{20}$$

$$\frac{1}{5} + \frac{1}{6} = \frac{6+5}{6\times 5} = \underline{\hspace{1.5cm}}$$

$$\frac{1}{6} + \frac{1}{7} = \frac{7+6}{6\times 7} = \underline{\hspace{1.5cm}}$$

$$\frac{1}{8} + \frac{1}{9} = \frac{9+8}{8\times 9} = \underline{\hspace{1.5cm}}$$

$$\frac{1}{10} + \frac{1}{11} = \underline{\hspace{1.5cm}} = \underline{\hspace{1.5cm}}$$

$$\frac{1}{12} + \frac{1}{13} = \underline{\hspace{1.5cm}} = \underline{\hspace{1.5cm}}$$

$$\frac{1}{2} + \frac{1}{2} = \frac{2+2}{2\times 2} = 1$$

$$\frac{1}{2} + \frac{1}{4} = \frac{4+2}{2\times 4} = \frac{3}{4}$$

$$\frac{1}{3} + \frac{1}{6} = \frac{6+3}{3\times 6} = \frac{1}{2}$$

$$\frac{1}{3} + \frac{1}{8} = \frac{8+3}{3\times 8} = \underline{\hspace{1.5cm}}$$

$$\frac{1}{4} + \frac{1}{8} = \frac{8+4}{4\times 8} = \underline{\hspace{1.5cm}}$$

$$\frac{1}{8} + \frac{1}{10} = \frac{10+8}{8\times 10} = \underline{\hspace{1.5cm}}$$

$$\frac{1}{12} + \frac{1}{15} = \underline{\hspace{1.5cm}} = \underline{\hspace{1.5cm}}$$

$$\frac{1}{15} + \frac{1}{20} = \underline{\hspace{1.5cm}} = \underline{\hspace{1.5cm}}$$

(2)

$$\frac{1}{1\times 2} = \frac{1\times 1}{1\times 2} = \frac{1}{2}$$

$$\frac{1}{1\times 2} + \frac{1}{2\times 3} = \frac{2\times 2}{2\times 3} = \frac{2}{3}$$

$$\frac{1}{1\times 2} + \frac{1}{2\times 3} + \frac{1}{3\times 4} = \frac{3\times 3}{3\times 4} = \underline{\hspace{1.5cm}}$$

$$\frac{1}{1\times 2} + \frac{1}{2\times 3} + \frac{1}{3\times 4} + \frac{1}{4\times 5} = \frac{4\times 4}{4\times 5} = \underline{\hspace{1.5cm}}$$

$$\frac{1}{1\times 2} + \frac{1}{2\times 3} + \frac{1}{3\times 4} + \frac{1}{4\times 5} + \frac{1}{5\times 6} = \underline{\hspace{1.5cm}} = \underline{\hspace{1.5cm}}$$

$$\frac{1}{1\times 2} + \frac{1}{2\times 3} + \frac{1}{3\times 4} + \frac{1}{4\times 5} + \frac{1}{5\times 6} + \frac{1}{6\times 7} = \underline{\hspace{1.5cm}} = \underline{\hspace{1.5cm}}$$

$$\frac{1}{1\times 2} + \frac{1}{2\times 3} + \frac{1}{3\times 4} + \frac{1}{4\times 5} + \frac{1}{5\times 6} + \frac{1}{6\times 7} + \frac{1}{7\times 8} = \underline{\hspace{1.5cm}} = \underline{\hspace{1.5cm}}$$

$$\frac{1}{1\times 2} + \frac{1}{2\times 3} + \frac{1}{3\times 4} + \frac{1}{4\times 5} + \frac{1}{5\times 6} + \frac{1}{6\times 7} + \frac{1}{7\times 8} + \frac{1}{8\times 9} = \underline{\hspace{1.5cm}} = \underline{\hspace{1.5cm}}$$

Have Fun with Math

Division Block with Basic Fractions

This is a chance 4 U 2 C how well you can divide with some of the basic fractions. See if you can complete the divisions in the following table in the allotted time. You are to find the quotient of the two fractions that locate each cell in the block; the divisor is in the horizontal row and the dividend is in the vertical column. Place your answers in the respective cells. The first two are done for you. (Examples: $\frac{3}{5} \div \frac{3}{4} = \frac{4}{5}$ and $\frac{3}{5} \div \frac{3}{5} = 1$.) To figure your score, subtract the total number wrong from the total number correct. Time is limited to 30 minutes.

	$\frac{3}{4}$	$\frac{3}{5}$	$\frac{2}{3}$	$\frac{1}{6}$	$\frac{1}{3}$	$\frac{1}{5}$	$\frac{5}{6}$	$\frac{1}{4}$	$\frac{1}{2}$	$\frac{4}{5}$
$\frac{3}{5}$	$\frac{4}{5}$	1								
$\frac{1}{3}$										
$\frac{1}{2}$										
$\frac{1}{5}$										
$\frac{2}{3}$										
$\frac{4}{5}$										
$\frac{5}{6}$										
$\frac{1}{4}$										
$\frac{1}{6}$										
$\frac{2}{5}$										

Scores: 0–20, Sad   21–40, Not So Good
41–60, Not So Bad   61–80, Pretty Darn Good
81–95, Almost Great   96–100, Bionic!

Have Fun with Math

Mini Fraction Rings

In the arrangements below, each number in the outer ring of a circle is the sum or product, as indicated, of the adjoining number in the inner ring and the number in the center circle. You are challenged to fill in the vacant spaces correctly. The first circle has been correctly filled in as an example.

1
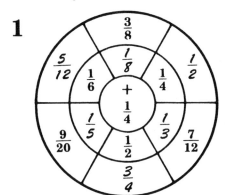

2
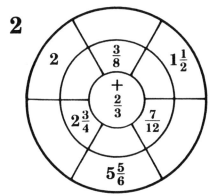

3
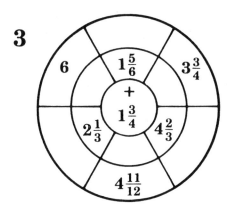

4
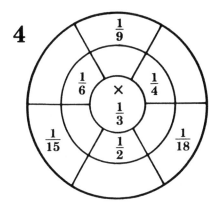

5
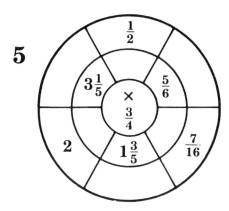

6
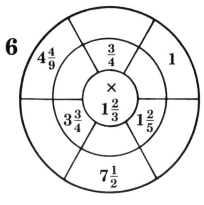

Have Fun with Math

Maxi Fraction Rings

In the diagram below, concentric rings enclose a circle containing a single fraction. This fraction is to act as an addend, subtrahend, multiplier, and divisor in combination with the numbers in the first, inner ring. The numbers in this first ring are to act as addends, minuends, multiplicands, and dividends. You are to find the sums, differences, products, and quotients of these numbers and write them in the respective ring segments. The answers have been provided for combinations in the top central section.

See if you can correctly fill in the answers for all the other sections. A perfect score is 28 correct answers.

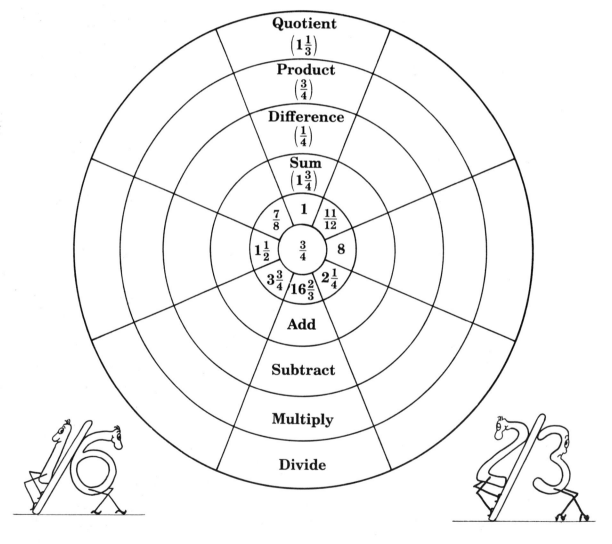

Have Fun with Math

Cross-Number Multiplication and Division Blocks with Fractions

Fill in the empty cells in the blocks below with numbers that make the multiplications and divisions work. The number in the lower right corner cell of each block should "check out" both vertically and horizontally.

1

$1\frac{1}{2}$	$\times$	$1\frac{1}{3}$	$=$	
$\times$	■	$\times$	■	$\times$
$1\frac{2}{3}$	$\times$	$1\frac{1}{5}$	$=$	
$=$	■	$=$	■	$=$
	$\times$		$=$	

2

$1\frac{1}{4}$	$\div$	$1\frac{1}{2}$	$=$	
$\div$	■	$\div$	■	$\div$
$3\frac{1}{3}$	$\div$	$1\frac{1}{4}$	$=$	
$=$	■	$=$	■	$=$
	$\div$		$=$	

3

$1\frac{1}{3}$	$\div$	$2\frac{2}{3}$	$=$	
$\div$	■	$\times$	■	$\div$
$3\frac{1}{5}$	$\times$	$1\frac{1}{4}$	$=$	
$=$	■	$=$	■	$=$
	$\div$		$=$	

4

$2\frac{4}{5}$	$\times$		$=$	$3\frac{1}{2}$
$\times$	■	$\times$	■	$\times$
	$\times$		$=$	
$=$	■	$=$	■	$=$
$9\frac{1}{3}$	$\times$	$4\frac{1}{2}$	$=$	

5

$2\frac{2}{3}$	$\div$		$=$	
$\div$	■	$\div$	■	$\div$
$3\frac{1}{5}$	$\div$	$2\frac{2}{5}$	$=$	
$=$	■	$=$	■	$=$
	$\div$		$=$	$\frac{3}{8}$

6

$2\frac{1}{2}$	$\times$		$=$	4
$\times$	■	$\div$	■	$\times$
	$\div$	$3\frac{1}{5}$	$=$	
$=$	■	$=$	■	$=$
11	$\times$		$=$	

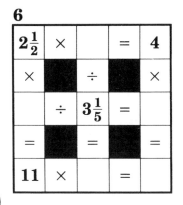

Have Fun with Math

Magic Multiplication Square Puzzles with Fractions

In a multiplication magic square, the products of numbers in each row, column, and diagonal are the same. The squares below are all partially completed multiplication magic squares with fractions. The first magic square has been completed for you. Study this square carefully. Then try to find the numbers that complete the five other magic multiplication squares.

1

5	$\frac{2}{5}$	$\frac{1}{2}$
$\frac{1}{10}$	1	10
2	$2\frac{1}{2}$	$\frac{1}{5}$

2

$\frac{1}{2}$		
	$2\frac{1}{2}$	$\frac{1}{4}$
		$12\frac{1}{2}$

3

$3\frac{1}{5}$		
$6\frac{2}{5}$		
$\frac{1}{5}$		$\frac{4}{5}$

4

		$\frac{5}{8}$
	$1\frac{1}{4}$	$12\frac{1}{2}$
$2\frac{1}{2}$		

5

	$\frac{4}{5}$	
	$3\frac{1}{5}$	
$\frac{2}{5}$	$12\frac{4}{5}$	

6

		$16\frac{2}{3}$
$8\frac{1}{3}$	$3\frac{1}{3}$	$1\frac{1}{3}$

Have Fun with Math

Cross-Number Puzzles with Fractions

You are given some of the numbers and all of the necessary arithmetical signs that lead to the correct horizontal and vertical totals. See if you can insert numbers in the empty spaces that will give the desired totals. There are no zeros. Make sure your solution for a puzzle works out both horizontally and vertically. The first puzzle has been solved as an example.

1

3	÷	1	−	$\frac{1}{2}$	=	$2\frac{1}{2}$
×		+		+		×
1	+	1	+	$\frac{1}{2}$	=	$2\frac{1}{2}$
−		+		+		÷
$\frac{1}{2}$	+	$\frac{1}{2}$	+	$1\frac{1}{2}$	=	$2\frac{1}{2}$
=		=		=		=
$2\frac{1}{2}$	+	$2\frac{1}{2}$	−	$2\frac{1}{2}$	=	$2\frac{1}{2}$

2

2	×		÷	1	=	$2\frac{2}{3}$
×		÷		×		+
	×		÷		=	
÷		−		+		−
	×		÷		=	3
=		=		=		=
$\frac{2}{3}$	+	$1\frac{1}{3}$	−		=	$\frac{2}{3}$

3

$\frac{3}{4}$	×	2	÷		=	1
×		×		×		×
	×		÷		=	
÷		÷		÷		+
	+		−		=	1
=		=		=		=
$\frac{1}{2}$	×		+	1	=	$1\frac{3}{4}$

4

$1\frac{1}{5}$	×		÷	$\frac{4}{5}$	=	$\frac{3}{5}$
+		+		÷		+
	÷		+		=	$1\frac{2}{5}$
+		−		+		−
	+		−		=	
=		=		=		=
3	−		−	$2\frac{1}{5}$	=	$\frac{2}{5}$

Have Fun with Math

Cross-Number Puzzles with Fractions and Signs of Operation

In the puzzles below, numbers are arranged to provide a given result, but most of the signs of operation are missing. You are to insert the signs of operation in the empty spaces that will give the indicated results with the given numbers. Make sure your solution works out both horizontally and vertically. The first puzzle has been solved as an example.

1

$\frac{1}{2}$	×	3	÷	1	=	$1\frac{1}{2}$
×		÷		×		+
4	×	$1\frac{1}{2}$	÷	2	=	3
+		+		−		−
2	×	$1\frac{1}{2}$	−	$\frac{1}{2}$	=	$2\frac{1}{2}$
=		=		=		=
4	−	$3\frac{1}{2}$	+	$1\frac{1}{2}$	=	2

2

3	×	$\frac{2}{3}$		3	=	$\frac{2}{3}$
$\frac{2}{3}$		2		$\frac{1}{3}$	=	$1\frac{2}{3}$
÷						
2		$1\frac{1}{3}$		$2\frac{2}{3}$	=	$\frac{2}{3}$
=		=		=		=
1		$2\frac{2}{3}$		$\frac{2}{3}$	=	3

3

$2\frac{1}{4}$		$\frac{1}{2}$	÷	$\frac{3}{4}$	=	$1\frac{1}{2}$
÷						
$\frac{3}{4}$		$1\frac{1}{2}$		$2\frac{1}{4}$	=	$\frac{1}{2}$
$\frac{3}{4}$		$\frac{1}{4}$		$\frac{1}{2}$	=	$1\frac{1}{2}$
=		=		=		=
4		3		$2\frac{1}{2}$	=	$3\frac{1}{2}$

4

2	÷	$\frac{2}{5}$		$1\frac{1}{5}$	=	6
×						
$1\frac{4}{5}$		$1\frac{1}{5}$		2	=	3
$2\frac{1}{5}$		$1\frac{3}{5}$		$\frac{4}{5}$	=	$1\frac{2}{5}$
=		=		=		=
$1\frac{2}{5}$		$3\frac{1}{5}$		3	=	$1\frac{3}{5}$

Have Fun with Math

What Do You Know about Fractions?

How well do you know how to use fractions? Here's a chance 4 U 2 find out. Select the answer from the list for each problem that you feel is correct. Write the letter of your choice in the space provided to the left of the problem. Time is limited to 15 minutes.

_______ 1. What part of 12 is a fourth of 8?
(a) $\frac{1}{4}$ (b) $\frac{1}{6}$ (c) $\frac{1}{3}$ (d) $\frac{2}{3}$ (e) Answer is not listed.

_______ 2. What part of 4 is half of 3?
(a) $\frac{1}{4}$ (b) $\frac{1}{2}$ (c) $\frac{3}{8}$ (d) $\frac{5}{8}$ (e) Answer is not listed.

_______ 3. What part of 5 is 3 less than half of 10?
(a) $\frac{1}{5}$ (b) $\frac{1}{2}$ (c) $\frac{2}{5}$ (d) $\frac{3}{5}$ (e) Answer is not listed.

_______ 4. What part of 6 is 2 more than 3?
(a) $\frac{1}{3}$ (b) $\frac{1}{2}$ (c) $\frac{2}{3}$ (d) $\frac{5}{6}$ (e) Answer is not listed.

_______ 5. Divide two thirds of 6 by four fifths of 10.
(a) $\frac{1}{2}$ (b) $\frac{1}{4}$ (c) $\frac{5}{6}$ (d) $\frac{4}{5}$ (e) Answer is not listed.

_______ 6. How much less is one third less than 3 than one fourth more than 4?
(a) $1\frac{3}{4}$ (b) $2\frac{1}{4}$ (c) $2\frac{5}{8}$ (d) $3\frac{1}{4}$ (e) Answer is not listed.

_______ 7. Divide 15 by a fifth and add 5.
(a) 8 (b) 20 (c) 40 (d) 80 (e) Answer is not listed.

_______ 8. What is the weight of a melon that weighs 3 kilograms and three quarters of its own weight?
(a) 12 kg (b) 9 kg (c) 4 kg (d) $3\frac{3}{4}$ kg (e) Answer is not listed.

_______ 9. A cabbage placed on a scale just balances the weight of four fifths of a cabbage of the same weight and four fifths of a kilogram. How much does the cabbage weigh?
(a) 3 kg (b) 4 kg (c) 5 kg (d) 6 kg (e) Answer is not listed.

_______ 10. Lois spends a quarter of her allowance on bus fare, a sixth on cosmetics, a sixth on hobbies, one twelfth on club activities, a third on clothes, and the remainder on school supplies. What part of her allowance does she spend on school supplies?
(a) $\frac{1}{12}$ (b) $\frac{1}{6}$ (c) $\frac{1}{4}$ (d) $\frac{1}{3}$ (e) Answer is not listed.

Scores:

0–1, Expired 2–3, Dying
4–5, Warm 6–7, Steaming
8–9, Hot 10, Volcanic

Secret Message Using Fractions

The answer to each problem in the list below represents a letter in the alphabet. When all the letters have been assembled in respective order, they form the words of a message. Using the alphabet-number chart to obtain the letters, see if you can determine the secret message.

A	B	C	D	E	F	G	H	I	J	K	L	M	N	O	P	Q	R	S	T	U	V	W	X	Y	Z
1	2	3	4	5	6	7	8	9	10	11	12	13	14	15	16	17	18	19	20	21	22	23	24	25	26

_ _ _ _   _ _ _   _ _ _ _   _ _ _ _   _ _ _ _ _   _ _ _ _ _ .

_____ Change $^{75}/_3$ to a whole number or mixed number.

_____ Lowest common denominator of $\frac{1}{3}$, $\frac{2}{5}$, $\frac{2}{3}$, and $\frac{4}{5}$.

_____ Number of 24ths in $\frac{7}{8}$.

_____ Numerator when $^{36}/_{48}$ is reduced to lowest terms.

_____ The sum of $\frac{1}{12}$, $\frac{1}{4}$, $\frac{1}{6}$, and $\frac{1}{2}$.

_____ Find the missing number: $4\frac{2}{3} = \frac{?}{3}$

_____ $1\frac{5}{6} + 2\frac{2}{3} + 3\frac{1}{2}$

_____ Subtract $7\frac{3}{4}$ from $8\frac{9}{12}$.

_____ Numerator when $7\frac{1}{3}$ is changed to an improper fraction.

_____ Denominator of largest fraction: $\frac{2}{3}$, $\frac{4}{5}$, $\frac{3}{4}$

_____ $7\frac{1}{5} \times \frac{5}{6}$

_____ Find the product of $11\frac{2}{3}$ and $1\frac{4}{5}$.

_____ $24\frac{1}{2} \div 1\frac{3}{4}$

_____ Quotient when $32\frac{1}{5}$ is divided by $1\frac{2}{5}$.

_____ $\frac{2}{3}$ of what number is 6?

_____ The sum of $14\frac{2}{3}$ and $17\frac{3}{4}$ is how much larger than $12\frac{5}{12}$?

_____ Twice what number is 16?

_____ Subtract $4\frac{1}{2}$ from the product of $4\frac{2}{3}$ and $3\frac{3}{4}$.

_____ The product of 18, 20, and 16 divided by the product of 32, 12, and 15.

_____ 35 is $1\frac{3}{4}$ of what number?

_____ $3\frac{3}{4} \times 4\frac{4}{5} \div 2\frac{1}{4}$

Have Fun with Math

Cross-Number Fractions Puzzle

Across

1. Denominator of the fraction $\frac{7}{12}$.
3. Number of 8ths when $2\frac{5}{8}$ is reduced to an improper fraction.
5. Least common denominator for $\frac{2}{3}$, $\frac{3}{8}$, and $\frac{5}{12}$.
6. $1\frac{1}{2} + 2\frac{2}{3} + 3\frac{3}{4} + 4\frac{1}{12}$
7. $16\frac{2}{3} + 23\frac{3}{4} - 3\frac{5}{12}$
9. $4\frac{4}{5} \times 13\frac{1}{3}$
11. $40\frac{1}{2} \div \frac{3}{16}$
14. 60 is $\frac{5}{6}$ of what number?
16. Find $\frac{3}{8}$ of 128.
18. $32\frac{1}{2} + 13\frac{7}{8} - 28\frac{3}{8}$
20. $14\frac{1}{2} \times 3\frac{3}{4} \times 1\frac{3}{5}$
22. Solve: $\dfrac{1\frac{7}{8} \times 4\frac{1}{5}}{2\frac{1}{4} - 1\frac{7}{8}}$
23. Divide the sum of $28\frac{3}{5}$ and $9\frac{4}{5}$ by $1\frac{3}{5}$.

Down

1. $14\frac{2}{5} \div 1\frac{1}{5}$
2. Divide $28\frac{3}{4}$ by $\frac{3}{8}$ and add $166\frac{1}{3}$ to the quotient.
3. Find $\frac{3}{8}$ of 56.
4. Solve: $\dfrac{12\frac{3}{5} \times 2\frac{1}{4}}{\frac{3}{5} \div 2\frac{2}{3}}$
8. 42 is $\frac{7}{12}$ of what number?
10. $8\frac{5}{6} + 7\frac{2}{3} - 12\frac{1}{2}$
12. Numerator of the fraction $\frac{1}{2}$.
13. $13\frac{1}{3} \times 11\frac{1}{5} \div 2\frac{1}{3}$
14. Numerator when $3\frac{1}{2}$ is changed to an improper fraction.
15. $78\frac{1}{4} + 57\frac{5}{6} + 75\frac{11}{12}$
17. From the product of $28\frac{1}{3}$ and $31\frac{1}{5}$ subtract 2.
19. $14\frac{2}{5} \times 5\frac{5}{8}$
21. To the sum of $13\frac{5}{6}$ and $27\frac{3}{4}$ add $32\frac{5}{12}$.

Have Fun with Math

Fun Test on Fractions

It's all in fun. After you read each question carefully, U R 2 write your answers in the spaces provided. Time is limited to 15 minutes.

1. Janis bought two candy bars for a cent and a quarter. At this rate, how much did she pay for one candy bar?

   Answer: _____

2. What number multiplied by half of itself will produce 50?

   Answer: _____

3. Which is correct: "The sum of ⅓ and ¼ are ⁵⁄₁₂" or "The sum of ⅓ and ¼ is ⁵⁄₁₂?"

   Answer: _____

4. How many quarter centimeter marks are there on one centimeter of a meter stick?

   Answer: _____

5. Eddy, who was hunting birds with his single-barrel shotgun, saw 12 doves sitting on a telephone line. He took careful aim and fired. If his shot killed ⅓ of the doves, how many of them were left?

   Answer: _____

6. How can you make 8 liters of corn from a ½-liter bag of corn?

   Answer: _____

7. If you have six pills and take one every half hour, how long will they last?

   Answer: _____

8. This and that is what part of this and that and a half more of this and that?

   Answer: _____

9. Which is worth more: ½ kilogram of $10 gold pieces or ¼ kilogram of $20 gold pieces?

   Answer: _____

10. Mrs. Smith had five large oranges that she divided equally among her two children. If neither child received more than one part of the oranges, how did she accomplish this?

    Answer: _____

Scores:

0–1, Frigid	2–3, Cool	4–5, Moderate
6–7, Warm	8–9, Hot	10, Torrid

Have Fun with Math

Mystic Square with Fractions

Solve each of the sixteen problems below. Then place the answers in the respective cells of the mystic square. When all the answers have been placed in their cells, find the sums of the rows, columns, and diagonal of answers. If the answers are all correct, all the sums will be the same.

Sum

1.	2.	3.	4.	
5.	6.	7.	8.	
9.	10.	11.	12.	
13.	14.	15.	16.	
Sum				

1. The number of 24ths in $\frac{3}{8}$.
2. $\frac{90}{108}$ reduced to lowest terms.
3. Express $\frac{34}{24}$ as a mixed number in lowest terms.
4. $2\frac{7}{12} + 4\frac{2}{3}$
5. $8\frac{5}{12} - 5\frac{5}{6}$
6. $14\frac{3}{5} \times \frac{5}{12}$
7. $25\frac{2}{3} \div 4\frac{2}{3}$
8. Add: $\frac{5}{12}$, $1\frac{1}{4}$, $\frac{1}{2}$, and $2\frac{1}{6}$.
9. Subtract $4\frac{5}{8}$ from $7\frac{1}{3}$ and add $2\frac{5}{24}$ to the difference.
10. Multiply $2\frac{2}{5}$ by $1\frac{9}{16}$.
11. Divide $14\frac{1}{4}$ by $4\frac{1}{2}$.
12. $5\frac{1}{3}$ is $\frac{4}{5}$ of what number?
13. $3\frac{3}{5} \times 2\frac{1}{3} \div 4\frac{1}{5}$
14. Find $\frac{5}{6}$ of $9\frac{2}{5}$.
15. Multiply the sum of $3\frac{1}{2}$ and $2\frac{13}{16}$ by $1\frac{1}{3}$.
16. Simplify: $\dfrac{1\frac{1}{5} \times 1\frac{3}{4}}{10 - 1\frac{3}{5}}$

Have Fun with Math

Cross-Number Review Puzzle
through Fractions

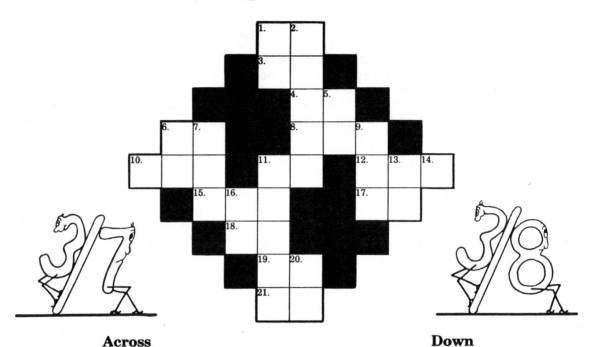

| **Across** | **Down** |

Across

1. Nearest number of 100's in 2,349.
3. Next consecutive number after 71.
4. 2,381 + 897 − 3,253
6. 50,274 ÷ 798
8. Find the product of 28 and 27.
10. 289 + 97 + 336 + 75
11. Number of 16ths in 2⅛.
12. 5⅝ × 4⅔ × 4⅘
15. 11⅔ × 20¼ ÷ ⁵/₁₂
17. From the sum of 21⅔ and 18¾ subtract 13⁵/₁₂.
18. 33⅓ is ⅚ of what number?
19. Subtract 1½ from the product of 7⅕ and 3⅛.
20. Solve: $\dfrac{11\frac{1}{5} \times 13\frac{1}{3}}{5\frac{7}{12} - 3\frac{1}{4}}$

Down

1. Add 9⅔ to the product of 3⅕ and 5⁵/₁₂.
2. Find the product of 1,793 and 18.
5. 41¼ is ¾ of what number?
6. Number of 8ths in 8⅝.
7. Subtract 9,176 from 9,551.
9. 5⅔ × 16⅞ × 6⅖
10. Divide the product of 5⅗ and 13⅓ by 10⅔.
11. Find the sum of 189; 34,867; 95; 1,659; 8; and 208.
13. Divide 10,449 by 387.
14. Solve: $\dfrac{48 \times 36 \times 105}{56 \times 45 \times 12}$
16. 13¾ + 7¹¹/₁₂ + 4⅙ + 28⅔ + 9½
20. Next consecutive even number after 12.

© 1988 J. Weston Walch, Publisher   *Have Fun with Math*

I can determine the size of numbers!

Part III
Decimals

Lineup with Decimals

Draw a straight line through any three numbers in a block that are in order of their size (smallest to largest or largest to smallest). The straight lines may be horizontal, vertical, or diagonal. It may be possible to draw more than one straight line in a block. A lineup in the first block has been drawn as an example. Try to find the lineups in the other blocks.

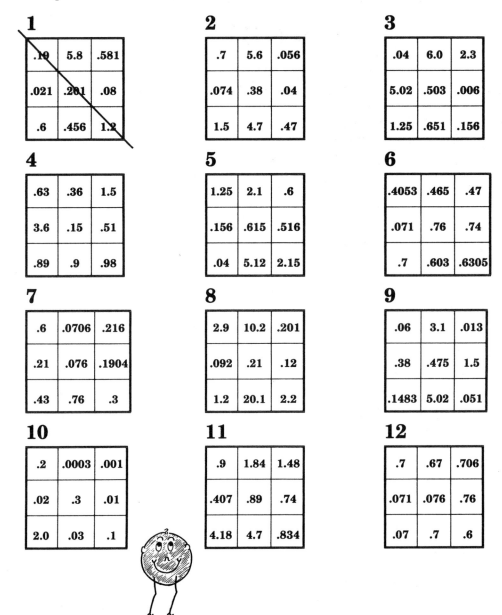

1

.19	5.8	.581
.021	.201	.08
.6	.456	1.2

2

.7	5.6	.056
.074	.38	.04
1.5	4.7	.47

3

.04	6.0	2.3
5.02	.503	.006
1.25	.651	.156

4

.63	.36	1.5
3.6	.15	.51
.89	.9	.98

5

1.25	2.1	.6
.156	.615	.516
.04	5.12	2.15

6

.4053	.465	.47
.071	.76	.74
.7	.603	.6305

7

.6	.0706	.216
.21	.076	.1904
.43	.76	.3

8

2.9	10.2	.201
.092	.21	.12
1.2	20.1	2.2

9

.06	3.1	.013
.38	.475	1.5
.1483	5.02	.051

10

.2	.0003	.001
.02	.3	.01
2.0	.03	.1

11

.9	1.84	1.48
.407	.89	.74
4.18	4.7	.834

12

.7	.67	.706
.071	.076	.76
.07	.7	.6

Have Fun with Math

Decimal Brain Stretchers

Following are 20 different series of numbers. You are to look for the pattern in a series and then fill in the next three numbers of that series. The first series has been completed as an example. Try stretching your brain on the remaining items. Time is limited to 30 minutes.

1. .1; .2; .3; .4; _.5_; _.6_; _.7_.
2. .1; .3; .5; .7; ____; ____; ____.
3. 1.0; .9; .8; .7; ____; ____; ____.
4. .3; 1.1; 1.9; 2.7; ____; ____; ____.
5. 9.6; 9.3; 8.9; 8.4; ____; ____; ____.
6. 10.0; 9.3; 8.6; 7.9; ____; ____; ____.
7. 7.8; 7.3; 6.8; 6.3; ____; ____; ____.
8. .06; .07; .09; .13; .21; ____; ____; ____.
9. .8; 2.1; 3.4; 4.7; ____; ____; ____.
10. .1; .2; .4; .7; 1.1; ____; ____; ____.
11. .02; .04; .08; .14; .22; ____; ____; ____.
12. .1; .2; .4; .8; 1.6; ____; ____; ____.
13. .5; .6; .9; 1.4; 2.1; ____; ____; ____.
14. 20.0; 19.8; 19.4; 18.6; ____; ____; ____.
15. 10.0; 9.9; 9.6; 9.1; 8.4; ____; ____; ____.
16. .1; .6; 1.6; 3.1; 5.1; ____; ____; ____.
17. 20.0; 19.8; 19.4; 18.6; ____; ____; ____.
18. 50; 25; 12.5; 6.25; ____; ____; ____.
19. .1; .02; .003; .0004; ____; ____; ____.
20. .1; .04; .007; .001; ____; ____; ____.

Scores:

0–3, Very Rough
8–10, Almost Rough
16–18, Smooth

4–7, Rough
11–15, Almost Smooth
19–20, Very Smooth

Have Fun with Math

Magic Addition Wheel Puzzles with Decimals

Try to rearrange the decimals from around each wheel at the left in the corresponding wheel at the right so that the numbers of the diameters (the numbers at each end of a diameter plus the number at the hub) of the corresponding wheel have the same sum.

1

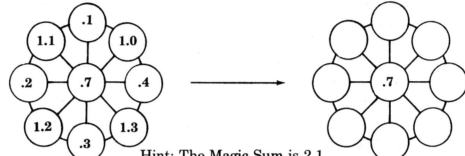

Hint: The Magic Sum is 2.1

2

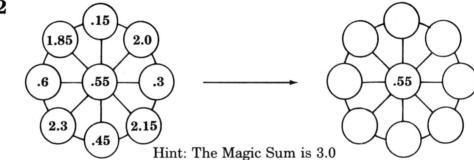

Hint: The Magic Sum is 3.0

3

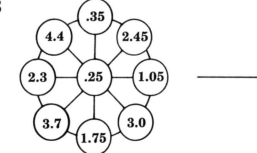

Have Fun with Math

Shooting Gallery with Decimals

Below is a shooting gallery with decimals. There are six targets filled with these numbers. You will be taking "shots" at the targets. A shot consists of circling a number in the target. A number is considered "hit" when you circle it. The object for each target is to provide six "hits" with a sum equal to the target number. The rules are as follows:

1. You get six shots at a target.
2. Each shot must hit a number.
3. All six shots must be totaled.
4. A number can be hit only once.

See if you can score winners on all the targets. You must plan your "shots" carefully.

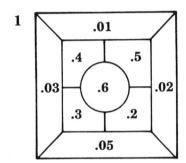

Target Number: 1

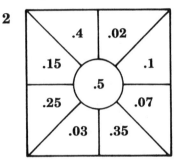

Target Number: 1

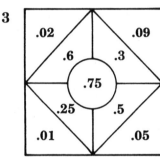

Target Number: 2

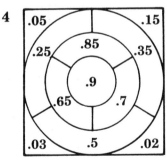

Target Number: 3

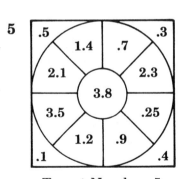

Target Number: 5

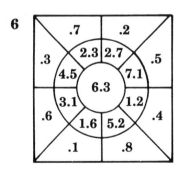

Target Number: 10

Have Fun with Math

Equalities and Inequalities with Decimals

Use the symbol < (is less than), > (is more than), or = (is equal to) that correctly fills each circle in the problems below. The first one has been completed as an example. Time is limited to 25 minutes.

(1) 17.8 − 4.2 (<) 9.6 + 6.7

(2) .7 + .7 ◯ 2.45 − 1.06

(3) 6.7 − 1.7 ◯ 1.68 + 3.12

(4) 9.1 − 3.78 ◯ 2.87 + 2.45

(5) .9 − .14 ◯ .17 + .59

(6) 10.0 − 7.37 ◯ 100.0 − 73.7

(7) 8.47 − 3.2 ◯ 3.3 + 1.97

(8) 2.85 + 1.87 ◯ 6.87 − 1.97

(9) 11.48 − 3.58 ◯ 13.53 − 5.63

(10) 12.38 − 3.47 ◯ 14.2 − 4.71

(11) 19.07 − 6.03 ◯ 9.39 + 3.62

(12) 5.67 + 3.18 ◯ 12.6 − 3.72

(13) 3.57 + 1.28 ◯ 8.61 − 3.76

(14) 16.72 − 3.19 ◯ 6.38 + 7.05

(15) 4.312 + 2.397 ◯ 9.919 − 3.209

(16) 1.487 − .182 ◯ .3768 + .5178

(17) 21.65 − 3.55 ◯ 12.42 + 5.59

(18) .483 − .206 ◯ 3.152 − 2.875

(19) 2.576 − 1.825 ◯ .8 − .053

(20) .825 + .368 ◯ 4.03 − 2.035

(21) .5361 + .86 ◯ 5.0 − 3.603

(22) 4.0 − 3.068 ◯ .032 + .9

(23) 3.8 − 3.14 ◯ .63 + .029

(24) 8.1 + 2.688 − 7.307 ◯ 7.01 − 4.309 + .78

(25) 3.3 + 7.88 − .093 ◯ 8.8 + 2.23 − .043

Scores: 0–4, Crawler   5–8, Shuffler   9–12, Walker
          13–17, Jogger   18–22, Runner   23–25, Sprinter

Have Fun with Math

Cross-Number Addition and Subtraction Blocks with Decimals

Fill in the empty cells in each of the blocks below with numbers that will make the additions and subtractions work. The number in the lower right corner cell of a block should "check out" both vertically and horizontally.

1

1.9	+	.09	=	
+	■	+	■	+
.08	+	2.3	=	
=	■	=	■	=
	+		=	

2

7.4	−	4.596	=	
−	■	−	■	−
5.024	−	3.9	=	
=	■	=	■	=
	−		=	

3

25.6	−	5.24	=	
+	■	+	■	+
1.64	−	.05	=	
=	■	=	■	=
	−		=	

4

1.357	+		=	
+	■	+	■	+
	+	3.09	=	3.133
=	■	=	■	=
	+	7.89	=	

5

	−	5.09	=	3.81
−	■	−	■	−
6.085	−		=	
=	■	=	■	=
	−		=	1.43

6

5.4	+		=	
−	■	−	■	−
	+	.038	=	
=	■	=	■	=
	+	2.902	=	6.4

Have Fun with Math

Magic Square Puzzles with Decimals

Magic square puzzles with decimals are like the magic square puzzles with whole numbers or fractions. The difference is that decimal numbers are used instead of whole numbers or fractions.

Some of the numbers in each puzzle below are missing. These missing numbers can be found, since the sums of the numbers in each column, row, and diagonal are the same. For example, the first puzzle was solved by noting that the sum of the numbers in one diagonal is 3.9 (1.56 + 1.3 + 1.04). The missing number in the cell in the middle vertical column was found by subtracting the sum of the two numbers in the column from the "magic sum" (3.9 less 1.3 + 2.34). The missing numbers in the other cells were found in a similar way.

Try solving the other puzzles on this sheet.

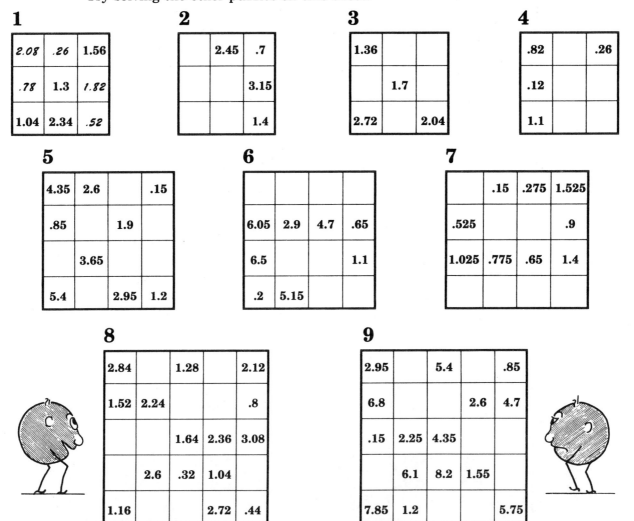

1

2.08	.26	1.56
.78	1.3	1.82
1.04	2.34	.52

2

	2.45	.7
		3.15
		1.4

3

1.36		
	1.7	
2.72		2.04

4

	.82		.26
.12		
1.1		

5

4.35	2.6		.15
.85		1.9	
	3.65		
5.4		2.95	1.2

6

6.05	2.9	4.7	.65
6.5			1.1
.2	5.15		

7

	.15	.275	1.525
.525			.9
1.025	.775	.65	1.4

8

2.84		1.28		2.12
1.52	2.24			.8
		1.64	2.36	3.08
	2.6	.32	1.04	
1.16			2.72	.44

9

2.95		5.4		.85
6.8			2.6	4.7
.15	2.25	4.35		
	6.1	8.2	1.55	
7.85	1.2			5.75

Have Fun with Math

Six-Pointed Magic Star Puzzle with Decimals

The characteristics of the magic star, as diagrammed below, are as follows:

1. Six rows with four numbers in a row; the six sums of the numbers in each of the six rows are equal.
2. Three rows with three numbers in a row; the three sums of the numbers in each of the three rows are equal.
3. Six triangles that form the points of the star, with three numbers in a triangle; the six sums of the three numbers in each of the six triangles are the same.
4. The three sums of the three numbers in each of the three rows and the sums of the three numbers in each of the six triangles are the same.

The numbers in this magic star are all decimals. Five of the thirteen decimal numbers that make up the star are given. From the five given numbers, and using the characteristics of the six-pointed magic star, you can find the other eight numbers. See if you can complete the numbers that make up the magic star. Check your results carefully to make sure that all the requirements for this six-pointed magic star are met.

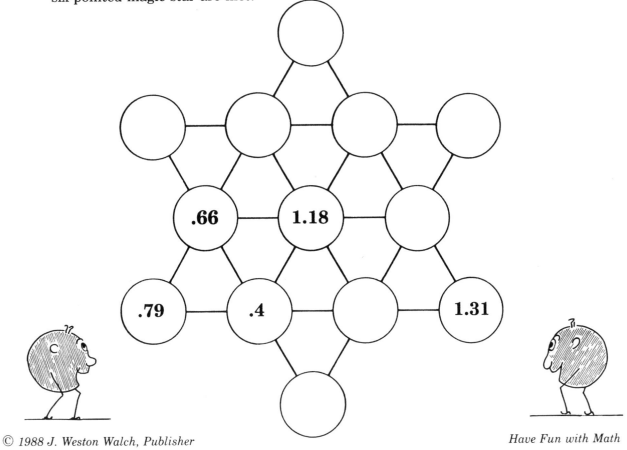

Have Fun with Math

Magic Multiplication Wheel Puzzles with Decimals

Try to rearrange the decimal numbers from around each wheel at the left in the corresponding wheel at the right so that the numbers of the diameters (the numbers at each end of a diameter plus the number at the hub) of the corresponding wheel have the same cumulative product.

1
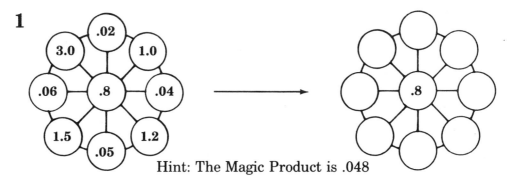
Hint: The Magic Product is .048

2
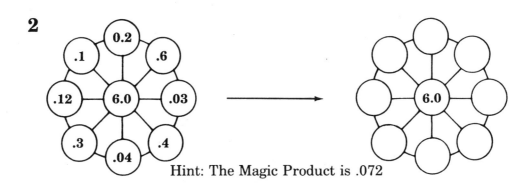
Hint: The Magic Product is .072

3
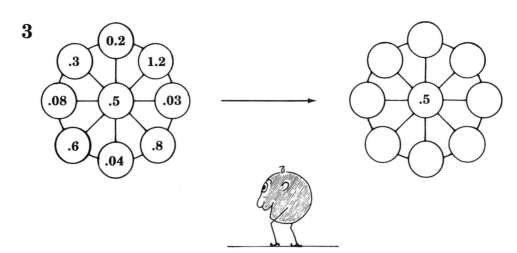

Have Fun with Math

Cross-Number Multiplication and Division Blocks with Decimals

Fill in the empty cells in each of the blocks below with numbers that will make the multiplications and divisions work. The number in the lower right corner cell of a block should "check out" both vertically and horizontally.

1

2.4	×	4.5	=	
×		×		×
1.5	×	3.4	=	
=		=		=
	×		=	

2

1.2	÷	2.5	=	
÷		÷		÷
.6	÷	.05	=	
=		=		=
	÷		=	

3

2.4	÷	1.25	=	
÷		×		÷
1.6	×	.2	=	
=		=		=
	÷		=	

4

.024	×		=	
×		×		×
	×	.7	=	
=		=		=
	×	8.4	=	5.04

5

.66	÷		=	
÷		÷		÷
	÷	.75	=	.08
=		=		=
	÷	.04	=	

6

	×	4.8	=	32.16
×		÷		×
.8	÷		=	
=		=		=
	×		=	321.6

Have Fun with Math

Magic Multiplication Squares with Decimals

In a multiplication magic square the products of the numbers in each row, column, and diagonal are the same. The squares below are all magic multiplication squares. The first magic square has been correctly completed as an example. Study this magic square carefully. Then try to find the decimal numbers that complete the other magic multiplication squares.

1

1.0	1.25	.1
.05	.5	5.0
2.5	.2	.25

2

.4		
	.8	
	.05	1.6

3

		5.0
	2.5	6.25
1.25		

4

.3		
3.0	.15	7.5

5

		.4
		12.8
1.6		.1

6

2.7		.3
		72.9
		24.3

Have Fun with Math

Decimal Rings

In the diagram below, concentric rings enclose a circle containing a single decimal number. This number is to act as an addend, subtrahend, multiplier, and divisor in combination with the numbers in the first, inner ring. The numbers in this first ring are to act as addends, minuends, multiplicands, and dividends. You are to find the sums, differences, products, and quotients of these numbers and write them in the respective ring segments. The answers have been provided for combinations in the top central section.

See if you can correctly fill in the answers for all the other sections. A perfect score is 28 correct answers.

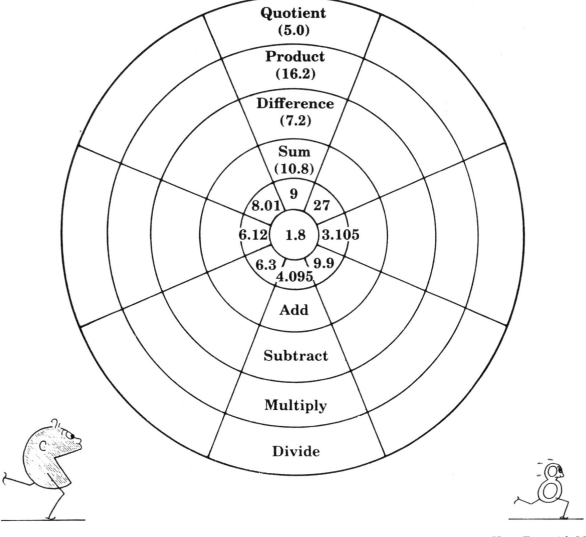

Cross-Number Puzzles with Decimal Numbers

You are given some of the decimal numbers and all of the necessary arithmetical signs that lead to correct horizontal and vertical totals. See if you can insert the numbers in the empty spaces to get the correct totals. There are no zeros. Make sure your solution to a puzzle works out both horizontally and vertically. The first puzzle has been solved as an example.

1

1	÷	.2	×	1.2	=	6
×		+		×		-
3.6	÷	1.2	×	.4	=	1.2
-		+		÷		-
2.4	-	1	+	.6	=	2
=		=		=		=
1.2	+	2.4	-	.8	=	2.8

2

1.2	×	.6	÷		=	1.8
-		+		÷		+
	÷		+		=	
+		+		+		+
	+		-		=	1
=		=		=		=
1.6	+		+	2.2	=	5

3

	×	3	÷	.5	=	1.5
×		÷		+		+
	×		÷		=	1.5
+		-		-		+
2	×		-		=	
=		=		=		=
3	+		-		=	4.5

4

4.5	×		÷		=	6
÷		×		-		-
1.5	+		+		=	
-		÷		+		+
	÷		+		=	2.5
=		=		=		=
2.5	+	4	-		=	5.5

Have Fun with Math

Cross-Number Puzzles with Decimals and Signs of Operation

In the puzzles below, decimal numbers are arranged to provide a given result, but most of the signs of operation are missing. You are to insert the signs of operation in the empty spaces that will give the indicated results. Make sure your solution to a puzzle works out both horizontally and vertically. The first puzzle has been solved as an example.

1

3	÷	1.5	−	1.5	=	.5
×	■	+	■	+	■	×
.5	+	1	+	.5	=	2
+	■	−	■	−	■	+
.5	+	.5	+	1.5	=	2.5
=	■	=	■	=	■	=
2	+	2	−	.5	=	3.5

2

1.2	×	.4		.8	=	.6
+	■		■		■	
.2		.2		.4	=	1.4
	■		■		■	
1.6		.2		.2	=	1.6
=	■	=	■	=	■	=
3		.4		2.2	=	.4

3

1	÷	.4		1.2	=	3
+	■		■		■	
1.8		.6		1	=	3
	■		■		■	
2.4		.6		.6	=	3.6
=	■	=	■	=	■	=
5.2		.4		2	=	3.6

4

2.5	÷	.5		.2	=	1
×	■		■		■	
.2		3		5	=	3
	■		■		■	
.5		1.5		.5	=	1.5
=	■	=	■	=	■	=
1		1		.5	=	2.5

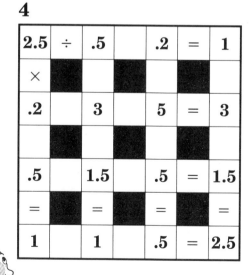

Have Fun with Math

Equal Fractions and Decimals

Circle the two numbers in each of the rows below that are equal. The first item has been completed for you as an example. Time is limited to 15 minutes.

1.	.001	(.1)	($\frac{1}{10}$)	$\frac{1}{100}$
2.	$\frac{1}{20}$	5.0	$\frac{1}{2}$	.05
3.	.25	$\frac{1}{2}$	$\frac{1}{4}$	.52
4.	$2\frac{1}{2}$	.4	.25	$\frac{2}{5}$
5.	.6	$\frac{3}{4}$	.65	$\frac{3}{5}$
6.	$7\frac{1}{2}$	.75	$\frac{3}{4}$	.075
7.	3.2	$\frac{8}{25}$	$3\frac{1}{5}$	.165
8.	.027	$2\frac{7}{10}$	$\frac{27}{100}$	2.7
9.	.19	$1\frac{9}{10}$	1.9	$9\frac{1}{10}$
10.	7.5	$\frac{3}{4}$	.075	$7\frac{1}{2}$
11.	6.25	.625	$6\frac{1}{2}$	$\frac{5}{8}$
12.	$\frac{7}{8}$	8.75	.875	$\frac{3}{4}$
13.	$5\frac{4}{5}$	5.8	.58	$\frac{5}{8}$
14.	.625	$\frac{1}{32}$	.0625	$\frac{1}{16}$
15.	4.3	.43	$\frac{43}{1000}$	$4\frac{3}{10}$
16.	$\frac{5}{8}$	$6\frac{3}{8}$	6.375	.6375
17.	.125	$\frac{1}{16}$	$\frac{1}{8}$	.8
18.	$\frac{1}{6}$	$.08\frac{1}{3}$	.625	$\frac{1}{12}$
19.	$.16\frac{2}{3}$	$\frac{1}{6}$	$.66\frac{2}{3}$	$\frac{1}{3}$
20.	.875	$\frac{5}{6}$	$.83\frac{1}{3}$	$\frac{2}{3}$
21.	.032	$3\frac{1}{5}$	.32	$\frac{8}{25}$
22.	$\frac{1}{30}$	$\frac{1}{3}$	$3\frac{1}{3}$	$.33\frac{1}{3}$
23.	$.66\frac{2}{3}$	$1\frac{2}{3}$	6.6	$\frac{2}{3}$
24.	$\frac{3}{200}$	.0015	.015	$\frac{3}{20}$
25.	$26\frac{1}{2}$	$2\frac{5}{8}$	2.625	26.25

Scores:

0–4, Very Sad — 5–8, Sad
9–12, Almost Sad — 13–17, Almost Glad
18–22, Glad — 23–25, Very Glad

Addition and Subtraction Rings with Fractions and Decimals

In the arrangements below, each number in the outer ring of a circle is the sum of the adjoining number in the inner ring and the number in the center circle. Conversely, each number in the inner ring of a circle is the difference when the number in the center circle is subtracted from the number in the adjoining outer ring. You are challenged to fill in the vacant spaces correctly using decimals. The first circle has been correctly filled in as an example.

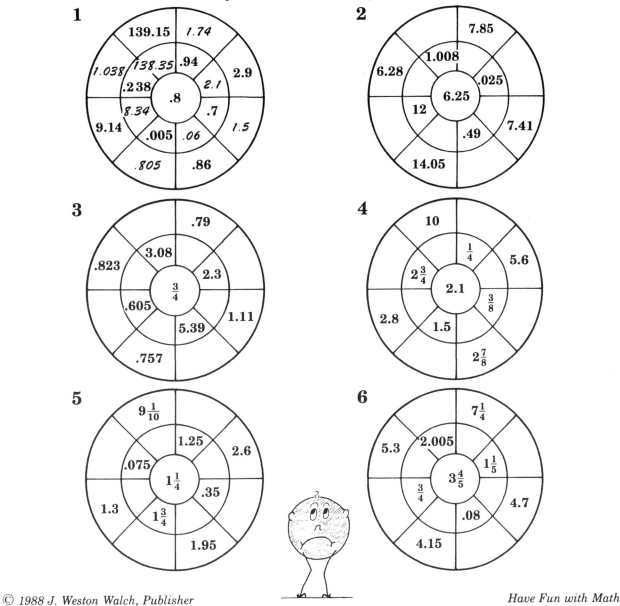

Have Fun with Math

Lineup with Fractions and Decimals

Draw a straight line through any three numbers in a block that are lined up in order of their size (smaller to larger or larger to smaller). The straight lines may be horizontal, vertical, or diagonal. It may be possible to draw more than one straight line in a block. The first block has been completed as an example.

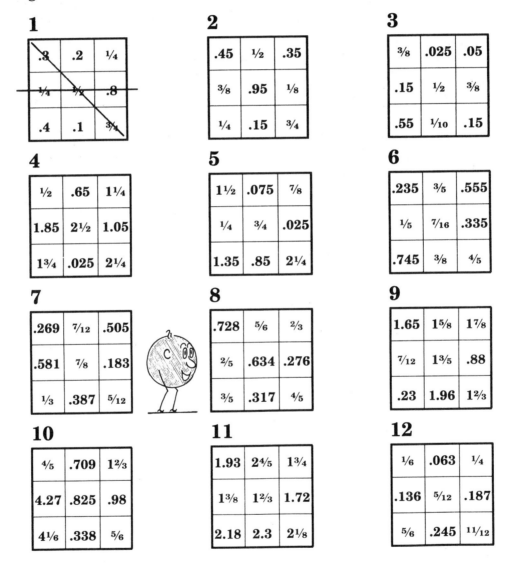

1

.3	.2	¼
¼	½	.8
.4	.1	¾

2

.45	½	.35
⅜	.95	⅛
¼	.15	¾

3

⅜	.025	.05
.15	½	⅜
.55	¹⁄₁₀	.15

4

½	.65	1¼
1.85	2½	1.05
1¾	.025	2¼

5

1½	.075	⅞
¼	¾	.025
1.35	.85	2¼

6

.235	⅗	.555
⅕	⁷⁄₁₆	.335
.745	⅜	⅘

7

.269	⁷⁄₁₂	.505
.581	⅞	.183
⅓	.387	⁵⁄₁₂

8

.728	⅚	⅔
⅖	.634	.276
⅗	.317	⅘

9

1.65	1⅝	1⅞
⁷⁄₁₂	1⅗	.88
.23	1.96	1⅔

10

⅘	.709	1⅔
4.27	.825	.98
4⅙	.338	⅚

11

1.93	2⅘	1¾
1⅜	1⅔	1.72
2.18	2.3	2⅛

12

⅙	.063	¼
.136	⁵⁄₁₂	.187
⅚	.245	¹¹⁄₁₂

Have Fun with Math

Multiplication and Division Rings with Fractions and Decimals

In the arrangements below, each number in the outer ring of a circle is the product of the adjoining number in the inner ring and the number in the center of the circle. Conversely, each number in the inner ring of a circle is the quotient when the adjoining number in the outer ring is divided by the number in the center of the circle. You are challenged to fill in the vacant spaces correctly using decimals. The first circle has been correctly filled in as an example.

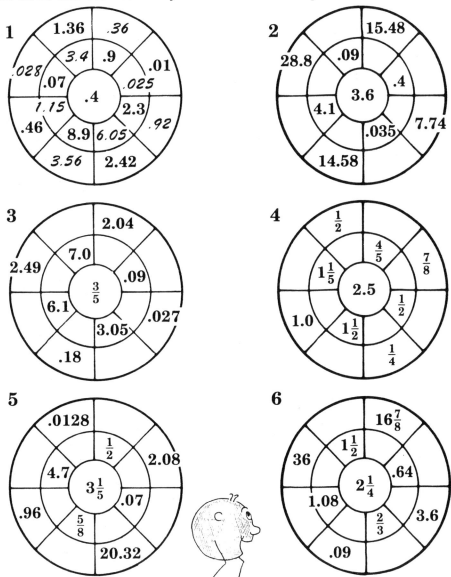

Have Fun with Math

Repeating Decimals

Decimals like .333 . . ., .666 . . ., and .3939 . . ., often written as .33$\overline{3}$, .66$\overline{6}$, and .39$\overline{39}$, which have a digit or a group of digits repeating endlessly, are called repeating decimals. The bar indicates the repeating sequence; the dots, although unnecessary, can be used to indicate that the sequence repeats endlessly.

Below are some fractions that provide repeating decimals. Satisfy yourself that the decimals do repeat endlessly. Carry divisions to six or more places.

$5/6$ = _____ $7/12$ = _____ $2/15$ = _____

$8/27$ = _____ $5/37$ = _____ $23/33$ = _____

Some fractions provide interesting decimal number patterns. Observe the results when such fractions are changed to decimals. Carry each of the following to six decimal places.

$1/9$ = _____ $1/99$ = _____

$2/9$ = _____ $2/99$ = _____

$3/9$ = _____ $5/99$ = _____

$4/9$ = _____ $8/99$ = _____

$5/9$ = _____ $10/99$ = _____

$6/9$ = _____ $16/99$ = _____

$7/9$ = _____ $56/99$ = _____

$8/9$ = _____ $75/99$ = _____

$1/11$ = _____ $1/999$ = _____

$2/11$ = _____ $2/999$ = _____

$3/11$ = _____ $5/999$ = _____

$4/11$ = _____ $8/999$ = _____

$5/11$ = _____ $16/999$ = _____

$6/11$ = _____ $56/999$ = _____

$7/11$ = _____ $75/999$ = _____

$8/11$ = _____ $90/999$ = _____

$9/11$ = _____ $175/999$ = _____

$10/11$ = _____ $587/999$ = _____

Have Fun with Math

Fun Test on Everyday Math

Below are ten problems you might expect to encounter during a day. Write each answer in the space provided below each problem. Test time is limited to 15 minutes.

1. You go to the market with eight deposit bottles valued at 12¢ each and buy groceries priced at $12.87. How much change do you get from a $20 bill?
   Answer: _____

2. Test your mental arithmetic (do not write the figures down to add them). How much is 36¢ and 69¢?   Answer: _____

3. You shop at a market and buy one each of these items:
   Coffee @ 2 jars for $5.79.   Soda @ 2 bottles for 89¢.
   Applesauce @ 2 cans for 85¢.   Creamed corn @ 3 cans for $1.49.
   How much is your bill?   Answer: _____

4. At your local market you get two merchant trading stamps, valued at a tenth of a cent each, for each 10¢ you spend. How much must you spend to get enough stamps for an electric can opener priced at $14.98?
   Answer: _____

5. Arriving at an airport, you plan in advance to make two local telephone calls (25¢ each), three suburban calls (40¢ each), and one long-distance call ($1.45). How many coins will you need for exact change?
   Answer: _____

6. You receive a yellow and blue sweater for your birthday and decide to exchange it. At the store you get a merchandise credit slip for $33.75. You select a shirt priced at $12.95 and also buy slacks for $29.85. How much cash must you pay out?   Answer: _____

7. On your first day at work as a clerk in a store, a customer buys an item for $4.79 and hands you a $20 bill. How many of each of the listed currency items must you return as change?
   Answer: $10 ( ); $5 ( ); $1 ( ); 25¢ ( ); 10¢ ( ); 5¢ ( ); 1¢ ( ).

8. To call a friend from a phone booth you need 95¢ for the first three minutes and 55¢ for each additional three minutes. You plan to talk for 15 minutes. What is the minimum number of coins you will need?
   Answer: _____

9. Suppose the clerk at a corner drug store specializes in illegible figures. He has just scribbled the amounts of your purchases at the right of a scrap of paper. What is their total?   Answer: _____
   1.74
   .89   2.64
   .37

10. Your bill at a restaurant is $4.65, and you decide to tip the waitress 90¢. Because you have only 20¢ in nickels, you give her six dollar bills and ask for change. The waitress has only two quarters in change. Without changing your plans, how do you solve this problem?   Answer: _____

Scores: 0–1, Frigid; 2–3, Cold; 4–5, Cool; 6–7, Warm; 8–9, Steaming; 10, Volcanic.

Have Fun with Math

Mystic Square with Fractions and Decimals

Solve each of the 16 problems in the list below. Then place the decimal equivalent answer for each problem in the respective cell of the square. When all the answers have been placed in their cells, find the sums of the rows of answers, columns of answers, and diagonal of answers. If the answers are all correct, all the sums will be the same.

Sum

1.	2.	3.	4.	
5.	6.	7.	8.	
9.	10.	11.	12.	
13.	14.	15.	16.	

Sum

1. $2\frac{3}{4}$ + 7.05 + $1\frac{5}{8}$ + 2.575
2. $7\frac{1}{4}$ − 5.85
3. .25 × $9\frac{1}{5}$
4. 29.38 ÷ $2\frac{3}{5}$
5. Find the sum of $1\frac{3}{8}$, 1.925, and $\frac{4}{5}$.
6. Determine the product of 5.7 and $1\frac{2}{3}$ and round to the nearest tenth.
7. Divide 40.85 by $4\frac{3}{4}$.
8. Subtract $3\frac{3}{8}$ from 10.175.
9. 8.725 − $3\frac{3}{5}$ + 2.575
10. $19\frac{2}{3}$ × .24 ÷ $\frac{4}{5}$ rounded to the nearest tenth.
11. 3.75 × $3\frac{1}{3}$ × .4 rounded to the nearest tenth.
12. 21.44 − ($6\frac{9}{10}$ + 4.14)
13. Find the product of $\frac{1}{5}$, 1.2, and $13\frac{1}{3}$ and round to the nearest tenth.
14. Determine the sum of $6\frac{3}{8}$, 1.6, and 4.225.
15. Find the difference between 25.58 and the sum of $9\frac{3}{50}$ and $3\frac{5}{12}$.
16. Divide the product of $3\frac{1}{3}$ and .24 by $1\frac{3}{5}$ and round to the nearest tenth.

Have Fun with Math

Cross-Number Decimals Puzzle

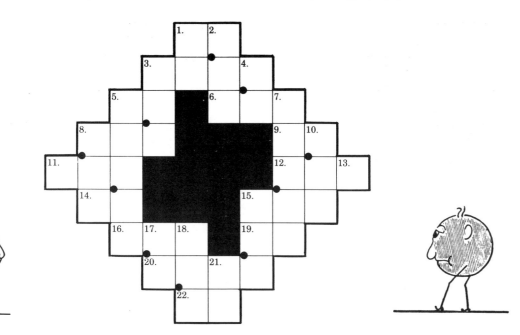

Across

1. Which is the larger: 3.5 or .53?
3. Write in figures: Four hundred and four tenths.
5. Round off 6.3399 to the nearest tenth.
6. 400.4 + 70.07 + 8.808 + 1.722
8. 1 − .128
9. 3.5 × 2.4
11. 8.4 ÷ .375
12. .58 is .8 of what number?
14. 2.44 × 25
15. 40⅜ + 56.025 + 27⅗
16. The product of 2.1 and 1⅕
19. Change ¹⁷/₂₅ to a decimal number.
20. 368.1 ÷ 50
22. Solve: $\dfrac{7.7 \times .08 \times 1.5}{.06 \times .35}$

Down

1. 3.076 + 19.95 + .974 + 6.0
2. 1.764 is .35 of what number?
3. 140.4 ÷ 3¼
4. Express 4⅘ as a decimal number.
5. Divide 33.706 by .05.
7. Subtract 12.72 from 200.
8. 13.135 − 4⅞
10. .16 × 26.5
11. Multiply 5⅓ by .375 and round to the nearest whole number.
13. Solve: $\dfrac{2.5 \times 3.6 \times .28}{.06 \times .24 \times 35}$
15. Round off 16.1512 to the nearest tenth.
17. Divide 142.5 by 25.
18. Number of times 4 is contained in 93.6.
21. Multiply 1.28 by 50.

Have Fun with Math

How Well Do You Know Decimals?

Do you think you know all about decimal numbers? Here's a chance for you to find out. Select the answer for each problem that you think is correct. Then place the letter of your choice in the space provided to the left of the problem. Time is limited to 15 minutes.

_____ 1. What part of 8 is 4 more than 3?
(a) .125 (b) .375 (c) .625 (d) .875 (e) Answer is not listed.

_____ 2. What decimal part of 4 is .4 of 2?
(a) .5 (b) .2 (c) 1.8 (d) 2.0 (e) Answer is not listed.

_____ 3. If .75 of a number is 1.2, what is the number?
(a) 1.6 (b) 2.4 (c) .24 (d) .9 (e) Answer is not listed.

_____ 4. What decimal part of 12 is 3 less than .6 of 15?
(a) .05 (b) .6 (c) .25 (d) .3 (e) Answer is not listed.

_____ 5. What decimal part of 5 is .5 of 6?
(a) .06 (b) .5 (c) .6 (d) .05 (e) Answer is not listed.

_____ 6. Divide 15 by .3 and add 15 to the quotient.
(a) 20 (b) 45 (c) 55 (d) 65 (e) Answer is not listed.

_____ 7. How much more is .3 less than 6 than .6 more than 3?
(a) 1.2 (b) 9.3 (c) 2.1 (d) .36 (e) Answer is not listed.

_____ 8. Add 20 to .5 and divide the sum by .5.
(a) 5 (b) 41 (c) 25 (d) 52 (e) Answer is not listed.

_____ 9. Find the sum of ½ of .4 and ¼ of .5.
(a) 1.75 (b) .127 (c) .375 (d) 3.75 (e) Answer is not listed.

_____ 10. Express the result of dividing .6 of 4 by .4 of 5 as a decimal fraction.
(a) 1.2 (b) .46 (c) 12 (d) .883 (e) Answer is not listed.

Scores:

0–1, Snorer	2–3, Sleeper
4–5, Dozer	6–7, Mover
8–9, Doer	10, Accomplisher

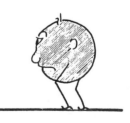

Have Fun with Math

Secret Message Using Decimals

The answer to each problem in the list below, when rounded off to the nearest whole number, represents a letter of the alphabet. When all the letters have been assembled in respective order, they form the words of a message. Using the alphabet-number chart to decode the letters, see if you can determine the secret message.

A	B	C	D	E	F	G	H	I	J	K	L	M	N	O	P	Q	R	S	T	U	V	W	X	Y	Z
1	2	3	4	5	6	7	8	9	10	11	12	13	14	15	16	17	18	19	20	21	22	23	24	25	26

_ _ _ _ _   _ _   _   _ _ _ _ _   _ _   _ _ _ _ _ _ _ .

_____ Which is the smallest: 21.3, 31.2, 132, or 13.2?

_____ Round off .09 to the nearest number of 12ths.

_____ 4.25 + .037 + 13.7 + .576 + 1.208

_____ 14.28 − 5.9

_____ 1.78 × 5.23

_____ 26.22 ÷ 1.38

_____ How many times is .3125 contained in 5/16?

_____ Find the sum of .6, 3.06, .826, 1.057, and 14.3.

_____ Subtract 5.837 from 21.05.

_____ Determine the product of 2.18 and 6.945.

_____ If 47.6 is the dividend and 3.87 is the divisor, find the quotient.

_____ 5.4 is .36 of what number?

_____ .15 × 9.6 ÷ .24

_____ Multiply 14¾ by 1.59.

_____ Subtract 6⅗ from the product of 2.4 and 6.5.

_____ Divide the sum of 8.02 and 132⅕ by 7.38.

_____ .76 of what number is 3.04?

_____ 2.1 × 1¼ ÷ .175

_____ $\dfrac{2.6 \times 1.4 \times .15}{.012 \times 3.5}$

Have Fun with Math

Cross-Number Review Puzzle through Decimals

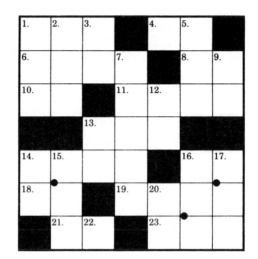

Across

1. Nearest number of thousands in 125,499.
4. Subtract 2,987 from 3,076.
6. Divide 123,027 by 69.
8. Least common denominator for $\frac{2}{3}$, $\frac{3}{4}$, and $\frac{5}{8}$.
10. Number of 12ths in $2\frac{1}{6}$.
11. $6\frac{1}{3} + 289\frac{1}{2} + 1005\frac{3}{4} + 34\frac{5}{12}$
13. $6\frac{2}{3} \times 5\frac{1}{4} \times 7\frac{1}{5}$
14. Which is the smallest: 9.634, 436.9, 6.349, or 36.49?
16. Divide 67.86 by 7.8.
18. $1\frac{7}{8} \times 8.8 \times 2\frac{2}{3}$
19. $1.44 \times 2\frac{3}{4} \div .16$
21. 10.8 is .45 of what number?
23. Solve: $\dfrac{6.3 \times .08 \times 1.6}{.04 \times .5 \times .12}$

Down

1. $3.2 \times 4\frac{2}{3} \times 7.5$
2. $13.8 \div .05$
3. $92.8 \times .625$
4. Numerator when $2\frac{2}{3}$ is changed to an improper fraction.
5. $8 + 34 + 689 + 103 + 82 + 7$
7. Multiply 359 by 88.
9. Nearest number of hundreds in 4,551.
12. $44\frac{4}{5} \div 1\frac{2}{5}$
13. $3\frac{3}{5} \times 6\frac{2}{3}$
14. Solve: $\dfrac{63 \times 96 \times 240}{12 \times 35 \times 54}$
15. Write as a decimal number: Three and forty-two hundredths.
16. Add 12.33 to the product of 7.65 and 9.8.
17. Change $7\frac{14}{25}$ to a decimal number.
20. 34.4 is .8 of what number?
22. $3\frac{1}{3} \times 5.6 \div 4\frac{2}{3}$

Have Fun with Math

We must be related!

1¢

Part IV
Percent

Equal Fractions, Decimals, and Percents

Each of the lines below has fraction, decimal, and percent expressions. You are to cross out the two expressions in each line that are *not* equal. Time is limited to 20 minutes. The first line has been solved as an example.

1.	~~1/20~~	1/2	50%	~~15%~~	.5
2.	2½%	.25	40%	¼	25%
3.	12½%	.125	⅛	.8	8%
4.	.33⅓	30%	33⅓%	3/100	⅓
5.	⅙	12%	.16⅔	1/12	16⅔%
6.	.66⅔	5/6	66⅔%	⅔	56%
7.	75%	¾	8½%	.75	3/40
8.	5/8	66⅔%	.625	7/12	62½%
9.	83⅓%	.67½	⅞	.83⅓	5/6%
10.	.875	83½%	⅞	5/6	87½%
11.	1/10	.001	10%	.1	1%
12.	.4	4%	.4%	40%	⅖
13.	700%	7/10	.07	70%	.7
14.	½%	1/25	1/200	5%	.005
15.	.16	⅙	16%	4/25	1.6%
16.	120%	1⅕	12%	.012	1.2
17.	5.3%	53%	.53	53/100	.0053
18.	.055	11/200	55%	5½%	.555
19.	.065	65%	6¼%	.65	13/20
20.	.062	.62	31/50	62%	6⅕
21.	5 5/9	55 5/9%	5/9	59%	.55 5/9
22.	17.5	1¾	175%	1.75	17½%
23.	3/50	.006	.6	3/500	.6%
24.	1⅗	160%	16.0	16%	1.6
25.	275%	.275	11/40	27½%	11/25

Scores:

0–4, Very Drab   5–8, Drab
9–12, Almost Drab   13–17, Almost Bright
18–22, Bright   23–25, Very Bright

Have Fun with Math

Lineup with Fractions, Decimals, and Percents

Draw a straight line through any three numbers in a block that are in order of their values (smaller to larger or larger to smaller). It may be possible to draw more than one straight line in a block. The straight lines may be horizontal, vertical, or diagonal. A lineup in the first block has been marked as an example. Try to find the lineups in the other blocks.

1

$3/4$	20%	$3/5$
.95	50%	.8
.45	$1/3$	70%

2

.2	$1/4$	28%
$1/3$	$1/10$	.3
12%	.35	16%

3

$1/2$	10%	$3/4$
15%	.12	20%
.3	$1/8$	.27

4

48%	.36	$2/3$
$1/6$	.2	24%
$3/8$	28%	.87

5

$9/10$	70%	80%
78%	.62	$3/4$
.875	$2/3$	.7

6

$5/8$	60%	$13/20$
57%	.7	$7/12$
.615	$2/5$	75%

7

6%	.37	$1/3$
.875	$2/3$	90%
$1/12$	10%	.15

8

$1/2$%	$1/2$	.05
.01	.4	12%
$1/10$	70%	.045

9

$14/25$	38%	$2/5$
.52	.6	35%
65%	$11/20$	.58

10

$1 3/4$	170%	1.6
42%	.12	$5/12$
.56	$3/5$	62%

11

.005	.2%	$3/20$
$3/500$	.4%	.01
.7%	.005	$1/5$

12

.3	$1/15$	22%
60%	$1/4$	.85
$1/3$	.05	20%

Have Fun with Math

Using a Six-Pointed Magic Star with Finding the Percent of a Number

Listed below the star diagram are twelve problems on finding a percent of a number. Round each answer to the nearest tenth. Place each answer in the circle of the star with the same number as the problem. If your answers are all correct, any four answers in a row will have the same total (53.8) as any other four answers in a row.

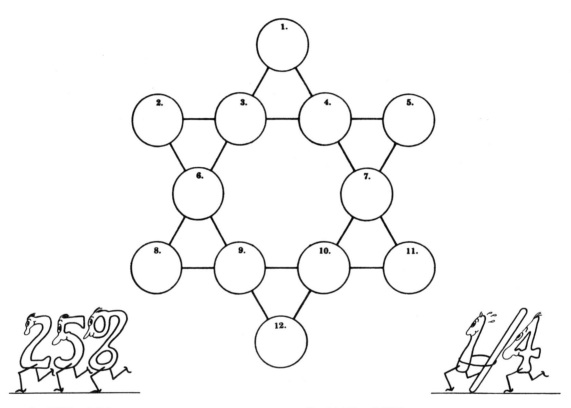

1. 25% of 86
2. 75% of 16.4
3. 20% of 96
4. 33⅓% of 50.7
5. 12½% of 43.2
6. 5% of 200

7. 2½% of 584
8. 6.2% of 50
9. 119% of 20
10. 83⅓% of 31.32
11. 16% of 5
12. 3.3% of 220

Have Fun with Math

Using a Five-Pointed Magic Star with Finding What Percent One Number Is of Another

Listed below the star diagram are ten problems on finding what percent one number is of another. Place each answer in the circle of the star with the same number as the problem. If your answers are all correct, any four answers in a row will total 100%.

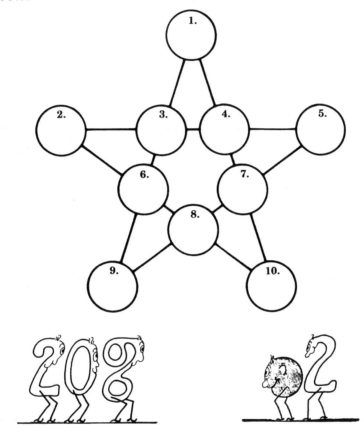

1. What percent of 125 is 62?
2. What percent of 50 is 20.7?
3. 2.52 is what percent of 56?
4. 42 is what percent of 250?
5. 14.92 is _____% of 40?

6. 15.24 is _____% of 120?
7. 43 is _____% of 500?
8. What percent of 400 is 83.6?
9. What percent of 18.5 is 6.142?
10. 32 is what percent of 128?

Have Fun with Math

Using a Six-Pointed Magic Star with Finding a Number When a Percent of It Is Known

Listed below the star diagram are twelve problems on finding a number when a percent of it is known. Place each answer in the circle of the star with the same number as the problem. If your answers are all correct, any four answers in a row will have the same total (201) as any other four answers in a row. Also, the sum of the three answers that make up any point of the star (128) is the same as the sum of the three answers that make up any other point of the star.

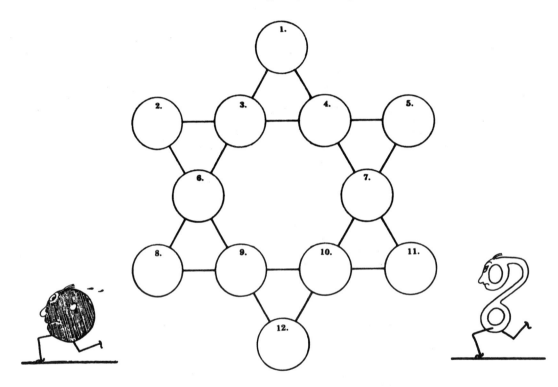

1. 10% of what number is 5.9?

2. 12 is 15% of what number?

3. 25% of what number is 9.5?

4. 1.55 is 5% of what number?

5. 100% of what number is 52?

6. 2 is 20% of what number?

7. 200% of what number is 90?

8. 2.35 is 2½% of what number?

9. 66⅔% of what number is 16?

10. 6.12 is 36% of what number?

11. 83⅓% of what number is 55?

12. 135.72 is 156% of what number?

Have Fun with Math

Percent Problem Chart

The chart below gives the three types of percent problems: (1) Finding the percent of a number (percentage and base given), (2) finding what percent one number is of another (base and percentage given), and (3) finding a number when a percent of it is known (percent and percentage given). The first problem has been done as an example. Try to find the other missing numbers. Time is limited to 20 minutes.

No.	Percent	Base	Percentage
1.	18%	46	*8.28*
2.		12	6
3.	36%		18
4.	6%	24	
5.	25%		6
6.		8	7
7.	3%	5,000	
8.		54	45
9.	6%		12
10.	83⅓%	582	
11.	120%		108
12.		38	38
13.	40%		12.6
14.		935	561
15.	4½%	624	
16.	60¾%	940	
17.		$34.00	$1.70
18.	2½%		2
19.	187½%		210
20.		10½	3½
21.	.5%		8
22.		25	13
23.	6%	$14.50	
24.	¾%	54	
25.		10	18

Scores:
0–4, Finished Last   5–8, Future Looks Bad
9–12, Wait Till Next Year   13–17, In the Playoffs
18–22, Super Bowler   23–25, Super Bowl Champ

Have Fun with Math

Mystic Square with Percent

Solve each of the 16 problems in the list below. Then place each answer in the cell of the square with the same number as the problem. When all the answers have been placed in the square, find the sums of the rows of answers, columns of answers, and diagonal of answers. If the answers are all correct, all the sums will be the same.

Sum

1.	2.	3.	4.	
5.	6.	7.	8.	
9.	10.	11.	12.	
13.	14.	15.	16.	
Sum				

1. Express 80% as a decimal number.
2. Numerator when 95% is expressed as a fraction and reduced to its simplest form.
3. Find 15% of 118.
4. 9.4 is what percent of 200, expressed as a decimal?
5. 7.55 is 50% of what number?
6. Express 730% as a decimal number.
7. Determine 33⅓% of 25.8 and round to the nearest tenth.
8. Percent, expressed as a decimal, when 126 is divided by 1,125.
9. 12⅜ is 125% of what number?
10. Find the percent, expressed as a decimal, that 14.7 is of 117.6.
11. What number is 2½% of 552?
12. Find 1¼% of 480.
13. 225% of what number is 36.9?
14. What number is 32% less than 5?
15. Find ½% of 420.
16. What percent gain, expressed as a decimal, is an increase from $180 to $216.54?

Have Fun with Math

How Well Do You Know Percent?

Do you think you know all about percent? Here's a chance for you to find out. Select the answer from the list for each question that you feel is correct. Circle your choice. Your time is limited to 15 minutes.

1. 6 is 50% more than what number?
   (a) 9   (b) 3   (c) 4   (d) 12   (e) Answer is not listed.

2. 60% less than what number is 8?
   (a) 10   (b) 16   (c) 48   (d) 20   (e) Answer is not listed.

3. 25 is what percent more than 10?
   (a) 50%   (b) 150%   (c) 200%   (d) 250%   (e) Answer is not listed.

4. This and that and half of this and that is what percent of this and that?
   (a) 150%   (b) 50%   (c) 100%   (d) 0%   (e) Answer is not listed.

5. 12 is 20% more than 50% of what number?
   (a) 8   (b) 12   (c) 20   (d) 28   (e) Answer is not listed.

6. 50% more than 40% of what number is 12?
   (a) 10   (b) 12½   (c) 25   (d) 50   (e) Answer is not listed.

7. 50% of 16 is 20% less than half of what number?
   (a) 24   (b) 20   (c) 40   (d) 64   (e) Answer is not listed.

8. 15 is what percent more than 25% of 20?
   (a) 50%   (b) 75%   (c) 100%   (d) 200%   (e) Answer is not listed.

9. If an advance from 10 to 20 is a gain of 100%, what percent loss is a decline from 20 to 10?
   (a) 50%   (b) 100%   (c) 200%   (d) 33⅓%   (e) Answer is not listed.

10. If a drop from 40 to 10 is a loss of 75%, what is the percent gain from 10 to 40?
    (a) 30%   (b) 75%   (c) 200%   (d) 400%   (e) Answer is not listed.

Scores:
0–1, Very Bitter	2–3, Bitter
4–5, Almost Bitter	6–7, Almost Sweet
8–9, Sweet	10, Very Sweet

Have Fun with Math

Cross-Number Percent Puzzle

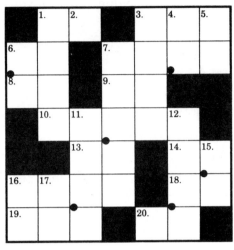

Across

1. Express eighteen hundredths as a percent.
3. How many hundredths are there in 135%?
6. Express 76% as a decimal.
7. Find 6% of $212.00.
8. Numerator when 92% is changed to a fraction.
9. 27 is what percent of 60?
10. Determine ½% of 5,225.
13. 3.36 is 16% of what number?
14. 62½% of 8⅘
16. $47.65 is 125% of what amount?
18. 15% less than that number which is 50% of 2.
19. 186 is 33⅓% less than what whole number?
20. 113.76 is what percent of 158?

Down

1. 800% of 204
2. Numerator when 32% is changed to a fraction.
3. 156.5 is 12½% of what number?
4. Number of hundredths in 37%.
5. Express ¹³⁄₂₅ as a percent.
6. Find 37½% of 19⅕.
7. 25% less than what number is 105.84?
11. What number is 75% of 829.2?
12. 27.91 is 5% of what number?
15. Find the number that is 45% less than 10.
16. 104 is what percent of 325?
17. 304.5 is 350% of what number?
20. Express 700% as a whole number.

Have Fun with Math

Secret Message Using Percent

The answer to each problem in the list below, when rounded off to the nearest whole number, represents a letter of the alphabet. When all the letters have been assembled in respective order, they form the words of a message. Using the alphabet-number chart to obtain the letters, see if you can decode the message.

A	B	C	D	E	F	G	H	I	J	K	L	M	N	O	P	Q	R	S	T	U	V	W	X	Y	Z
1	2	3	4	5	6	7	8	9	10	11	12	13	14	15	16	17	18	19	20	21	22	23	24	25	26

_ .

_____   Number of hundredths in .23.

_____   Express .15 as a percent.

_____   Change 72% to a number of 25ths.

_____   Numerator when 55% is changed to a fraction.

_____ $9/100$ changed to a percent.

_____   Find 20% of 95.

_____   4 is what percent of 400?

_____   What number is 75% of 4?

_____   12 is 80% of what number?

_____   Determine $6\frac{1}{2}$% of 200.

_____   35% of what number is 5.6?

_____   Find .2% of 500.

_____   Percent expressed when $3\frac{1}{2}$ is divided by 25.

_____   3 is $33\frac{1}{3}$% of what number?

_____   What percent is 35 of 235?

_____   Determine $6\frac{1}{4}$% of 225.

_____   5.8 is 39% of what number?

_____ $11\frac{3}{4}$ is what percent of 196?

_____   Find $4\frac{1}{2}$% of 412.

_____   32.5 is 155% of what number?

_____ $5\frac{1}{4}$ is what percent of 175?

_____   What number is 4.8% of $62\frac{1}{2}$?

_____   6 is 20% more than what number?

_____ $14\frac{1}{4}$ is 25% less than what number?

_____   What percent reduction is a price change from $220 to $178?

© 1988 J. Weston Walch, Publisher

Have Fun with Math

Cross-Number Review Puzzle through Percent

Across

1. Nearest number of thousands in 29,498.
3. Subtract 2,987 from 3,043.
4. Divide 6,786 by 87.
5. $22\frac{2}{5} \times 16\frac{7}{8}$
6. Least common denominator for $\frac{1}{4}$, $\frac{3}{8}$, $\frac{1}{6}$, and $\frac{2}{3}$.
8. Find the product of 4.8 and 6.125.
10. $26\frac{1}{4}$ is .625 of what number?
12. $94\frac{1}{3} + 169.3 + 207\frac{3}{4} + 79\frac{1}{6} + 136.45$
14. Express $\frac{8}{25}$ as a percent.
15. Find 3% of $138.00.
17. 152.46 is what percent of 423.5?
18. 34.2 is 360% of what number?
19. $12\frac{1}{2}$% less than what number is 56?

Down

1. Find the product of 36 and 719.
2. Number of hundredths in 96%.
4. Find .7% of 11,000.
5. 5.13 is 15% of what number?
6. $7 + 37 + 148 + 63 + 9$
7. $11\frac{2}{3} \times 4\frac{4}{5} \div 1\frac{1}{6}$
8. Change .465 to nearest number of 5ths.
9. Number of times that 7.8 is contained in 725.4.
11. Divide 45 by $\frac{5}{6}$ and multiply the quotient by 45.1.
13. $\dfrac{35 \times 48 \times 84}{18 \times 28 \times 40}$
16. Subtract 8.55 from the sum of $7\frac{3}{4}$ and $2\frac{2}{5}$.
18. 276.96 is what percent of 288.5?

Have Fun with Math

So you're a couple
of squares?

Part V

Powers and Roots

Interesting Number Patterns with Squares

The results of certain arithmetical operations with numbers that include squares may surprise you. Complete the following expressions by filling in the blanks to observe the patterns.

---

(1)

$1^2 = 0 \times 8 + 1 =$ _____

$3^2 = 1 \times 8 + 1 =$ _____

$5^2 = 3 \times 8 + 1 =$ _____

$7^2 = 6 \times 8 + 1 =$ _____

$9^2 = 10 \times 8 + 1 =$ _____

$11^2 = 15 \times$ _____

$13^2 = 21 \times$ _____

$15^2 = 28 \times$ _____

$17^2 =$ _____

$19^2 =$ _____

(2)

$1 =$ ___^{2}

$1 + 3 =$ ___^{2}

$1 + 3 + 5 =$ ___^{2}

$1 + 3 + 5 + 7 =$ ___^{2}

$1 + 3 + 5 + 7 + 9 =$ ___^{2}

$1 + 3 + 5 + 7 + 9 + 11 =$ ___^{2}

$1 + 3 + 5 + 7 + 9 + 11 + 13 =$ ___^{2}

$1 + 3 + 5 + 7 + 9 + 11 + 13 + 15 =$ ___^{2}

$1 + 3 + 5 + 7 + 9 + 11 + 13 + 15 + 17 =$ ___^{2}

$1 + 3 + 5 + 7 + 9 + 11 + 13 + 15 + 17 + 19 =$ ___^{2}

---

(3)

$2^2 - 1^2 = 4 - 1 =$ _____

$3^2 - 2^2 = 9 - 4 =$ _____

$4^2 - 3^2 = 16 - 9 =$ _____

$5^2 - 4^2 = 25 - 16 =$ _____

$6^2 - 5^2 = 36 - 25 =$ _____

$7^2 - 6^2 = 49 - 36 =$ _____

$8^2 - 7^2 = 64 - 49 =$ _____

$9^2 - 8^2 = 81 - 64 =$ _____

$10^2 - 9^2 = 100 - 81 =$ _____

$11^2 - 10^2 =$ _____

(4)

$(3 \times 1) + 1 = 4 =$ ____^{2}

$(4 \times 2) + 1 = 9 =$ ____^{2}

$(5 \times 3) + 1 = 16 =$ ____^{2}

$(6 \times 4) + 1 = 25 =$ ____^{2}

$(7 \times 5) + 1 = 36 =$ ____^{2}

$(8 \times 6) + 1 =$ ____ $=$ ____^{2}

$(10 \times 8) + 1 =$ ____ $=$ ____^{2}

$(14 \times 12) + 1 =$ ____ $=$ ____^{2}

$(20 \times 22) + 1 =$ ____ $=$ ____^{2}

$(34 \times 36) + 1 =$ ____ $=$ ____^{2}

(5)

$1^2 =$ _____

$11^2 =$ _____

$111^2 =$ _____

$1111^2 =$ _____

$11111^2 =$ _____

$111111^2 =$ _____

$1111111^2 =$ _____

$11111111^2 =$ _____

$111111111^2 =$ _____

Have Fun with Math

More Interesting Number Patterns with Squares

Complete the following arithmetical expressions by filling in the blanks so that you can observe the resulting number patterns. Perhaps you can apply the principles of these patterns to the multiplications of certain numbers. If so, you should be able quickly to write the product to any of the multiplication problems listed at the bottom of the page. Place your answers in the spaces provided.

(A)

$1 \times 3 = (2 - 1) \times (2 + 1) = 2 \times 2 - 1 = 2^2 - 1 = $ _____

$2 \times 4 = (3 - 1) \times (3 + 1) = 3 \times 3 - 1 = 3^2 - 1 = $ _____

$3 \times 5 = (4 - 1) \times (4 + 1) = 4 \times 4 - 1 = 4^2 - 1 = $ _____

$4 \times 6 = (5 - 1) \times (5 + 1) = 5 \times 5 - 1 = 5^2 - 1 = $ _____

$5 \times 7 = (6 - 1) \times (6 + 1) = 6 \times 6 - 1 = $ _____

$6 \times 8 = (7 - 1) \times (7 + 1) = 7 \times 7 - 1 = $ _____

$7 \times 9 = (8 - 1) \times (8 + 1) = 8 \times 8 - 1 = $ _____

$8 \times 10 = (9 - 1) \times (9 + 1) = 9 \times 9 - 1 = $ _____

$14 \times 16 = (15 - 1) \times (15 + 1) = $ _____

$19 \times 21 = (20 - 1) \times (20 + 1) = $ _____

$49 \times 51 = (50 - 1) \times (50 + 1) = $ _____

$99 \times 101 = (100 - 1) \times (100 + 1) = $ _____

(B)

$8 \times 12 = (10 - 2) \times (10 + 2) = 100 - 4 = $ _____

$13 \times 17 = (15 - 2) \times (15 + 2) = 225 - 4 = $ _____

$18 \times 22 = (20 - 2) \times (20 + 2) = 400 - 4 = $ _____

$24 \times 26 = (25 - 1) \times (25 + 1) = 625 - 1 = $ _____

$23 \times 27 = (25 - 2) \times (25 + 2) = 625 - 4 = $ _____

$7 \times 13 = (10 - 3) \times (10 + 3) = 100 - 9 = $ _____

$12 \times 18 = (15 - 3) \times (15 + 3) = $ _____

$22 \times 28 = (25 - 3) \times (25 + 3) = $ _____

$46 \times 54 = (50 - 4) \times (50 + 4) = $ _____

(C)

$1\frac{1}{2} \times 2\frac{1}{2} = 2 \times 2 - \frac{1}{4} = $ _____

$2\frac{1}{2} \times 3\frac{1}{2} = 3 \times 3 - \frac{1}{4} = $ _____

$3\frac{1}{2} \times 4\frac{1}{2} = 4 \times 4 - \frac{1}{4} = $ _____

$4\frac{1}{2} \times 5\frac{1}{2} = 5 \times 5 - \frac{1}{4} = $ _____

$5\frac{1}{2} \times 6\frac{1}{2} = $ _____

$7\frac{1}{2} \times 8\frac{1}{2} = $ _____

$9\frac{1}{2} \times 10\frac{1}{2} = $ _____

$14\frac{1}{2} \times 15\frac{1}{2} = $ _____

$19\frac{1}{2} \times 20\frac{1}{2} = $ _____

Examples to Solve:

1. $29 \times 31 = $ _____
2. $39 \times 41 = $ _____
3. $59 \times 61 = $ _____
4. $28 \times 32 = $ _____
5. $79 \times 81 = $ _____
6. $38 \times 42 = $ _____
7. $48 \times 52 = $ _____
8. $58 \times 62 = $ _____
9. $78 \times 82 = $ _____
10. $27 \times 33 = $ _____
11. $37 \times 43 = $ _____
12. $57 \times 63 = $ _____
13. $26 \times 34 = $ _____
14. $36 \times 44 = $ _____
15. $25 \times 35 = $ _____
16. $75 \times 85 = $ _____
17. $6\frac{1}{2} \times 7\frac{1}{2} = $ _____
18. $8\frac{1}{2} \times 9\frac{1}{2} = $ _____
19. $14\frac{1}{2} \times 15\frac{1}{2} = $ _____
20. $24\frac{1}{2} \times 25\frac{1}{2} = $ _____

Have Fun with Math

Powers and Roots You Should Know About

The ability correctly to fill in the blanks of the following chart, and solve the related items, paves the way for much of the understanding necessary to work with the powers and roots of numbers. Do your best.

Square Root	Number	Squared	Cubed	4th Power	5th Power
1.000	1	1	1	1	1
1.414	2				
1.732	3				
	4		64		1,024
	5	25		625	
	6				
	7		343		16,807
2,828	8			4,096	
	9	81			
	10				
	11				
	12				
	13				
	14				
	15				
	16				
	17				
	18				
	19				
	20				
	21	441			
	22				
	23				
	24				
	25				

When the chart has been filled in, use it to help complete the following:

a. $2^3 = 2 \times 2 \times 2 =$ _____

b. $\sqrt[3]{8} = \sqrt[3]{2 \times 2 \times 2} =$ _____

c. $2^4 = 2 \times 2 \times 2 \times 2 =$ _____

d. $\sqrt[3]{16} = \sqrt[3]{2 \times 2 \times 2 \times 2} =$ _____

e. $3^3 = 3 \times 3 \times 3 =$ _____

f. $\sqrt[5]{243} = \sqrt[5]{3 \times 3 \times 3 \times 3 \times 3} =$ _____

g. $5^4 =$ _____

h. $\sqrt[3]{216} =$ _____

i. $7^3 =$ _____

j. $\sqrt[4]{1,296} =$ _____

k. $\sqrt{324} =$ _____

l. $(\frac{1}{2})^3 =$ _____

m. $\sqrt[3]{\frac{1}{8}} =$ _____

An Alternate Method for Doing Square Roots

Would you like a method for doing square root that still gives you the correct answer in spite of some arithmetical errors? There is such a method for finding the square root of a number, and it is no more laborious than the commonly accepted method. The example that follows illustrates the method.

Find the square root of 6,045.

Make a guess of the root, say 70. This guess is "fairly close" to the actual root, but any guess will do. Test your guess by dividing into 6,045.

$6,045 \div 70 = 86.36$ (correct to two decimal places).

Since $6,045 = 70 \times 86.36$, the square root of 6,045 must be about midway between 70 and 86.36, or about $\frac{1}{2} (70 + 86.36)$, which is 78.18. Thus, the second guess of the square root is 78.18.

Now do the division process a second time.

$6,045 \div 78.18 = 77.3216$ (correct to four decimal places).

$\frac{1}{2} (78.18 + 77.3216) = 77.7508$. Thus the third guess is 77.7508.

Do the division process a third time.

$6,045 \div 77.7508 = 77.7484$ (correct to four decimal places).

$\frac{1}{2} (77.7508 + 77.7484) = 77.7496$ (correct to four decimal places).

77.750 is the desired root of 6,045 and it is correct to three decimal places. Satisfy yourself that this answer is correct by extracting the square root of 6,045 using the conventional method.

The above method of finding the square root of a number takes about the same time as does the conventional method. It has the advantage that arithmetical errors are less of a worry. Errors lengthen the work, but each fresh step continues to bring the solver nearer the desired root, whereas in the conventional method, one slip near the beginning makes the rest of the work meaningless.

Using the alternate method for finding the square root of a number, determine the square roots of the following numbers (solve correct to three decimal places):

1. 13 _____   6. 9.87 _____

2. 76 _____   7. 8,598 _____

3. 159 _____   8. 54.75 _____

4. 17.8 _____   9. 20,925 _____

5. 678 _____   10. 478.69 _____

Some Special Square and Square Root Problems

Following are some special problems with which to practice finding squares and square roots. All the problems have answers that are whole numbers. Solve the problems by finding the squares of the numbers under the square root signs and then extracting the square root of their sums or differences, as indicated. Place the answers in the spaces provided.

1. $\sqrt{12^2 + 5^2}$ = _____

2. $\sqrt{15^2 + 8^2}$ = _____

3. $\sqrt{24^2 + 7^2}$ = _____

4. $\sqrt{21^2 + 20^2}$ = _____

5. $\sqrt{35^2 + 12^2}$ = _____

6. $\sqrt{40^2 + 9^2}$ = _____

7. $\sqrt{53^2 - 28^2}$ = _____

8. $\sqrt{61^2 - 11^2}$ = _____

9. $\sqrt{65^2 - 33^2}$ = _____

10. $\sqrt{65^2 - 16^2}$ = _____

11. $\sqrt{73^2 - 55^2}$ = _____

12. $\sqrt{85^2 - 77^2}$ = _____

13. $\sqrt{60^2 + 25^2}$ = _____

14. $\sqrt{51^2 - 45^2}$ = _____

15. $\sqrt{84^2 + 13^2}$ = _____

16. $\sqrt{89^2 - 39^2}$ = _____

17. $\sqrt{84^2 + 35^2}$ = _____

18. $\sqrt{95^2 - 76^2}$ = _____

19. $\sqrt{140^2 + 51^2}$ = _____

20. $\sqrt{277^2 - 115^2}$ = _____

21. $\sqrt{224^2 + 207^2}$ = _____

22. $\sqrt{337^2 - 175^2}$ = _____

23. $\sqrt{272^2 + 225^2}$ = _____

24. $\sqrt{377^2 - 352^2}$ = _____

25. $\sqrt{572^2 + 315^2}$ = _____

Have Fun with Math

Finding the Square Root of a Number by Factoring

The square roots of selected whole numbers that are perfect squares can be found by factoring these numbers. To do that, follow these steps:

1. List all the prime factors of the number in order of size, keeping them under the square root sign.
2. For each two equal factors under the square root sign, one of them can be placed outside the sign.
3. When all the factors have been removed to outside the square root sign, multiply them together. The resulting product will be the desired square root of the number.

Examples:

1. $\sqrt{144} = \sqrt{2 \times 2 \times 2 \times 2 \times 3 \times 3} = 2 \times 2 \times 3 = 12$
2. $\sqrt{225} = \sqrt{3 \times 3 \times 5 \times 5} = 3 \times 5 = 15$
3. $\sqrt{324} = \sqrt{2 \times 2 \times 3 \times 3 \times 3 \times 3} = 2 \times 3 \times 3 = 18$
4. $\sqrt{1,521} = \sqrt{3 \times 3 \times 13 \times 13} = 3 \times 13 = 39$
5. $\sqrt{1,936} = \sqrt{2 \times 2 \times 2 \times 2 \times 11 \times 11} = 2 \times 2 \times 11 = 44$
6. $\sqrt{2,916} = \sqrt{2 \times 2 \times 3 \times 3 \times 3 \times 3 \times 3 \times 3} = 2 \times 3 \times 3 \times 3 = 54$
7. $\sqrt{7,056} = \sqrt{2 \times 2 \times 2 \times 2 \times 3 \times 3 \times 7 \times 7} = 2 \times 2 \times 3 \times 7 = 84$

All the square roots of the numbers listed below can be found by using the factoring method. Place factors and answers in the spaces provided.

1. $\sqrt{576}$ = _____
2. $\sqrt{784}$ = _____
3. $\sqrt{1,024}$ = _____
4. $\sqrt{1,225}$ = _____
5. $\sqrt{1,764}$ = _____
6. $\sqrt{2,025}$ = _____
7. $\sqrt{3,025}$ = _____
8. $\sqrt{3,136}$ = _____
9. $\sqrt{3,969}$ = _____
10. $\sqrt{4,225}$ = _____

11. $\sqrt{4,356}$ = _____
12. $\sqrt{5,184}$ = _____
13. $\sqrt{6,084}$ = _____
14. $\sqrt{7,056}$ = _____
15. $\sqrt{11,025}$ = _____
16. $\sqrt{27,225}$ = _____
17. $\sqrt{30,625}$ = _____
18. $\sqrt{50,625}$ = _____
19. $\sqrt{63,504}$ = _____
20. $\sqrt{99,225}$ = _____

Have Fun with Math

More Square Roots with Factoring

By remembering the values for $\sqrt{2}$, $\sqrt{3}$, $\sqrt{5}$, $\sqrt{6}$, $\sqrt{7}$, and $\sqrt{10}$, the square root of many numbers can be determined.

Remember: $\sqrt{2} = 1.414$ $\sqrt{3} = 1.732$ $\sqrt{5} = 2.236$
$\sqrt{6} = 2.449$ $\sqrt{7} = 2.646$ $\sqrt{10} = 3.162$

You proceed this way:

1. List all the prime factors of the number in order of size, keeping them under the square root sign.
2. For each two equal factors under the square root sign, one can be placed outside the sign.
3. When all the factors but a 2, 3, 5, 6, 7, or 10 have been removed to outside the square root sign, multiply them together. Then multiply this product by the square root of the number that remains under the sign. The result will be the desired square root of the number.

Examples:

1. $\sqrt{18} = \sqrt{3 \times 3 \times 2} = 3\sqrt{2} = 3 \times 1.414 = 4.242$
2. $\sqrt{12} = \sqrt{2 \times 2 \times 3} = 2\sqrt{3} = 2 \times 1.732 = 3.464$
3. $\sqrt{20} = \sqrt{2 \times 2 \times 5} = 2\sqrt{5} = 2 \times 2.236 = 4.472$
4. $\sqrt{24} = \sqrt{2 \times 2 \times 6} = 2\sqrt{6} = 2 \times 2.449 = 4.898$
5. $\sqrt{28} = \sqrt{2 \times 2 \times 7} = 2\sqrt{7} = 2 \times 2.646 = 5.292$
6. $\sqrt{40} = \sqrt{2 \times 2 \times 10} = 2\sqrt{10} = 2 \times 3.162 = 6.324$
7. $\sqrt{175} = \sqrt{5 \times 5 \times 7} = 5\sqrt{7} = 5 \times 2.646 = 13.23$
8. $\sqrt{360} = \sqrt{2 \times 2 \times 3 \times 3 \times 10} = 6\sqrt{10} = 6 \times 3.162 = 18.97$
9. $\sqrt{3,675} = \sqrt{3 \times 5 \times 5 \times 7 \times 7} = 5 \times 7 \times \sqrt{3} = 35 \times 1.732 = 60.62$

All the square roots of the numbers listed below can be found by using the factoring method illustrated. Round off the answers to two decimal places and put them in the spaces provided.

1. $\sqrt{63} = 3\sqrt{7} =$ _____
2. $\sqrt{72} =$ _____
3. $\sqrt{75} =$ _____
4. $\sqrt{80} =$ _____
5. $\sqrt{96} =$ _____
6. $\sqrt{216} =$ _____
7. $\sqrt{250} =$ _____

8. $\sqrt{252} =$ _____
9. $\sqrt{500} =$ _____
10. $\sqrt{640} =$ _____
11. $\sqrt{675} =$ _____
12. $\sqrt{882} =$ _____
13. $\sqrt{1,000} =$ _____

14. $\sqrt{1,575} =$ _____
15. $\sqrt{2,205} =$ _____
16. $\sqrt{2,646} =$ _____
17. $\sqrt{2,700} =$ _____
18. $\sqrt{3,528} =$ _____
19. $\sqrt{4,800} =$ _____
20. $\sqrt{20,000} =$ _____

Have Fun with Math

Using a Six-Pointed Magic Star with Powers of Numbers

Listed below the star diagram are twelve arithmetical expressions involving powers of numbers. Place the numerical value of each expression in the circle of the star with the same number as the problem. If your answers are all correct, any four answers in a row will have the same total (1,390).

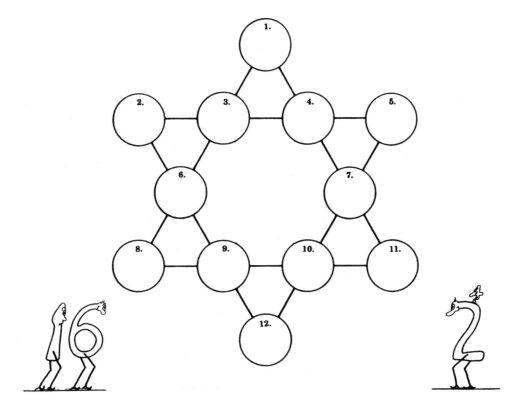

1. $14^2 - 2^3 + 2^1$
2. 1^5
3. $25^2 + 4^3 + 5^1$
4. $5^4 + 2^3 - 2^1$
5. 4^3
6. $19^2 + 2^4 + 2^1$

7. $4^4 - 3^1$
8. $10^2 + 3^3$
9. $21^2 + 1^2$
10. $8^3 - 3^2 + 2^1$
11. $18^2 - 2^3$
12. $23^2 + 3^3 + 3^2 + 3^1$

Have Fun with Math

Using a Magic Triangle with Roots of Numbers

Listed below the triangle diagram are eighteen arithmetical expressions involving roots of numbers. Place the numerical value of each expression in the circle of the triangle with the same number as the problem. If your answers are all correct, the seven answers on each of the three sides of the triangle will have the same sum (72.5).

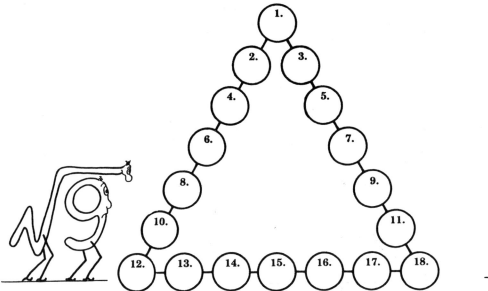

1. $\sqrt{4}$

2. $\sqrt{123.21}$

3. $\sqrt{21.16}$

4. $\sqrt{408.04}$

5. $\sqrt{187.69}$

6. $\sqrt{361} \div \sqrt{.01}$

7. $\sqrt{484} + \sqrt{.64}$

8. $10\frac{2}{5} + \sqrt[3]{8}$

9. $\sqrt[3]{27} + 13.3$

10. $\sqrt{36} + \sqrt{1.44}$

11. $\sqrt{100} - \sqrt{.04}$

12. $\sqrt{\frac{1}{4}} + \sqrt{.04}$

13. $\sqrt{72\frac{1}{4}}$

14. $\sqrt{400} + \sqrt{2.25}$

15. $\sqrt{300 + 9.76}$

16. $\sqrt{9^2 + 12^2}$

17. $\sqrt{34 + .81}$

18. $\sqrt{9} + \sqrt{.09}$

Have Fun with Math

Mystic Square with Squares and Square Roots

Find the numerical value of each of the sixteen expressions listed below. Then place the value of each expression in the respective cells of the square. When all the numerical values are in the square, find the sums of the rows of numbers, columns of numbers, and diagonal of numbers. If the numerical values of the expressions are all correct, all the sums will be the same.

Sum

1.	2.	3.	4.	
5.	6.	7.	8.	
9.	10.	11.	12.	
13.	14.	15.	16.	

Sum

1. $4^2 + 2.5^2 + .5^2$

2. $\sqrt{30.25}$

3. $2^2 - .2$

4. $\sqrt{761.76}$

5. $3.9^2 - 1.1^2$

6. $4^2 + 1.2^2 - .2^2$

7. $\sqrt{361 + 3.81}$

8. $\sqrt{3.9^2 + 8^2}$

9. $4.4^2 + 1.2^2$

10. $2.65 \div .5^2$

11. $3.5^2 + .2^2 + .1^2$

12. $4^2 - \sqrt{.09}$

13. $\sqrt{2.9^2 - 2^2}$

14. $\sqrt{625} + \sqrt{.81}$

15. $5^2 - \sqrt{.64}$

16. $\sqrt{7.5^2 - 2.1^2}$

Have Fun with Math

Cross-Number Powers and Roots Puzzle

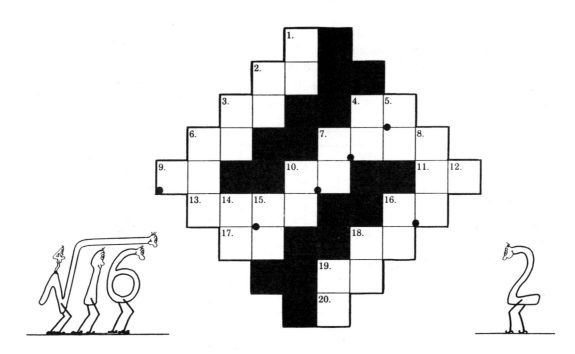

Across

1. The square of $\sqrt{5}$.
2. 3^3
3. The square root of 256.
4. $\sqrt{32.49}$
6. 2^5
7. Find the square root of 14 correct to three decimal places.
9. Determine the square of .6.
10. The square root of 11.56.
11. $18^2 - 15^2$
13. $\sqrt{204}$ (2 decimal places)
16. $\sqrt{5.76} + \sqrt{40.96}$
17. $\sqrt{6,600 + 625}$
18. $2^6 - 6^2 + 1^3$
19. $\sqrt{85^2 - 77^2}$
20. $\sqrt[4]{16}$

Down

1. $\sqrt{95^2 - 76^2}$
2. $5^2 + 1^2$
3. $6 \div \sqrt{\frac{1}{4}}$
4. $2^5 + 5^2$
5. $\sqrt{54.76}$
6. The square of 19.
7. $16^2 - 15^2 + 3^1$
8. Find the square root of 88,804.
9. The cube root of .027.
10. $\sqrt{404 + 1,040}$
12. $\sqrt{64} + \sqrt{.81} + \sqrt{.01}$
14. $\sqrt{2,304}$
15. $\sqrt{2.4^2 + .7^2}$
16. $\sqrt{80^2 + 39^2}$
18. $\sqrt{432.64} + \sqrt{27.04}$
19. $8 \div .5^2$

Have Fun with Math

Secret Message Reviewing through Powers and Roots

The numerical values of each item in the list below, when rounded off to the nearest whole number, represent letters of the alphabet. When all the letters have been assembled in respective order, they form the words of a message. Using the alphabet-number chart to obtain the letters, see if you can decode the message.

A	B	C	D	E	F	G	H	I	J	K	L	M	N	O	P	Q	R	S	T	U	V	W	X	Y	Z
1	2	3	4	5	6	7	8	9	10	11	12	13	14	15	16	17	18	19	20	21	22	23	24	25	26

_ _ _ _ _ _ _ _ _   _ _ _ _ _ _   _

_ _ _ _ _   _ _ _ _ _ _   _ _ _ _ _   _ _ _ _ _ .

_____ Nearest number of hundreds in 1,951.

_____ Subtract 198 from 203.

_____ One less than 6 is how many more than one less than 3?

_____ Subtract 1,673 from the sum of 753 and 928.

_____ $12{,}838 \div 917$

_____ Sum of three consecutive whole numbers after 3.

_____ Average of 8, 21, 5, 17, and 9.

_____ Numerator when $3\frac{3}{4}$ is changed to an improper fraction.

_____ $12\frac{2}{3} - 5\frac{8}{12}$

_____ $3\frac{3}{4} \times 6\frac{2}{3}$

_____ $3\frac{5}{6} + 7\frac{2}{3} + 8\frac{7}{12}$

_____ $50\frac{2}{5} \div 2\frac{4}{5}$

_____ $3\frac{1}{8}$ is $\frac{5}{8}$ of what number?

_____ $\frac{2}{3} \times 1\frac{1}{8} \div \frac{3}{4}$

_____ $.211 + 2.309 + .08 + 1.4$

_____ $57.72 - 39.416 + .696$

_____ $.04 \times .8 \times 31.25$

_____ $4.8 \times 5\frac{1}{4} \div 1.4$

_____ 8.4 is .56 of what number?

_____ How many times is .375 contained in $\frac{3}{8}$?

_____ $\dfrac{6.3 \times 1.5 \times .32}{.03 \times 5.6 \times 4.5}$

_____% .16 changed to percent.

_____% 5 is what percent of 500?

_____ Numerator when 88% is changed to a fraction.

_____ Find $12\frac{1}{2}\%$ of 40.

_____ 1.12 is 28% of what number?

_____ 27.6 is 20% more than what number?

_____ 6.75 is 25% less than what number?

_____ $\sqrt{385}$

_____ 2^3

_____ $\sqrt{116.3 + 52.7}$

_____ 1^4

_____ $29^2 - 21^2$

_____ $2.4^2 + 1.8^2 - 1^2$

Have Fun with Math

Cross-Number Review Puzzle through Powers and Roots

Across

1. Nearest number of thousands in 51,501.
3. 4,083 − 3,986
5. Lowest common denominator for ⅞, ⅔, and ⁵⁄₁₂.
6. 287,766 ÷ 657
7. 7½ + 23.105 + 4⅝ + 35.6 + 2¾
9. 2⅓ × 19.2 ÷ .8
10. 22.4 is what decimal part of 32?
11. $\dfrac{2.1 \times .18 \times 2.5}{.05 \times 4.5 \times .3}$
13. 1.89 is .4% of what number?
15. What number is 5% of 82.8?
17. $(⅕)^2$
18. $\sqrt{9,604}$
19. $\sqrt{130^2 - 126^2}$

Down

1. Multiply 377.5 by 14.4.
2. $\sqrt[3]{8}$
3. ⅔ of what number is 62?
4. $3^2 + 4^3 + 5^1$
5. 18¾ × 14⅔
6. 65.73 + 241.8 + 109.536 + 68.304 + 2.07
8. Numerator when ⁴⁰⁄₉₆ is reduced to lowest terms.
11. $\sqrt{14,448.04}$
12. 36.32 is ⅘ of what number?
14. $\sqrt{35.6 + 13.4}$
15. $\dfrac{63 \times 56 \times 60}{45 \times 96}$
16. 4.8 ÷ 2⅔
19. 6.504 is what percent of 216.8?

Have Fun with Math

We're interdependents!

Part VI
Metric Measure

Making Linear Measurements

A piece of copper wire has been cut into 20 pieces as shown below. Using a ruler with a metric scale, measure each of the 20 pieces and record the measurements in the respective spaces provided for the numbered pieces. Find the sum of the lengths of all the pieces to determine the length of the original wire in number of centimeters. Make all measurements to nearest millimeter.

_____ 1.

_____ 2.

_____ 3.

_____ 4.

_____ 5.

_____ 6.

_____ 7.

_____ 8.

_____ 9.

_____ 10.

_____ 11.

_____ 12.

_____ 13.

_____ 14.

_____ 15.

_____ 16.

_____ 17.

_____ 18.

_____ 19.

_____ 20.

_____ Sum

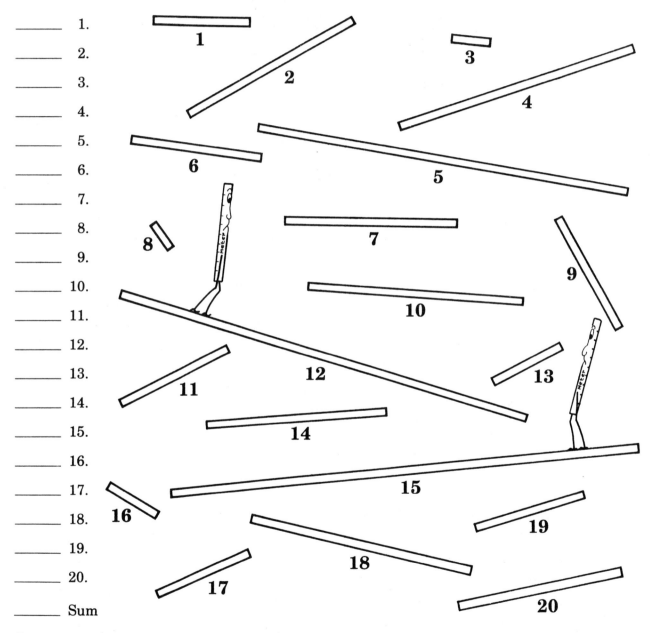

Have Fun with Math

Lineup with Metric Linear Measurement Equivalents

Draw a straight line through any three equal measurements in a block. It may be possible to draw more than one straight line in a block. The straight lines may be horizontal, vertical, and/or diagonal.

1

5 hm	5 m	50 cm
50 dm	.05 hm	5 dam
500 mm	50 dm	.5 m

2

.05 hm	500 mm	5 cm
50 cm	5 dm	½ m
5 km	½ dam	50 mm

3

20 mm	2 cm	.2 dam
2 dm	.02 m	.002 km
.002 hm	20 dm	2 cm

4

6 dm	³⁄₅ m	60 cm
.06 km	.6 dam	6 m
600 mm	60 dm	³⁄₅ hm

5

250 dm	.25 km	25 dm
25 cm	2.5 hm	¼ dam
.25 hm	25 m	250 cm

6

1,200 cm	120 dam	1,200 dm
12,000 mm	1.2 hm	12 m
12 dam	120 m	1.2 km

7

300 dm	.3 hm	3 km
3 dam	30 cm	30 m
.3 km	300 m	3 hm

8

20 dam	200 dm	20 hm
200 cm	2,000 m	2,000 mm
2 km	20 dm	200 m

9

11 cm	.011 dam	110 mm
11 dam	110 dm	1,100 cm
1,100 m	11 hm	.11 km

10

.05 km	500 cm	5 dam
50 m	5 hm	5,000 cm
½ hm	5,000 mm	5 km

11

.2 cm	2 dm	20 mm
2 km	.002 m	.2 hm
.02 hm	.2 dam	2 mm

12

20 dam	.02 hm	.2 km
.002 km	200 cm	2 m
2,000 mm	20 dm	2 hm

Have Fun with Math

How Long? How Wide? How Far?

Here's a chance 4 U 2 C how well you can estimate metric linear measure. Pick from the four measures after each item the one that is the best estimate. Write the letter of your choice in the space provided at the left of the problem. Time is limited to 15 minutes.

_____ 1. Length of a toothpick.
   a. 136 mm   b. 21 cm   c. 68 mm   d. 18 mm

_____ 2. Length of a sheet of notebook paper.
   a. 14 dm   b. 82 mm   c. 54 cm   d. 28 cm

_____ 3. Length of a new wooden pencil.
   a. 19 cm   83 mm   c. 38 cm   d. 19 dm

_____ 4. Length of a medium-size paper clip.
   a. 7 dm   b. 3½ mm   c. 35 mm   d. 25 cm

_____ 5. Overall length of a newborn baby.
   a. 23 dm   b. 92 mm   c. 125 cm   d. 46 cm

_____ 6. Breadth of an average-size car.
   a. 60 cm   b. 2 m   c. 120 cm   d. 1 m

_____ 7. Breadth of a highway driving lane.
   a. 200 cm   b. 38 dm   c. 6 m   d. 76 dm

_____ 8. Length of a table knife.
   a. 11 dm   b. 44 cm   c. 88 mm   d. 22 cm

_____ 9. Approximate distance from New York to San Francisco.
   a. 960,000 m   b. 2,400 km   c. 4,800 km   d. 9,600 km

_____ 10. Approximate mean distance across Lake Michigan.
   a. 112 km   b. 224 km   c. 56,000 m   d. 22,400 m

Scores:
0–1, Very Short	2–3, Short
4–5, Almost Short	6–7, Almost Long
8–9, Long	10, Very Long

Have Fun with Math

Using a Magic Triangle with Metric Linear Measure

Listed below the triangle diagram are fifteen problems on metric linear measure. Express all answers in number of meters, placing the answer for each problem in the circle of the triangle with the same number as the problem. If your answers are all correct, any six answers in a row will have a total of 1,000 meters (1 km).

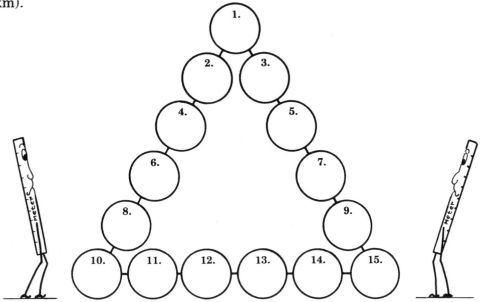

1. Change 4 dam 7 m to number of meters.
2. 1 hm 9 dam 2 m = _____ m.
3. Find ⅚ of 3 hm 9 dam 6 m.
4. What length is .75 of 164 m?
5. Take 62½% of 160 m.
6. Add 2 hm 2 m 3 dm to 5 dam 8 m 7 dm.
7. Subtract 1 hm 3 dam 7 dm from 3 hm 6 dam 8 m 7 dm.
8. Multiply 8 dam 8 m 2 dm 5 cm by 4.
9. Divide 1 km 7 hm 2 dam by 8.
10. 1 dam 9 m 2 dm is ⅘ of what distance?
11. 1 hm 2 m 5 cm + 1 hm 5 dam 7 dm + 5 dam 4 m 2 dm 5 cm.
12. Take 2 hm 3 m 2 dm 5 cm from the sum of 2 hm 8 m 5 dm and 1 hm 4 dam 7 dm 5 cm.
13. Subtract 2 dam 5 m 7 dm from 8 dam 2 m 5 dm and multiply the difference by 5.
14. Add 1 hm 6 m 4 dm to 4 hm 6 dm and divide the sum by 3.
15. 2 dam 4 m 5 dm is 35% of what distance?

Have Fun with Math

Determining the Largest Metric
Area Measurements

Circle the largest metric area measurement in each of the following rows of measurements. Reminders: 1 a (are) = 100 m^2; 1 ha (hectare) = 100 a; 1 km^2 = 100 ha. Time is limited to 15 minutes.

1. (1 m^2)	20 dm^2	10,000 mm^2
2. 400 cm^2	40 dm^2	1 m^2
3. 100,000 mm^2	2 m^2	150 dm^2
4. 300 dm^2	25,000 cm^2	4 m^2
5. 3 dm^2	250 cm^2	35,000 mm^2
6. 2,000,000 mm^2	300 dm^2	2.5 m^2
7. 12.4 m^2	2,480 cm^2	496,000 mm^2
8. 900 cm^2	4.5 dm^2	18,000 mm^2
9. 10 dm^2	.05 m^2	50 cm^2
10. .92 dm^2	82 cm^2	9,500 mm^2
11. 4.5 m^2	350 dm^2	25,000 cm^2
12. .0005 km^2	600 m^2	70,000 dm^2
13. .06 km^2	80,000 m^2	7 ha
14. 80 a	6,000 m^2	.7 ha
15. .03 a	500 dm^2	4 m^2
16. 50 ha	250 a	1 km^2
17. 3.5 ha	35 a	3,500 m^2
18. 5,000 m^2	.025 km^2	5 ha
19. 3 km^2	1,500,000 m^2	20,000 a
20. 1.5 km^2	250 ha	20,000 a

Scores:

0–3, Flip Flub   4–6, Flub
7–10, Almost a Flub   11–14, Almost a Hot Shot
15–17, Hot Shot   18–20, Super Hot Shot

Have Fun with Math

What Size Area?

Here's a chance 4 U 2 C how well you can estimate metric area. Pick the area measurement that represents the best estimate for each item. Then write the letter of your choice in the space provided at the left of the problem. Time is limited to 15 minutes.

_____ 1. An average-size table napkin.
   a. 110 cm^2 b. 11 dm^2 c. 4.4 m^2 d. 44 dm^2

_____ 2. A playing card for the game of bridge.
   a. 50 cm^2 b. 5 dm^2 c. 200 cm^2 d. 500 mm^2

_____ 3. The top of a card table.
   a. 280 cm^2 b. 700 cm^2 c. 7 m^2 d. 70 dm^2

_____ 4. A sheet of typing paper.
   a. 24 dm^2 b. 60 cm^2 c. 240 cm^2 d. 6 dm^2

_____ 5. The top of a soda pop can.
   a. 290 mm^2 b. 1,160 mm^2 c. 29 cm^2 d. 116 cm^2

_____ 6. The top of a double bed.
   a. 272 dm^2 b. 2,720 cm^2 c. 1,088 dm^2 d. 8 m^2

_____ 7. A large city lot.
   a. 1,860 m^2 b. 45.6 a   c. 2 ha   d. 465 m^2

_____ 8. Home plate for baseball.
   a. 56 dm^2 b. 140 cm^2 c. 14 dm^2 d. 5,600 cm^2

_____ 9. A football playing field.
   a. 200 a   b. 50 a   c. 500 m^2 d. 6 m^2

_____ 10. The state of Rhode Island.
   a. 3,120,000 m^2 b. 3,120 km^2 c. 12,480 km^2 d. 78,000 ha

Scores:
0–1, Very Minus   2–3, Quite Minus
4–5, Some Minus   6–7, Some Plus
8–9, Quite Plus   10, Very Plus

Have Fun with Math

Using a Six-Pointed Magic Star with Metric Measure of Area

Listed below the star diagram are twelve problems on metric measure of area. Express all answers in number of square meters, placing the answer for each problem in the circle of the star with the same number as the problem. If your answers are all correct, any four answers in a row will have a sum of 1,000 m^2.

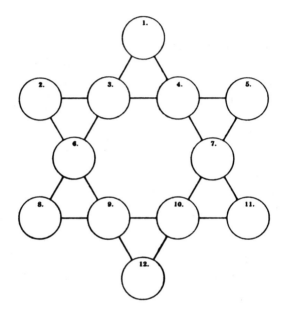

1. Change 3 dam^2 91 m^2 to number of square meters.
2. 15,700 dm^2 = _____ m^2.
3. .000265 km^2 = _____ m^2.
4. 3,430,000 cm^2 = _____ m^2.
5. 235,000,000 mm^2 = _____ m^2.
6. Take ⅚ of 364 m^2 80 dm^2.
7. Find the sum of 89 m^2 30 dm^2 and 97 m^2 70 dm^2.
8. Find the product of 5 m and 8 m.
9. Multiply 52 m^2 62 dm^2 50 cm^2 by 8.
10. Divide 4.6 km^2 by 10,000.
11. Multiply 2 m^2 46 dm^2 87 cm^2 50 mm^2 by 32.
12. 88 m^2 50 dm^2 is 75% of what area?

Have Fun with Math

Matching Metric Volume
Measurement Equivalents

In the two lists below, each measurement in the right-hand column is equivalent to a measurement in the left-hand column. When you locate the equivalent measurement in the right-hand column, place its letter in the blank space in front of the item it matches in the left-hand column. Time is limited to 15 minutes.

Reminders: 1 dm^3 = 1,000 cm^3 = 1 l (liter); 1 cm^3 of water = 1 g (gram); 1 dm^3 of water = 1 l (liter) of water = 1 kg (kilogram).

_____ 1. 1 cm^3	A. 1,600 mm^3
_____ 2. 1,000 cm^3	B. .25 cm^3
_____ 3. 1 m^3	C. 5 m^3
_____ 4. 5,000,000 cm^3	D. 750 dm^3
_____ 5. 25,000 dm^3	E. 15 l (liters)
_____ 6. .05 m^3	F. .035 cm^3
_____ 7. 1.6 cm^3	G. 1,000 mm^3
_____ 8. 36 mm^3	H. 12 g (grams)
_____ 9. 6.3 dm^3	I. .03 m^3
_____ 10. .0008 m^3	J. 50,000 cm^3
_____ 11. 250 mm^3	K. 700,000 mm^3
_____ 12. ¾ m^3	L. 1 dm^3
_____ 13. .002 dm^3	M. 2,300,000 cm^3
_____ 14. 35 mm^3	N. .036 cm^3
_____ 15. 30,000 cm^3	O. 2,000 mm^3
_____ 16. .7 dm^3	P. 1,000 dm^3
_____ 17. 2.3 m^3	Q. 6,300,000 mm^3
_____ 18. 12 cm^3 of water	R. 2.7 kg (kilogram)
_____ 19. 15 dm^3	S. 25 m^3
_____ 20. 2.7 dm^3 of water	T. 800 cm^3

Scores:

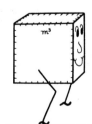

0–3, Super Blooper   4–7, Blooper
8–10, Blooping Trooper   11–15, Trooper
16–18, Super Trooper   19–20, Colossal Trooper

Have Fun with Math

Using a Five-Pointed Magic Star with Metric Measure of Volume

Listed below the star diagram are ten problems on metric measure of volume. Express all answers in number of cubic centimeters, placing the answers for each problem in the circle of the star with the same number as the problem. If your answers are all correct, any four answers in a row will have a sum of 1,000 cm^3 (1 liter or 1 dm^3).

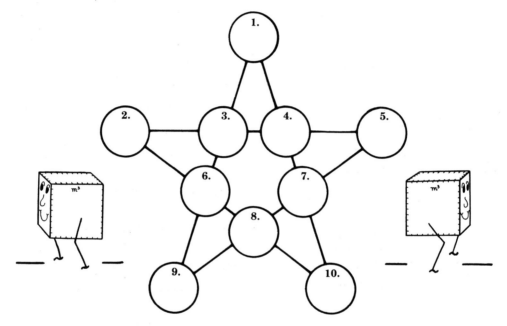

1. Change 300 cm^3 88,000 mm^3 to number of cubic centimeters.

2. 500 cm^3 17,000 mm^3 = _____cm^3.

3. .000155 m^3 = _____cm^3.

4. 69,000 mm^3 = _____cm^3.

5. Take ⅘ of 323 cm^3 750 mm^3.

6. The sum of 14 cm^3 638 mm^3 and 11 cm^3 362 mm^3.

7. Multiply 16 cm^3 500 mm^3 by 12.

8. Divide 604 cm^3 800 mm^3 by 5.4.

9. Multiply the sum of 15 cm^3 250 mm^3 and 38 cm^3 625 mm^3 by 8.

10. 34½% of a liter is equal to what volume in cm^3?

Have Fun with Math

Metric Measure of Capacity Equivalents

Each of the rows below has four measurements that are equivalents and one that is not an equivalent. Cross the measurement that is *not* equal to the other four measurements in each of the twenty rows. As an example, the non-equivalent measure in the first row has been crossed out. Time is limited to 20 minutes.

Reminder: 1 cm^3 or 1 ml of H_2O = 1 g (gram); 1 dm^3 or 1 l of H_2O = 1 kg (kilogram).

1. 130 cl	1,300 ml	13 dl	.013 hl	~~1.3 dal~~
2. .3 l	3,000 ml	30 dl	.03 hl	300 cl
3. .01 dal	10 cl	100 ml	.001 kl	1 dl
4. 7 ml	.00007 cl	.07 dl	.007 l	.0007 dal
5. 200 dal	2,000 l	20,000 hl	2 kl	200,000 cl
6. .04 kl	400 dl	4 dal	.4 l	4,000 cl
7. 250 dl	.025 kl	25 l	.25 hl	2,500 ml
8. 65 cl	.65 l	6,500 ml	.0065 hl	6.5 dl
9. .096 dl	.96 dal	960 cl	.0096 kl	9.6 l
10. .022 kl	220 dal	22 l	2,200 cl	.22 hl
11. 4.2 kl	420 dal	420,000 ml	42,000 dl	42 hl
12. 1.8 dal	18,000 cl	1,800 cl	18 l	.018 kl
13. 270 dl	27,000 ml	.027 kl	2.7 hl	2,700 cl
14. 8.8 dl	.088 dal	.0088 hl	.88 l	.0088 kl
15. 126 dl	.126 dal	1,260 ml	.00126 kl	.0126 hl
16. .00078 kl	780 ml	.078 hl	7.8 dl	.78 l
17. 5 dm^3	50 cl	5 l	5,000 ml	.005 kl
18. .00067 kl of H_2O	.067 l of H_2O	.0067 dal of H_2O	67 ml of H_2O	67 g (grams)
19. 800 g (grams)	.8 l of H_2O	800 ml of H_2O	.0008 kl of H_2O	80 dl of H_2O
20. 210 cl of H_2O	.0021 kl of H_2O	2.1 kg	21 l of H_2O	2,100 ml of H_2O

Scores: 0–3, Chug!   4–8, Chug! Chug!   9–12, Start
13–15, Warmed Up   16–18, In Gear   19–20, Away!!!

Have Fun with Math

How Much?

Here's a chance 4 U 2 C how well you can estimate metric capacities. Pick the capacity measure that represents your best estimate for each item. Then write the letter of your choice in the space provided at the left of the problem. Time is limited to 15 minutes.

_____ 1. Standard measuring cup.
    a. 474 ml   b. 1 l   c. 237 ml   d. 74 cl

_____ 2. Gasoline tank of a medium-size car.
    a. 150 l   b. 750 cl   c. 15 hl   d. 75 l

_____ 3. Teaspoon.
    a. 15 ml   b. 50 ml   c. 20 cl   d. 75 l

_____ 4. Can of soda pop.
    a. 14 dl   b. 355 ml   c. 71 cl   d. 3 dal

_____ 5. Drinking glass.
    a. 95 cl   b. 296 ml   c. 592 ml   d. 48 cl

_____ 6. Thimbleful.
    a. 36 ml   b. 5 dl   c. 24 cl   d. 12 ml

_____ 7. Oil drum.
    a. 1,900 cl   b. 340 l   c. 5 hl   d. 190 l

_____ 8. Water bucket.
    a. 228 cl   b. 114 dl   c. 228 dl   d. 23 l

_____ 9. Large cider jug.
    a. 15 l   b. 72 dl   c. 38 dl   d. 2 hl

_____ 10. Standard 25-meter competitive swimming pool.
    a. 464 kl   b. 96,800 l   c. 200 hl   d. 1,856 kl

Scores:
0–1, No Show   2–3, Needs Time
4–5, Shows Promise   6–7, Could Arrive
8–9, Right There   10, Real Whiz

    Have Fun with Math

Using a Magic Wheel with Metric Measure of Capacity

Listed below the wheel diagram are seventeen problems on metric measure of capacity. Express all answers in number of liters, placing the answer for each problem in the circle of the wheel with the same number as the problem. If your answers are all correct, any five answers in a row will have a sum of 1,000 liters (1 kl).

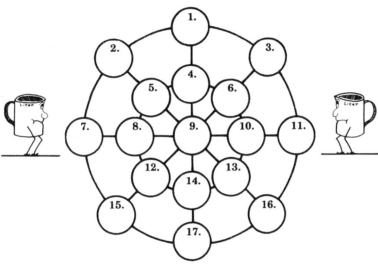

1. Change 1 hl 6 dal 2 l to number of liters.
2. Number of liters in 3 hl.
3. 3 hl 6 dal 9 l = _____ l.
4. ⅘ of 4 hl 3 dal 2 l 5 dl.
5. What capacity is .375 of 2 hl 4 dal 8 l?
6. Find 37% of 5 hl.
7. Add 8 dal 3 l 4 dl to 3 hl 8 l 6 dl.
8. Subtract 3 kl 8 hl 7 dal 9 l from 4 kl 1 hl 1 dal.
9. Multiply 1 dal 8 l 1 dl 2 cl 5 ml by 8.
10. Divide 2 kl 4 hl 9 dal 6 l by 12.
11. .24 of 1 hl.
12. Subtract 5 hl 6 dal 9 l 4 dl from the sum of 3 hl 7 dal 4 l 5 dl and 4 hl 4 dal 8 l 9 dl.
13. 1 hl 3 l 7 cl + 1 dal 9 l 9 dl + 2 hl 3 cl.
14. Subtract 1 hl 6 l 8 cl from 1 hl 1 dal 8 l 5 dl 8 cl and multiply the difference by 5.6.
15. Add 5 dal 4 l 7 dl 4 cl to 1 hl 5 l 6 cl and divide the sum by 3.4.
16. Number of dm³ in .139 kl.
17. 7 dal 4 l 7 dl 9 cl is 27% of what capacity?

Determining the Smallest Metric Weight Measurements

Circle the smallest metric weight measurement in each of the following 20 rows of measurements. The first one has been done as an example. Time is limited to 15 minutes.

Reminders: 1 t (ton) = 1,000 kg; 1 l (liter) of H_2O = 1 dm^3 = 1 kg.

1. 140 cg	.0014 kg	(.14 g)
2. 90 mg	.09 dg	.009 dag
3. 25 cg	2,500 mg	.025 hg
4. .9 dag	9,000 mg	9 dg
5. .31 dag	.0031 hg	310 cg
6. 80 mg	.008 dag	.8 cg
7. 200 dg	.02 hg	20,000 mg
8. 5 kg	5,000 dag	5.00 hg
9. 9.9 hg	99,000 cg	99 g
10. 3 g	30 cg	.03 hg
11. .004 kg	4 dag	400 dg
12. 44 g	440 dg	4,400 mg
13. 500 dg	5 g	50 dag
14. 7,000 mg	70 g	.7 hg
15. .3 t	300,000 dg	300 kg
16. .52 hg	5.2 dag	520 cg
17. 85 cm^3 of H_2O	.085 kg	8.5 g
18. 36,000 mg	3.6 l of H_2O	.36 kg
19. 170 dg	1.7 g	17 ml of H_2O
20. 1.2 hg	1.2 dm^3 of H_2O	12 kg

Scores:
0–3, Very Bitter   4–7, Bitter
8–10, Almost Bitter   11–15, Almost Sweet
16–18, Sweet   19–20, Very Sweet

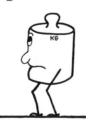

Have Fun with Math

How Heavy? How Light?

Here's a chance 4 U 2 C how well you can estimate metric weights. Pick the weight measurement that represents your best estimate for each item. Then write the letter of your choice in the space provided to the left of the problem. Time is limited to 15 minutes.

_____ 1. New wooden pencil.
  a. 14 g b. 35 dg c. 380 dg d. 7 g

_____ 2. Welterweight boxer.
  a. 19,000 g b. 65 kg c. 380 hg d. 130 kg

_____ 3. Medium-size paper clip.
  a. 12 dg b. 24 cg c. 6 dg   d. 60 mg

_____ 4. Newborn baby.
  a. 34 hg b. 17 kg c. 136 g   d. 68 hg

_____ 5. Orange of average size.
  a. 23 dag b. 69 hg c. 9,200 g d. 92 dag

_____ 6. Medium-size car.
  a. 3,900 kg b. 6,500 hg c. 1,300 kg d. 52,000 dag

_____ 7. Loaf of bread.
  a. 128 dag b. 17 hg c. 68 dag d. 340 g

_____ 8. Regular-size candy bar.
  a. 1,775 cg b. 142 g c. 284 dg d. 71 g

_____ 9. Mid-size carton of milk.
  a. 450 g b. 9 hg c. 360 dag d. 18 hg

_____ 10. Can of soda pop.
  a. 34 dag b. 170 g c. 68 dag d. 425 dg

Scores:

0–1, Very Light 2–3, Light
4–5, Almost Light 6–7, Almost Heavy
8–9, Heavy   10, Very Heavy

Have Fun with Math

Using a Mystic Square with Metric Measure of Weight

Express the answers to each of the sixteen problems listed below the mystic square diagram in number of grams. Place the answers in the respective cells of the square. When all the answers are in the cells, find the sums of the rows and columns of answers. If the answers are all correct, the sums will be the same.

Sum

1.	2.	3.	4.	
5.	6.	7.	8.	
9.	10.	11.	12.	
13.	14.	15.	16.	
Sum				

1. Change 4 hg 6 dag 9 g to number of grams.
2. 6 dag 1 g = _____ g.
3. ⅝ of 1 hg 4 dag 4 g.
4. What weight is ¹⁹⁄₂₅ of 5 hg?
5. Find 3.7% of 4 kg.
6. Add 4 dag 5 cl to 2 hg 8 dag 3 l 9 dl 5 cl.
7. Subtract 8 hg 5 g from 1 kg 9 dag 8 g.
8. Multiply 3 dg 7 cg 6 mg by 625.
9. Divide 2 kg 2 hg 9 dag 6 g 8 dg by 8.7.
10. .206 of 1 kg.
11. 7 dag 6 cg 2 mg + 8 g 3 cg 8 mg + 1 hg 9 dg.
12. Subtract 4 dag 9 g from the sum of 3 hg 9 g 8 cg and 9 dag 9 dg 2 cg.
13. Add 4 g 8 dg 5 mg to 1 dag 7 cg and multiply the sum by 8.
14. Subtract 3 kg 7 hg 1 g 6 dg from 5 kg 1 dag 4 dg and divide the difference by 3.2.
15. Weight of .438 dm³ of water.
16. 1 dag 5 g 6 dg 4 cg is 46% of what weight?

Have Fun with Math

How Hot? How Cold?

Here's a chance 4 U 2 C how well you can estimate Celsius temperatures. Pick the temperature measure that represents your best estimate for each item. Then write the letter of your choice in the space provided at the left of the problem. Time is limited to 15 minutes.

_____ 1. A very hot day.
     a. 103°C   b. 83°C   c. 38°C   d. 8°C

_____ 2. Boiling point of water.
     a. 212°C   b. 100°C   c. 32°C   d. 10°C

_____ 3. Freezing point of water.
     a. 0°C   b. 32°C   c. 100°C   d. 212°C

_____ 4. Wintertime at the North Pole.
     a. 0°C   b. 40°C   c. −100°C   d. −40°C

_____ 5. Oven temperature for baking a cake.
     a. 350°C   b. 98°C   c. 180°C   d. 18°C

_____ 6. A person's normal body temperature.
     a. 74°C   b. 98°C   c. 18°C   d. 37°C

_____ 7. Comfortable temperature at which to set home thermostat.
     a. 75°C   b. 20°C   c. 45°C   d. 60°C

_____ 8. Melting point of copper.
     a. 1,085°C   b. 543°C   c. 2,170°C   d. 272°C

_____ 9. Temperature of a person with a dangerously high fever.
     a. 40°C   b. 30°C   c. 20°C   d. 10°C

_____ 10. Suggested temperature for a competitive swimming pool.
     a. 62°C   b. 45°C   c. 26°C   d. 16°C

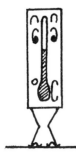

Scores:

0–1, Very Cold   2–3, Cold
4–5, Almost Cold   6–7, Almost Hot
8–9, Hot   10, Very Hot

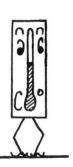

Have Fun with Math

Cross-Number Metric Measure Puzzle

Across

1. Change 4¾ dm to number of mm.
4. Express 32,000 m in number of km.
6. Number of meters in ⅝ of a km.
7. How many mm^2 in .837 cm^2?
8. 22 m^2 39 dm^2 = _____ dm^2.
10. 60 m^2 is what part of an are?
11. Number of m^3 when 21 m^3 965 dm^3 940 cm^3 is added to 52 m^3 884 dm^3 60 cm^3.
14. Weight in number of grams of 435 cm^3 of water.
16. Weight in number of kilograms of 627 liters of water.
18. What percent of 6 kl is 3,360 l?
19. Number of metric tons in 9,250 kg.

Down

1. Express the weight of 4 cl 6 ml of fresh water in number of grams.
2. Number of meters in 72,200 cm.
3. Number of grams in .552 kg.
4. Change .33 hl to number of liters.
5. Express .027 hg as number of dg.
7. Difference in number of mm between 7.02 m and 6.931 m.
9. Number of grams when 1 hg 8 dag 2 g is divided by 5.
11. How many cubic meters in 75,000 dm^3?
12. 8,690,000 cm^3 = _____ m^3.
13. Express 5 hl 2 dal 2 l as number of liters.
14. 2,250 g is what percent of 5 kg?
15. Change 36,000,000 mm to number of km.
17. Number of liters when 1 dag 8 l 7 dl 5 cl is multiplied by 4.

Have Fun with Math

Secret Message Using Metric Measure

The answer to each problem in the list below represents a letter of the alphabet. When all the letters have been assembled in respective order, they form the words of a message. Using the alphabet-number chart to obtain the letters from the answers, see if you can decode the message.

A	B	C	D	E	F	G	H	I	J	K	L	M	N	O	P	Q	R	S	T	U	V	W	X	Y	Z
1	2	3	4	5	6	7	8	9	10	11	12	13	14	15	16	17	18	19	20	21	22	23	24	25	26

_ _ _ _ _ _ _ _ _ _ _ _ _ _ _ _

_ _ _ _ _ _ _ _ _ .

_____ Change 1 dam 3 m to number of meters.

_____ 500 dm^2 = _____ m^2.

_____ How many cubic meters in 1,000,000,000 mm^3?

_____ 19,000 ml = _____ l.

_____ Change .021 kg to number of g.

_____ Find the number of cm when 5 cm 4 mm is added to 1 dm 2 cm 6 mm.

_____ Number of cm when 1 cm 25 mm is multiplied by 4.

_____ Number of km^3 when 22 km^3 500 hm^3 is divided by 2½.

_____ Number of liters when 2 l 3 dl 7 cl 5 ml is multiplied by 8.

_____ Number of kg in 2% of a ton.

_____ Find the number of meters in ⅔ of 1 dam 2 m.

_____ How many m^2 in 80% of 6 m^2 25 dm^2?

_____ 9 dm^3 900 cm^3 is .45 of what number of dm^3?

_____ Number of dl in 48% of 3 dal 1 l 2 dl 5 cl.

_____ Find the number of grams in ⅝ of 1 dag 4 g 4 dg.

_____ Subtract 2 km 7 hm from 4 km 2 hm and divide by 5 to find number hm.

_____ Product of 125 dam and 40 hm as number of km^2.

_____ Number of cm^3 when 1 cm^3 250 mm^3 is multiplied by 12.

_____ Sum of 2 kl 7 hl 2 dal 4 l and 3 kl 2 hl 7 dal 6 l in number of kl.

_____ Number of grams when 1 hg 2 dag 4 g 8 dg is divided by 7.8.

_____ Liters of capacity in a container whose volume is .018 m^3.

_____ Express 150,000 dm^2 as number of ares.

_____ 2 dg 8 cg is 4% of how many g?

_____ How many kg are there in 18 dm^3 of fresh water?

_____ Multiply 312 kg 500 g by 16 and express the result in number of tons.

_____ Number of kg in a bucket holding 1 dal 9 l of fresh water.

_____ Express .19 km^2 as number of hectares.

How far?
How many?
How much?

Have Fun with Math

Cross-Number General Review Puzzle through Metric Measure

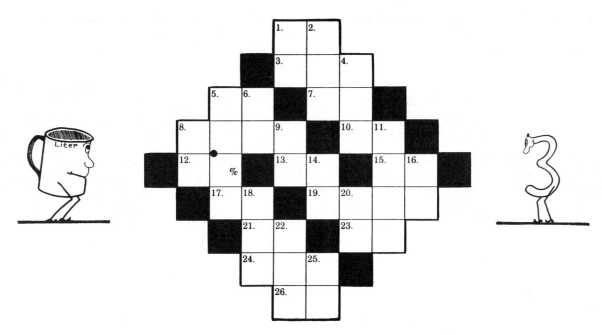

Across

1. Divide 45,312 by 768.
3. Average of 71, 124, 1,043, 239, and 108.
5. $5\frac{1}{3} + 3\frac{5}{12} + 7\frac{1}{4}$
7. $16\frac{4}{5} \times 2\frac{11}{12} \div 2\frac{1}{3}$
8. Subtract 49.795 from the product of 3.78 and 14.6.
10. $\dfrac{4.2 \times .15 \times 3.2}{3.5 \times 1.2 \times .02}$
12. 23.76 is what percent of 52.8?
13. 2.79 is 4.5% of what number?
15. Numerical value of 2^6.
17. $\sqrt{51^2 - 45^2}$.
19. 53 m² 65 dm² = _____ dm²
21. Number of liters when 2 dal 8 l 7 dl 6 cl 2 ml is added to 4 dal 3 l 2 dl 3 cl 8 ml.
23. Number of grams when 6 hg 5 dag 6 g is divided by 8.
24. Express 288 dm³ as number of l.
26. Weight in number of kg of .084 m³ of water.

Down

1. $33\frac{1}{8}$ is $\frac{5}{8}$ of what number?
2. Find the square root of 831,744.
4. $111\frac{1}{4} \times 6.4$
5. Change 13 m² 52 dm² to number of square meters.
6. Number of liters when 4 dal 2 l 7 dl 4 cl is added to 2 dal 6 l 2 dl 6 cl.
8. 18.9 is 35% of what number?
9. $\dfrac{27 \times 16 \times 35}{28 \times 15}$
11. 4 m 6 dm 6 cm 2 mm = _____ mm.
14. Find 16% of $156\frac{1}{4}$.
16. Number of grams when 7 g 5 dg is multiplied by 6.
18. $6^3 + 16^2$
20. 1,042.53 ÷ 27.435
22. Number of mm³ when 1 cm³ 440 mm³ is divided by 5.
25. Nearest number of ten thousands in 844,879.

Have Fun with Math

Part VII
Perimeters, Areas, and Volumes

Here come
those crazy
solids!

Finding the Area of "Old Shadowface"

Find the total area of the outline of "Old Shadowface" as diagrammed below. Don't forget to subtract the hole in the head. The fourteen figures that make up the face include triangles, rectangles, trapezoids, and a circle. Each unit of grid represents 3 centimeters; use pi = 3.14.

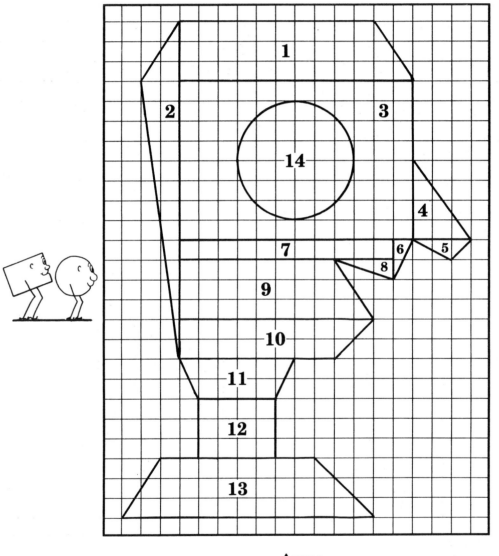

Areas

1. _____	5. _____	9. _____	13. _____
2. _____	6. _____	10. _____	14. _____
3. _____	7. _____	11. _____	*Total Area*
4. _____	8. _____	12. _____	_____

Have Fun with Math

Finding Perimeters and Areas from Grid Measurements

Find the perimeter (P) and area (A) of each figure below from dimensions read from the grid lines. Each grid unit represents 1 cm. An edge of a sheet of paper or dividers can be used to transfer distance to the horizontal or vertical grid lines for measurement. Solve to nearest whole unit; use pi = 3.14.

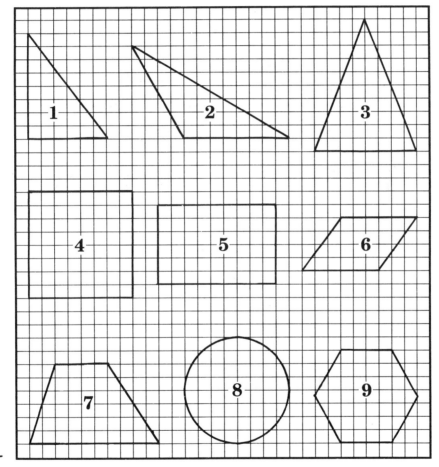

1. P = _____
   A = _____

2. P = _____
   A = _____

3. P = _____
   A = _____

4. P = _____
   A = _____

5. P = _____
   A = _____

6. P = _____
   A = _____

7. P = _____
   A = _____

8. P = _____
   A = _____

9. P = _____
   A = _____

Have Fun with Math

Using a Six-Pointed Magic Star with Plane Figures

Listed below are twelve problems on finding a dimension of a plane figure. Write the correct answers in the circles of the star with the same number as the problem. If your answers are all correct, any four in a row will have the same sum. Express all answers in number of centimeters; use pi = 3.14.

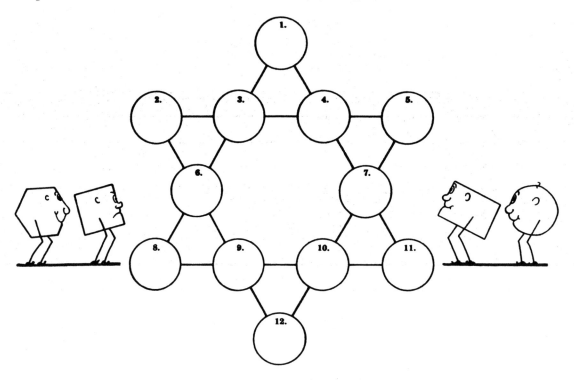

1. Length of a side of a square whose perimeter is 100 cm.
2. Altitude of a triangle whose base is 48 cm and whose area is 816 cm^2.
3. Length of a side of a square whose area is 529 cm^2.
4. Length of a leg of a right triangle with area of 294 cm^2 and other leg of 28 cm.
5. Width of a rectangle whose length is 30 cm and whose perimeter is 104 cm.
6. Altitude of a parallelogram whose area is 228 cm^2 and whose base is 19 cm.
7. Diameter of a circle whose area is 530.66 cm^2.
8. Perimeter of a rectangle whose area is 96 cm^2 and whose width is 12 cm.
9. Radius of a circle whose circumference is 106.76 cm.
10. Length of one side of a regular hexagon whose perimeter is 90 cm.
11. Length of side of a regular hexagon with altitude of 24.25 cm and area of 2,037 cm^2.
12. Perimeter of a rectangle whose area is 82.5 cm^2 and whose width is 7.5 cm.

Have Fun with Math

Finding the Volumes and Surface Areas of Solid Figures

Find the volume (V) and total surface area (A) of each of the figures below from the given dimensions. Solve to the nearest whole unit; use pi = 3.14.

1 Cube

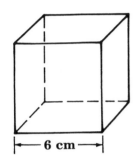

6 cm

2 Rectangular Solid

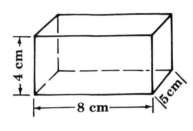

4 cm 8 cm 5 cm

3 Right Cylinder

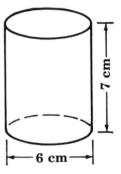

7 cm 6 cm

4 Right Cylindrical Cone   **5** Right Pyramid

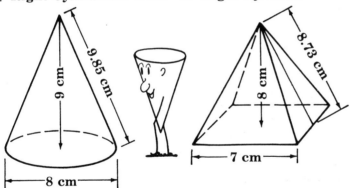

9 cm 9.85 cm 8 cm 8.73 cm 7 cm 8 cm

6 Sphere

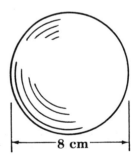

8 cm

Volumes and Surface Areas:

1. V = _____
   A = _____

2. V = _____
   A = _____

3. V = _____
   A = _____

4. V = _____
   A = _____

5. V = _____
   A = _____

6. V = _____
   A = _____

Have Fun with Math

Finding the Volume of Robby the Robot

Find the volume of Robby the Robot from the dimensions given in the diagram below. Solve to the nearest whole unit; use pi = 3.14.

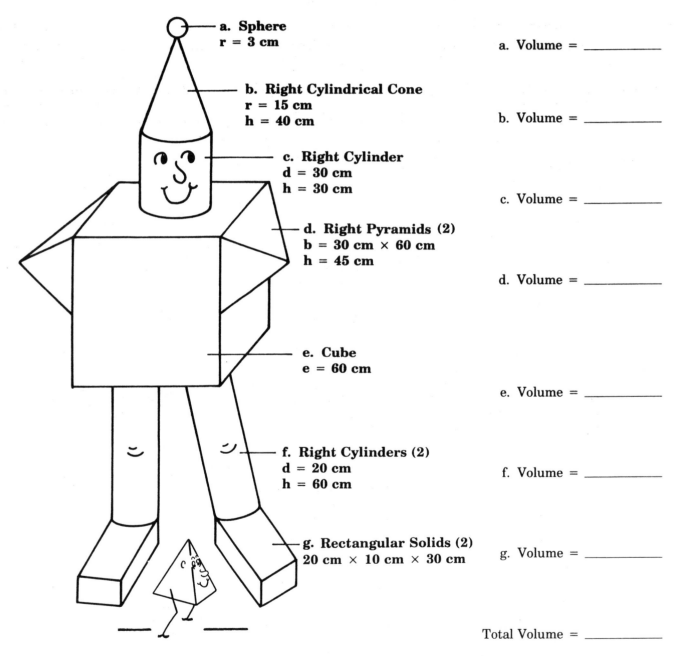

a. Sphere
r = 3 cm

a. Volume = _____

b. Right Cylindrical Cone
r = 15 cm
h = 40 cm

b. Volume = _____

c. Right Cylinder
d = 30 cm
h = 30 cm

c. Volume = _____

d. Right Pyramids (2)
b = 30 cm × 60 cm
h = 45 cm

d. Volume = _____

e. Cube
e = 60 cm

e. Volume = _____

f. Right Cylinders (2)
d = 20 cm
h = 60 cm

f. Volume = _____

g. Rectangular Solids (2)
20 cm × 10 cm × 30 cm

g. Volume = _____

Total Volume = _____

Have Fun with Math

Using a Five-Pointed Magic Star
with Solid Figures

Below are ten problems on finding a dimension of a solid figure. Write the correct answers in the circles of the star diagram with the same number as the problem. If all your answers are correct, any four in a row will have the same sum. Express all answers in number of centimeters; use pi = 3.14.

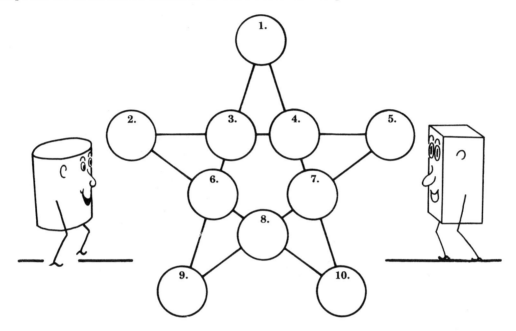

1. Length of the edge of a cube whose volume is 27,000 cm³.
2. Length of a rectangular solid with height of 25 cm, width of 20 cm, and volume of 19,500 cm³.
3. Height of a right cylinder whose base is 314 cm² and whose volume is 7,222 cm³.
4. Height of a regular pyramid with base area of 900 cm² and volume of 5,100 cm³.
5. Radius of a sphere that will exactly fit into a cube having an edge of 42 cm.
6. Length of the edge of a cube whose total surface area is 1,176 cm².
7. Height of a right cylindrical cone whose radius is 30 cm and whose volume is 24,492 cm³.
8. Radius of a sphere whose surface area is 5,024 cm².
9. Radius of a right cylindrical cone with height of 100 cm and volume of 113,982 cm³.
10. Length of one side of the base of a regular four-sided pyramid with height of 30 cm and volume of 7,290 cm³.

Have Fun with Math

Cross-Number Puzzle: Perimeters, Areas, and Volumes

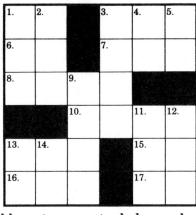

(Solve all problems to nearest whole number; use pi = 3.14.)

Across

1. Number of dm in the perimeter of a rectangle 7¼ dm by 4¾ dm.
3. Area in number of cm^2 of a square whose side is 15 cm.
6. Perimeter in number of m of a triangle having two equal sides of 15½ m and a third side of 17 m.
7. Area in number of m^2 of a parallelogram with a length of 35 m and an altitude of 19 m.
8. Number of dm^2 in the area of a trapezoid with bases of 42 dm and 65 dm and an altitude of 26 dm.
10. Area in number of dm^2 of a circle whose diameter is 72 dm.
13. Surface area in number of cm^2 of a cube whose edge is 8 cm.
15. Surface area in number of dm^2 of a rectangular solid 2 dm wide, 3½ dm long, and 4 dm high.
16. Volume in number of dm^3 of a cone whose diameter is 12 dm and whose height is 15 dm.
17. Volume in number of cm^3 of a sphere whose radius is 2½ cm.

Down

1. Area of a triangle in number of m^2 if the length of the base is 30⅛ m and the altitude is 16 m.
2. Surface area in number of cm^2 of a sphere whose radius is 6.2 cm.
3. Volume in number of cm^3 of a rectangular solid 29 cm long, 15 cm wide, and 6 cm high.
4. Length in dm of a rectangle whose width is 14½ dm and whose area is 377 dm^2.
5. Length in cm of the side of a square whose area is 3,025 cm^2.
9. Area in number of dm^2 of a trapezoid with bases of 197 dm and 180.8 dm and altitude of 50 dm.
11. Volume of a pyramid in number of cm^3 when the height is 12 cm and base is 164 cm^2.
12. Perimeter in number of m of a rectangle 167.5 m wide and 325 m long.
13. Height in number of dm of a pyramid with a volume of 17,500 dm^3 and a base area of 1,500 dm^2.
14. Diameter in cm of a circle whose area is 5,806 cm^2.

Have Fun with Math

Secret Message: Review through Perimeters, Areas, and Volumes

The answers to each problem in the list below, when rounded off to the nearest whole number, represent letters of the alphabet. When all the letters have been assembled in respective order, they form the words of a message. Using the alphabet-number chart to obtain the letters, see if you can decode the message.

A	B	C	D	E	F	G	H	I	J	K	L	M	N	O	P	Q	R	S	T	U	V	W	X	Y	Z
27	28	29	30	31	32	33	34	35	36	37	38	39	40	41	42	43	44	45	46	47	48	49	50	51	52

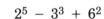

__ __ __ __ __ __ __ __ __ __ __ __ __ __ __ __ __ __ __ __ __ .

_____ From the product of 29 and 45 subtract the sum of 478 and 787.

_____ If 3,239 is the dividend and 79 is the divisor, find the quotient.

_____ Average of 48, 14, 51, 29, and 63.

_____ $5\frac{2}{3} + 9\frac{1}{2} + 18\frac{1}{12} + 6\frac{3}{4}$

_____ $11\frac{5}{8}$ is $\frac{3}{8}$ of what number?

_____ $2\frac{1}{8} \times 13\frac{1}{3} \div \frac{5}{6}$

_____ Number of times that 3.76 is contained in 101.52.

_____ Add 76.94 to 25.083 and subtract 56.023 from the sum.

_____ $\dfrac{4.5 \times 9.3 \times 1.12}{.12 \times 3.5 \times 3.6}$

_____ Find $18\frac{3}{4}\%$ of 240.

_____ % 175.5 is what percent of 650?

_____ $7\frac{1}{2}\%$ of what number is 2.7?

_____ $2^5 - 3^3 + 6^2$

_____ $\sqrt{35^2 - 21^2}$

_____ $\sqrt{900} + \sqrt{225} + \sqrt{16}$

_____ Number of cubic meters in 31,000,000 cm³.

_____ Number of grams in $\frac{4}{5}$ of 4 dag 7 g 5 dg.

_____ Number of meters when 4 m 7 dm 5 cm is multiplied by 8.

_____ Area of a triangle in dm² when base is 15 dm and altitude is 4 dm.

_____ Circumference in number of cm of a circle whose radius is 6.5 cm.

_____ Perimeter in number of cm of a square whose area is 100 cm².

_____ Volume in m³ of right cylinder with radius 2 m and height 2.5 m.

Have Fun with Math

Cross-Number Review Puzzle
through Perimeters, Areas, and Volumes

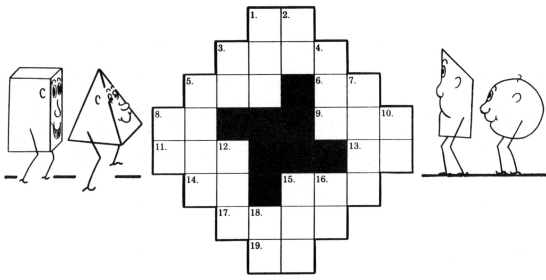

(Solve all problems to nearest whole number; use pi = 3.14.)

Across

1. From the product of 237 and 69 subtract 16,309.
3. $6.186 + 53.734 + 486.4 + 304.78 + 386.9$
5. $13\frac{1}{2} \times 11\frac{1}{4} \div \frac{5}{8}$
6. Average of $38\frac{3}{4}$, 40.245, $31\frac{1}{2}$, 62.88, and $36\frac{5}{8}$.
8. 3.6 is 15% of what number?
9. $2^5 + 3^4 + 4^3 + 5^2$
11. Change 7 l 6 dl 5 cl to number of cl.
13. Multiply 3 kg 2 hg 5 dag by 4 and express the product as number of kg.
14. Length of the perimeter in cm of a square whose area is 256 cm².
15. Area in number of cm² of a circle whose diameter is 23 cm.
17. Volume in cm³ of a regular pyramid with height of 27 cm and base side of 32 cm.
19. Surface area in number of dm² of rectangular solid 5 dm by 4 dm by 3 dm.

Down

1. Volume of a right cylinder in dm³ if the radius is 4 dm and height is 8.42 dm.
2. Length in dm of a rectangle with width of 27 dm and area of 1,161 dm².
3. $\dfrac{1.4 \times .36 \times 1.5}{.045 \times 1.2}$
4. $\sqrt{708,964}$
5. $28.8 \times 85\frac{5}{8}$
7. Change 2 kg 1 dag 5 g to number of g.
8. 18 is $\frac{2}{3}$ of what number?
10. Subtract $36\frac{5}{12}$ from the sum of $31\frac{3}{4}$ and $27\frac{2}{3}$.
12. Number of mm when $3\frac{3}{5}$ m is subtracted from 4.149 m.
15. Find 36% of 1,150.
16. Radius in number of cm of a sphere whose surface area is 3,215 cm².
18. Radius in number of cm of a circle whose circumference is 182 cm.

Have Fun with Math

They need us!

Part VIII
Miscellaneous Materials

A Written Direction Test

This page is to remain face down on your desk top until your teacher tells you it is time to begin work. Follow all of the directions on this sheet very carefully. You are not to look around the room or ask any questions. Time limit is 15 minutes.

1. Read everything on this page before doing anything else.
2. Write your name on the line at the top of this sheet.
3. In the block at the right, number the lines from 1 to 9, putting the numbers at the left end and immediately above the respective lines.
4. Place a period behind and near the bottom of each number in the block.
5. Select three consecutive digits between 1 and 9; arrange them in descending order of value on line 1.
6. Reverse the order of the digits you have written on line 1 to form a new number. Place this new number on line 2 with the digits directly below the digits of the number on the line above.
7. Subtract the number formed by the digits on line 2 from the number formed by the digits on line 1. Place the difference on line 3 so that the digits are aligned with the digits on the other two lines.
8. Reverse the order of the digits on line 3 and place them on line 4 so they are aligned with the digits of the number on the line above.
9. Add the number formed by the digits on line 4 to the number formed by the digits on line 3. Place this sum on line 5, keeping the digits of this number aligned with the digits above.
10. Write the number 20 on line 6 so the digits of this number are directly below the two right-hand digits of the number on line 5.
11. Multiply the number formed by the digits on line 5 by the number on line 6. Place this product on line 7.
12. Divide the product you have placed on line 7 by 3 and enter the quotient on line 8.
13. If the number you have entered on line 8 is 7,260, draw a circle around it; if the number is not 7,260, go back to item 5 and check your work.
14. When you feel you have correctly completed item 13, place an *X* on line 9; then raise your hand to get the attention of your teacher. When the teacher recognizes you, take your hand down and wait patiently for others to finish.
15. Now that you are about to finish reading carefully, do only items 1 and 2. Then turn this page face down on your desk and wait quietly for others to complete the test.

Have Fun with Math

Number Circus

Number combinations sometimes produce unusual results. See for yourself by carefully following the directions for each item below. Repeat each item using different numbers to be certain the process described really works.

1. Write any even whole number. Add 14. Multiply by 2. Subtract 8. Divide by 4. Subtract one half the original number. The result will always be 5.

2. Write any whole number of two or more digits. Reverse the digits to form a new number. Subtract the smaller of the two numbers from the larger. Divide the difference by 9. There will never be a remainder.

3. Write any three digits. Multiply the first by 2; then add 5 and multiply by 5. Add the second digit and multiply the sum by 10. Add the third digit and subtract 250. The result will be the three digits in order.

4. Write a prime number greater than 3. Square it. Add 17. Divide by 12. The remainder will always be 6.

5. Write any three digits in consecutive order. Reverse the three digits to form a new number. Subtract the smaller number from the larger. The result will always be 198.

6. Write a three-digit whole number in which there is a difference of two or more between the first and third digits. Reverse the order of digits to form a new number. Subtract the smaller number from the larger. Reverse the difference. Add the difference and the number formed by reversing it. The sum will always be 1,089.

7. Write any three-digit whole number. Now write the same digits alongside the first three, forming a six-digit number. This number will always be divisible by 7, 11, and 13.

8. Write any whole number. Square it. Square the next larger whole number. Subtract the smaller square from the larger square. The original number can be found by subtracting 1 and taking half the difference.

9. Write any two consecutive whole numbers. Add the two consecutive numbers and circle this sum. Square each of the two consecutive numbers and subtract the smaller square from the larger. The difference between the two squares will be the sum of the two consecutive numbers that you have circled.

10. Write any even number. Divide the number by 2. Square the quotient. Write the nearest whole number above and the nearest whole number below this square. You will have three numbers; the original even number and the other two. The sum of the squares of the two smaller numbers will always be equal to the square of the larger number.

Mathematical Word Puzzle

The array of letters below includes twenty-five basic mathematical words in addition to the two words already marked. These words are arranged horizontally, vertically, and diagonally. See how many of the words you can find. Mark the words by circling them as illustrated.

O	A	H	N	V	W	P	G	I	D	X	V	D	I	V	I	D	E	A	E
K	W	D	I	F	F	E	R	E	N	C	E	I	C	U	R	B	T	D	Q
A	E	U	D	X	I	J	A	J	Q	C	D	V	G	B	E	O	F	Y	U
M	P	R	O	V	A	L	M	W	B	P	N	I	C	M	Z	L	O	F	O
D	N	U	M	E	R	A	T	O	R	H	K	S	G	O	A	J	I	T	T
B	X	U	K	Y	L	Y	J	Q	A	X	S	O	D	M	F	R	C	G	I
E	S	D	E	N	O	M	I	N	A	T	O	R	I	A	E	L	I	Y	E
M	U	L	T	I	P	L	I	C	A	N	D	C	Z	W	F	T	H	Z	N
B	E	C	L	T	Z	M	R	N	O	P	E	R	C	E	N	T	E	K	T
V	S	Q	U	A	R	E	U	I	M	D	C	H	R	Q	R	K	S	R	B
M	D	N	U	N	W	E	H	J	U	F	I	T	V	Y	I	E	J	S	F
D	K	H	C	O	Q	M	T	L	L	T	G	V	K	S	R	O	Q	U	M
Q	P	L	P	E	R	C	E	N	T	A	G	E	I	A	T	Y	Z	B	U
L	I	T	E	R	A	U	P	X	I	T	D	U	S	D	M	F	P	T	L
O	R	N	W	R	I	Q	S	V	P	O	G	D	S	V	E	N	T	R	T
J	W	F	T	U	X	E	H	S	L	R	Y	L	E	A	Z	N	Z	A	I
G	X	B	G	F	R	A	C	T	I	O	N	V	Q	N	O	A	D	H	P
E	U	F	P	D	I	J	T	R	E	K	P	W	H	C	D	Y	N	E	L
S	U	Z	A	G	C	S	F	B	R	C	I	K	B	J	M	D	X	N	Y
H	P	R	O	D	U	C	T	L	M	B	W	N	I	N	U	E	N	D	G

Have Fun with Math

Rapid Multiplication with Certain Pairs of Two-Digit Numbers

This sheet explains a method of rapid multiplication that can be used for finding the products of certain pairs of two-digit numbers. You can learn to tell at a glance that 63×67 is equal to 4,221, or that 84×86 is equal to 6,424.

The following rule for finding the product applies to any pair of two-digit numbers whose unit digits have a sum of 10 and whose tens digits are the same. The first part of the product is the product of the common tens digit and the next consecutive number after that tens digit. The second part of the product (written as two digits) is the product of the two units digits. Remember that the rule applies only to the certain pairs of numbers described.

> *Example*: 48×42 is found as follows: 4×5 is 20; 8×2 is 16; the product is 2,016.

> *Example*: 71×79 is found as follows: 7×8 is 56; 1×9 is 09; the product is 5,609.

Using the illustrated method, write the products for the problems below in the spaces provided.

1. $72 \times 78 =$ _____
2. $16 \times 14 =$ _____
3. $73 \times 77 =$ _____
4. $91 \times 99 =$ _____
5. $52 \times 58 =$ _____
6. $94 \times 96 =$ _____
7. $74 \times 76 =$ _____
8. $43 \times 47 =$ _____

9. $83 \times 87 =$ _____
10. $42 \times 48 =$ _____
11. $61 \times 69 =$ _____
12. $44 \times 46 =$ _____
13. $22 \times 28 =$ _____
14. $17 \times 13 =$ _____
15. $49 \times 41 =$ _____
16. $36 \times 34 =$ _____
17. $51 \times 59 =$ _____

18. $29 \times 21 =$ _____
19. $68 \times 62 =$ _____
20. $52 \times 58 =$ _____
21. $33 \times 37 =$ _____
22. $81 \times 89 =$ _____
23. $32 \times 38 =$ _____
24. $93 \times 97 =$ _____
25. $84 \times 86 =$ _____

Rapid Multiplication with Two Numbers Ending in 5's

The product of pairs of numbers ending in 5's can be found with mental computation by applying the following rules: (1) For the first digits of the product, multiply the numbers formed by the digits to the left of the 5's (in the multiplier and the multiplicand) and add one half their sum, disregarding any fraction. (2) If the sum of the numbers formed by the digits to the left of the 5's is even, then the last two digits of the product are 25; if the sum is odd, then the last two digits of the product are 75.

Example: Multiply 45 × 65. 4 × 6 is 24; one half the sum of 4 and 6 is 5; the sum of 24 and 5 is 29. Annex 25 (the sum of 4 and 6 is even). The product is 2,925.

Example: Multiply 45 × 75. 4 × 7 is 28; one half the sum of 4 and 7 is 5 (disregarding the fraction); the sum of 28 and 5 is 33. Annex 75 (the sum of 4 and 7 is odd). The product is 3,375.

Example: Multiply 115 × 45. 11 × 4 is 44; one half the sum of 11 and 4 is 7 (disregarding the fraction); the sum of 44 and 7 is 51. Annex 75 (the sum of 11 and 4 is odd). The product is 5,175.

Using the illustrated method, write the products for the problems below in the spaces provided.

1. 65 × 25 = _____
2. 45 × 85 = _____
3. 95 × 35 = _____
4. 75 × 55 = _____
5. 65 × 25 = _____
6. 85 × 25 = _____
7. 75 × 45 = _____
8. 125 × 75 = _____

9. 35 × 65 = _____
10. 85 × 35 = _____
11. 55 × 35 = _____
12. 55 × 85 = _____
13. 95 × 85 = _____
14. 75 × 85 = _____
15. 95 × 65 = _____
16. 135 × 35 = _____
17. 115 × 205 = _____

18. 25 × 75 = _____
19. 55 × 45 = _____
20. 95 × 75 = _____
21. 75 × 65 = _____
22. 95 × 55 = _____
23. 35 × 75 = _____
24. 105 × 45 = _____
25. 225 × 85 = _____

Have Fun with Math

Rapid Multiplication with Numbers Having the Same Tens Digits

The product of any two two-digit numbers having the same tens digits can be found with mental computation by applying the following rules: (1) Add the whole of one number to the unit digit of the other and multiply by the common tens digit. (2) Annex a zero to the result; to this number add the product of the two unit digits.

Example: Multiply 64 × 67. 64 plus 7 is 71; 71 × 6 is 426. Annex 0 to 426, making it 4,260; add 4 × 7 (28), making it 4,288. The product is 4,288.

Example: Multiply 93 × 98. 93 plus 8 is 101; 101 × 9 is 909. Annex 0 to 909, making it 9,090; add 3 × 8 (24), making it 9,114. The product is 9,114.

After studying the examples above, write the products for the problems below in the spaces provided.

1. 14 × 18 = _____

2. 29 × 23 = _____

3. 65 × 69 = _____

4. 58 × 51 = _____

5. 54 × 59 = _____

6. 82 × 85 = _____

7. 67 × 68 = _____

8. 39 × 33 = _____

9. 84 × 88 = _____

10. 17 × 16 = _____

11. 46 × 49 = _____

12. 43 × 47 = _____

13. 45 × 42 = _____

14. 91 × 96 = _____

15. 56 × 53 = _____

16. 89 × 82 = _____

17. 73 × 75 = _____

18. 61 × 66 = _____

19. 58 × 51 = _____

20. 36 × 39 = _____

21. 92 × 97 = _____

22. 26 × 28 = _____

23. 74 × 76 = _____

24. 75 × 77 = _____

25. 93 × 99 = _____

Have Fun with Math

Rapid Computation with Certain Fractions

Below are two shortcuts for sharpening your mental arithmetic with fractions. The first is a method for adding any two fractions with numerators of 1; the second is a method for squaring any number ending in ½.

Adding Fractions with Numerators of 1

To add two fractions having numerators of 1, write the sum of the denominators over the product of the denominators. Reduce if necessary.

Example: $\dfrac{1}{3} + \dfrac{1}{5} = \dfrac{3+5}{3\times5} = \dfrac{8}{15}$

Example: $\dfrac{1}{6} + \dfrac{1}{8} = \dfrac{6+8}{6\times8} = \dfrac{14}{48}$
$= \dfrac{7}{24}$

1. ½ + ⅓ = _____

2. ⅓ + ¼ = _____

3. ¼ + ⅕ = _____

4. ½ + ⅙ = _____

5. ½ + ⅕ = _____

6. ½ + ⅛ = _____

7. ⅕ + ⅙ = _____

8. ⅕ + ⅛ = _____

9. ¼ + ¹⁄₁₂ = _____

10. ⅛ + ¹⁄₁₂ = _____

Squaring Numbers Ending in ½

To square any number ending in ½, multiply the number by itself increased by 1 and annex ¼.

Example: $(4½)^2 = (4 \times 5) + ¼ = 20¼$

Example: $(11½)^2 = (11 \times 12) + ¼ = 132¼$

11. $(2½)^2 = $ _____

12. $(3½)^2 = $ _____

13. $(5½)^2 = $ _____

14. $(6½)^2 = $ _____

15. $(8½)^2 = $ _____

16. $(12½)^2 = $ _____

17. $(15½)^2 = $ _____

18. $(20½)^2 = $ _____

19. $(25½)^2 = $ _____

20. $(50½)^2 = $ _____

Have Fun with Math

Rapid Computation Quiz

This quiz stresses rapid mental computation. After you have looked at a problem, write the answer in the space to the left of the problem. Time is limited to 3 minutes.

_____ 1. 48 × 75

_____ 2. 32 × 99

_____ 3. 6,400 ÷ 25

_____ 4. 68 × 72

_____ 5. 125 × 41

_____ 6. 7.6 × 1,000

_____ 7. ¼ + ⅕

_____ 8. ¾ ÷ ⅔

_____ 9. 46 × 1.5

_____ 10. 5 − .055

_____ 11. 3.95 + 1.08

_____ 12. 870 ÷ .001

_____ 13. 475 × .02

_____ 14. 24 ÷ .25

_____ 15. 9 is 5% of what number?

_____ 16. 87½% of 40

_____ 17. 9 is what percent of 36?

_____ 18. $.12^2$

_____ 19. 20.5^2

_____ 20. $\sqrt{12,100}$

Scores:

0–3, Deceased	4–7, Little Hope	8–10, Struggling Hard
11–15, Quite Alive	16–18, Feeling Good	19–20, Top of the World

Have Fun with Math

Fun Test on Thought Questions
with Easy Numbers

Below are some math questions that should make you think. Read each question carefully and see if you can select the correct answer from the list provided. Place the letter of your response in the space at the left of the problem. Time is limited to 15 minutes.

_____ 1. How many months of the year have 30 days?
(a) 11   (b) 12   (c) 4   (d) 7   (e) Answer is not listed.

_____ 2. If a young steer on three legs weighs 300 kg, what will this steer weigh when it stands on all four legs?
(a) nothing   (b) 200 kg   (c) 300 kg   (d) 400 kg   (e) Answer is not listed.

_____ 3. Divide 10 by one half and add 3. What is the answer?
(a) 8   (b) 13   (c) 20   (d) 23   (e) Answer is not listed.

_____ 4. The children of Mr. and Mrs. Allen consist of two pairs of twins. How many children do Mr. and Mrs. Allen have?
(a) 2   (b) 3   (c) 4   (d) 6   (e) Answer is not listed.

_____ 5. If it takes 3 minutes to cook an egg in boiling water, how many minutes will it take to cook 3 eggs?
(a) 1 minute   (b) 6 minutes   (c) 9 minutes
(d) 12 minutes   (e) Answer is not listed.

_____ 6. If a half-liter jar holds 100 marbles, how many marbles would there be in an empty two-liter plastic jar?
(a) 400   (b) 200   (c) 100   (d) none   (e) Answer is not listed.

_____ 7. You have three pills and take one every half hour. How long will the three pills last?
(a) ½ hour   (b) 1 hour   (c) 1½ hour   (d) 2 hours
(e) Answer is not listed.

_____ 8. If the life expectancy of the average person is 67 years, how many birthdays would an average person have?
(a) none   (b) 1   (c) 66   (d) 67   (e) Answer is not listed.

_____ 9. If there are 12 20-cent stamps in a dozen, how many 10-cent stamps are there in a dozen?
(a) 6   (b) 12   (c) 24   (d) 36   (e) Answer is not listed.

_____ 10. A farmer fenced a square plot of ground. When he had finished, he noted that there were five fence posts on each of the four sides. How many posts were used to fence the plot?
(a) 10   (b) 15   (c) 16   (d) 20   (e) Answer is not listed.

Scores: 0–1, Strike Three   2–3, Flied Out
4–5, Sacrifice   6–7, Hit
8–9, Three-Bagger   10, Home Run!

Have Fun with Math

Fun Test on Math Riddles

Here's a chance to test your skill with some math riddles. Read each riddle carefully; some are tricky. Write your answer in the space provided below each item. Time is limited to 15 minutes.

1. How long will an eight-day clock run without winding?
   Answer: _____

2. How far can a person walk into a park?
   Answer: _____

3. Three cows ahead of a cow, three cows behind a cow, and two cows in the middle. How many cows are there altogether?
   Answer: _____

4. What is the difference between a new dime and an old quarter?
   Answer: _____

5. What one-digit number increases in value when it is turned upside down?
   Answer: _____

6. Why can't an Englishman's hand be 12 inches long?
   Answer: _____

7. What can you put in a bucket to make it weigh less?
   Answer: _____

8. What digit becomes zero when you take half of it?
   Answer: _____

9. When you add to it, it gets smaller and smaller; when you take away from it, it gets larger and larger. What is it?
   Answer: _____

10. If Jamie has a shirt for every day of the month, what is the least number of shirts he can have?
    Answer: _____

Scores:

0–1, In the Rough	2–3, Sand Trapped
4–5, Below Par	6–7, Par
8–9, Birdie	10, Hole in One!

Have Fun with Math

Fun Test on Catchy Math Questions

Here are some catchy math questions for you to try. Read each question carefully; try not to get "caught." Write your answer in the space provided below the question. Time is limited to 15 minutes

1. I have two new coins with a total value of 35 cents. One of the coins is not a dime. What are the two coins?

   Answer: _____

2. You are a jailer with 38 prisoners and all but 8 escape. How many prisoners do you have left?

   Answer: _____

3. Subtract 15 from the consecutive numbers between 5 and 9.

   Answer: _____

4. Can an Olympic high jumper, who can clear a height of 2.2 meters, jump as high as a house?

   Answer: _____

5. Mauler Ned, a prize fighter, works during the day as a butcher. If he weighs 95 kilograms at night standing on one foot, what does he weigh during the day standing on both feet?

   Answer: _____

6. How can you place eight pieces of candy in three cups so there is an odd number of pieces in each cup?

   Answer: _____

7. If two men dig two holes in one day, can one man dig half a hole in half a day?

   Answer: _____

8. Over what area can a horse graze with a rope ten meters long tied firmly around its neck?

   Answer: _____

9. If five cats can catch five mice in five minutes, how many cats will it take to catch ten mice in ten minutes?

   Answer: _____

10. How can you make seven even without adding or subtracting a number from it?

    Answer: _____

Scores:

0–1, Very Bad Day	2–3, Bad Day
4–5, Almost a Bad Day	6–7, Almost a Good Day
8–9, Good Day	10, Very Good Day

Have Fun with Math

Fun Test with General Math Problems

How good are you at solving general math problems? Here's a chance to find out. There are 5 possible answers given for each of the 10 problems below. Select your desired response and write its letter in the space provided at the left of each problem. Time is limited to 15 minutes.

_____ 1. What number multiplied by half itself will provide a product of 50?
(a) 10   (b) 15   (c) 20   (d) 25   (e) Answer is not listed.

_____ 2. How many half-meter cubic blocks will it take to equal a one-meter cube?   (a) 2   (b) 4   (c) 6   (d) 16   (e) Answer is not listed.

_____ 3. A student who divided a number by 5, instead of multiplying, got 12 as an answer. What should the answer have been?   (a) 300
(b) 60   (c) 30   (d) 180   (e) Answer is not listed.

_____ 4. If a turkey weighs 6 kg plus one third its own weight, how much does the turkey weigh?   (a) 9 kg   (b) 12 kg   (c) 15 kg
(d) 18 kg   (e) Answer is not listed.

_____ 5. If a clock strikes the hours and half-hours, how many strikes will it make in one day?   (a) 280   (b) 180   (c) 156   (d) 90
(e) Answer is not listed.

_____ 6. Janis is thinking of a number. If she multiplies it by 2 and decreases it by 3, the result will be the original number. What number is Janis thinking of?   (a) 2   (b) 3   (c) 4   (d) 5   (e) Answer is not listed.

_____ 7. How many half-decimeter squares does it take to make a square meter?   (a) 4   (b) 40   (c) 400   (d) 4,000   (e) Answer is not listed.

_____ 8. If it takes 12 minutes to saw a log into 3 pieces, how long will it take to saw a log of the same size into 6 pieces, at the same rate?
(a) 12 min   (b) 24 min   (c) 30 min   (d) 32 min   (e) Answer is not listed.

_____ 9. If the diameter of a nickel was placed over the word *approximately*, starting with the first letter, how many letters would be covered?
(a) all of them   (b) 8 letters   (c) all but 4 letters   (d) all but 3 letters   (e) Answer is not listed.

_____ 10. Fencing that encloses a square lot is fixed on upright posts 4 meters apart. If each side of the lot is 20 meters long, how many posts are necessary to fence the lot?   (a) 28   (b) 24   (c) 22
(d) 20   (e) Answer is not listed.

Scores:

0–1, Didn't Finish   2–3, Lapped
4–5, Left Behind   6–7, In the Pack
8–9, Just Nosed Out   10, Four-Minute Mile

Have Fun with Math

Fun Test on Everyday Math

The problems on this sheet are about everyday math. See how many correct answers you can select. Place the letter of your choice in the space provided at the left of the problem. Time is limited to 15 minutes.

_____ 1. Assume a billion dollars is to be divided equally among 200 million people. How much should each person receive? (a) 5¢ (b) 50¢ (c) $5 (d) $50 (e) $500

_____ 2. If the tax rate is $7.50 per $100, what would be the annual tax on property assessed at $50,000? (a) $3.75 (b) $37.50 (c) $375.00 (d) $3,750.00 (e) $37,500.00

_____ 3. If the water rate is 40¢ per cubic meter, what would be the monthly cost of watering a lawn for half an hour per day, assuming the sprinkler system disburses 200 liters per minute? (a) $144.00 (b) $72.00 (c) $36.00 (d) $7.20 (e) $3.60

_____ 4. How long should it take a person to walk a distance of 5 kilometers without dawdling? (a) 5 minutes (b) 9 minutes (c) 18 minutes (d) 36 minutes (e) 45 minutes

_____ 5. You are planning to serve lemonade to a gathering of 100 young people. If you want each person to be served 2 glasses, how much lemonade should you provide? (a) 10 liters (b) 15 liters (c) 25 liters (d) 50 liters (e) 100 liters

_____ 6. In making change from a dollar bill for a 39¢ purchase, what is the least number of coins that can be used? (a) 3 (b) 4 (c) 5 (d) 6 (e) 7

_____ 7. At 6¢ a kilowatt-hour, what would be the cost of burning a 100-watt light bulb continuously for a month? (a) 43.2¢ (b) $2.16 (c) $4.32 (d) $8.64 (e) $43.20

_____ 8. About how many nickels could you hold in both your hands cupped together? (a) 300 (b) 150 (c) 75 (d) 50 (e) 25

_____ 9. The distance from the earth to the sun is about 150,000,000 kilometers. This would be approximately how many times the diameter of the earth? (a) 120 (b) 600 (c) 1,200 (d) 6,000 (e) 12,000

_____ 10. If gas is supplied at the rate of $6 per 100 cubic meters, what would be the cost per month of operating a heater that burns 6 cubic meters per hour for 8 hours per day? (a) $86.40 (b) $172.80 (c) $17.28 (d) $8.64 (e) $4.32

Scores:
0–1, Completely Lost   2–3, Missing
4–5, Almost Missing   6–7, Almost Sharp
8–9, Sharp   10, Very Sharp

Have Fun with Math

Thought Stinkers

Do you read a problem carefully before you try to decide on a solution? Here's a chance to find out. Place the letter of your answer in the space to the left of each problem. Time is limited to 15 minutes.

_____ 1. How many cubic meters of dirt in a hole 2 meters deep, 2½ meters long, and 1½ meters wide?   (a) none   (b) 3.25 m^3 (c) 7.5 m^3 (d) 23.5 m^3 (e) Answer is not listed.

_____ 2. What number is 45 less than by the same amount as it is more than 39?   (a) 40   (b) 46   (c) 50   (d) 51   (e) Answer is not listed.

_____ 3. In a box of 3 dozen oranges, all but 4 of each dozen are good. How many oranges in the box are bad?   (a) 8   (b) 16   (c) 24   (d) 32   (e) Answer is not listed.

_____ 4. If a farmer has 5 haystacks in one field and 3 haystacks in a second field, how many haystacks does he have putting them all together?   (a) 0   (b) 1   (c) 2   (d) 8   (e) Answer is not listed.

_____ 5. 4 months of the year have 30 days; 7 months have 31 days. How many months of the year have 28 days?   (a) 9   (b) 1   (c) 11   (d) 12   (e) Answer is not listed.

_____ 6. A dog in a box weighs 8 kg 750 g. If the box alone weighs 750 g, how much does the dog weigh?   (a) 8 kg   (b) 9½ kg   (c) 8¾ kg   (d) 9,500 g   (e) Answer is not listed.

_____ 7. It takes 5 salesmen 5 days to sell 5 cars. At this same rate, how long will it take 1 salesman to sell 1 car?   (a) 25 days   (b) 15 days   (c) 10 days   (d) 1 day   (e) Answer is not listed.

_____ 8. Mr. and Mrs. Blackwood have 5 sons, and each son has 1 sister. How many people are in the Blackwood family?   (a) 6   (b) 8   (c) 10   (d) 12   (e) Answer is not listed.

_____ 9. Jill's height is 1 m 66 cm. To get a better view of a parade, she stood on a box that was 34 cm high. How tall was Jill then?   (a) 166 cm   (b) 190 cm   (c) 2 m   (d) 210 cm   (e) Answer is not listed.

_____ 10. An ancient Roman senator was born on May 31 of 35 B.C. Unusual as it may seem, he died on May 31 of A.D. 35. How old was this Roman senator when he died?   (a) 71   (b) 70   (c) 69   (d) 51   (e) Answer is not listed.

Scores:

0–1, Super Stinker   2–3, Stinker
4–5, Almost a Stinker   5–6, Almost a Thinker
7–8, Thinker   10, Super Thinker

Have Fun with Math

A Test for Math Wizards

Can we call you "The Supreme Wizard" today? Here's a chance to find out. After each of the 10 questions below there are 5 possible answers. Place the letter of your answer in the space provided to the left of each question. Time for the quiz is limited to 15 minutes.

_____ 1. The number of marbles in a basket doubles every minute. The basket is full of marbles in 10 minutes. When was the basket half full?
(a) in 4 minutes   (b) in 5 minutes   (c) in 8 minutes
(d) in 9 minutes   (e) Answer is not listed.

_____ 2. The combined ages of a family of five total 88. The two youngest are 8 and 10 years old. What was the total of the family's combined ages 8 years ago?   (a) 38   (b) 40   (c) 48   (d) 56   (e) Answer is not listed.

_____ 3. A boy started to climb a sand dune from a given point. If each time he takes a step forward he slips a half-step backward, how many steps will he have to take to reach a point 5 full steps ahead of his starting point?   (a) 7
(b) 8   (c) 9   (d) 10   (e) Answer is not listed.

_____ 4. What is the next number in the following series: 2, 6, 15, 31, 56, . . . ?
(a) 92   (b) 80   (c) 71   (d) 64   (e) Answer is not listed.

_____ 5. If it takes 1 minute to make each cut, how long will it take to cut a 5-meter pole into 4 pieces?   (a) 2 minutes   (b) 4 minutes
(c) 5 minutes   (d) 6 minutes   (e) Answer is not listed.

_____ 6. If April 15 falls on Wednesday, what day of the week is the last day of April?   (a) Monday   (b) Wednesday   (c) Friday
(d) Sunday   (e) Answer is not listed.

_____ 7. The fencing that encloses a square lot is fixed on upright posts placed 4 meters apart. If 20 posts are necessary to fence the lot, what is its area?
(a) 256 m^2 (b) 400 m^2 (c) 576 m^2 (d) 1,024 m^2 (e) Answer is not listed.

_____ 8. Debbie and Jason both work. Debbie is off every third day; Jason is off every fifth day. Both are off this Thursday. What is the next day of the week both will be off work together?   (a) Friday   (b) Sunday
(c) Tuesday   (d) Wednesday   (e) Answer is not listed.

_____ 9. I plan to drive a distance of 2 kilometers at the rate of 60 km/hr. If I drive the first kilometer at 30 km/hr, at what speed must I drive the next kilometer?   (a) 60 km/hr   (b) 90 km/hr   (c) 120 km/hr
(d) 150 km/hr   (e) Answer is not listed.

_____ 10. Before going on a vacation, Robin was asked how long she would be away. She answered, "The day before yesterday I was able to say that I would start a week from tomorrow. As of today, I'm not coming back until two weeks from the day after tomorrow." How many days does Robin expect to be away?   (a) 7   (b) 9   (c) 11   (d) 13   (e) Answer is not listed.

Scores: 0–1, Commoner   2–3, Beginning Apprentice   4–5, Apprentice
6–7, Almost a Wizard   8–9, Wizard   10, The Supreme Wizard

Have Fun with Math

Straight Line Designs

Using a straight edge and pencil, you can draw straight lines between the points on circle diagrams, like the ones below, to create many interesting designs. Shading with different colored pencils adds to the designs. Using these circle diagrams, see if you can produce two of the designs shown above. Then try to create other designs of your own.

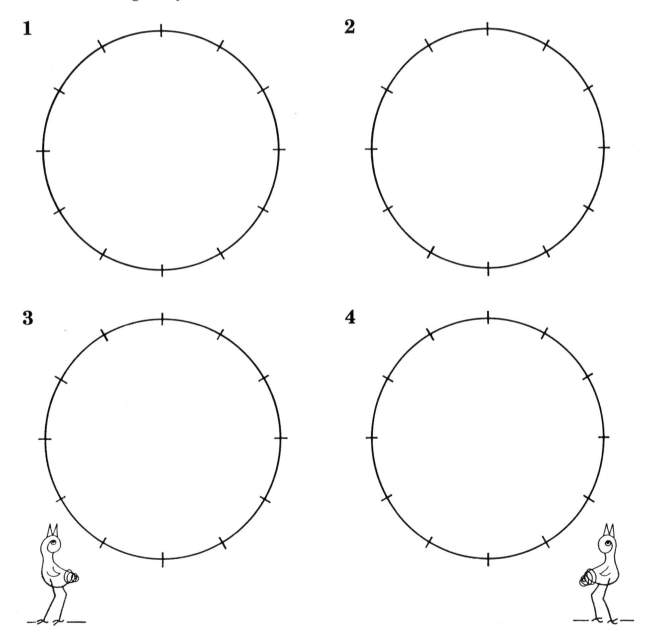

Have Fun with Math

Line Puzzles

 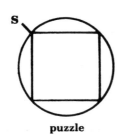 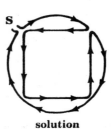 

puzzle   solution

Above is a line puzzle and its solution. The object of the puzzle is to start at **s** and trace the entire figure with a pencil in one continuous line. Rules are as follows: (1) You can't lift your pencil from the paper after starting; (2) you can't trace over any part of a line in the puzzle more than once; and (3) you can't cross over any line. Following the rules, try to solve the puzzles below. Not all of them have solutions. Colored pencils help in tracing paths.

1

2
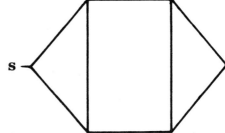

3
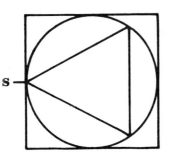

4
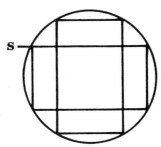

5
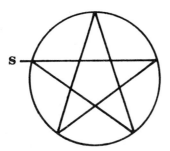

6
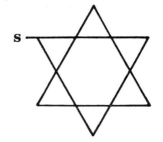

More Line Puzzles

Try to solve the puzzles below by starting at the specified point (**s**) and tracing the entire figure with one continuous line. Remember the rules: (1) You can't lift your pencil from the paper after starting; (2) you can't trace over any part of a line in the puzzle more than once; and (3) you can't cross over any line. Not all the puzzles have a solution. You may wish to use colored pencils for your tracings.

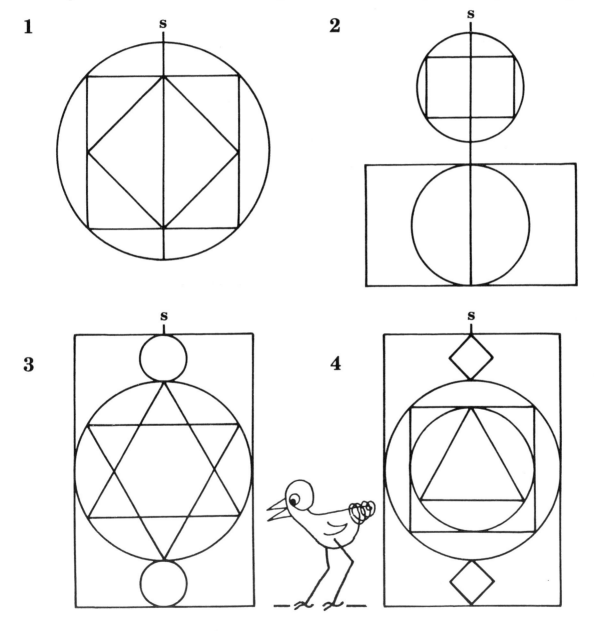

Have Fun with Math

Observation Test

Below are four overlapping figures; a circle, a triangle, a square, and a pentagon. Each figure contains a number of X's. See if you can correctly answer each of the ten questions about the X's and the figures. Place your answers in the spaces provided to the left of the questions.

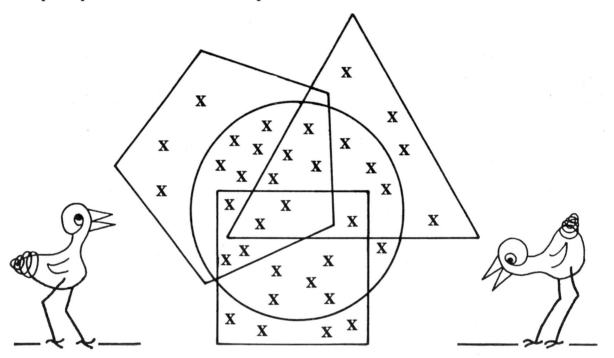

How many X's are there:

_____ 1. In all of the figures?
_____ 2. In the circle, but not in the triangle, square, or pentagon?
_____ 3. In the square, but not in the circle, pentagon, or triangle?
_____ 4. In the pentagon, but not in the circle, triangle, or square?
_____ 5. Common to the circle and the square, but not in the pentagon or triangle?
_____ 6. Common to the circle and the triangle, but not in the square or pentagon?
_____ 7. Common to the pentagon and the square, but not in the triangle or circle?
_____ 8. Common to the circle, triangle, and pentagon, but not in the square?
_____ 9. Common to the triangle, circle, and square, but not in the pentagon?
_____ 10. Common to the circle, triangle, square, and pentagon?

Have Fun with Math

Toothpick Math

Five toothpick puzzles are provided on this sheet. Get twenty-four toothpicks; then try to solve the puzzles. You can show your solutions in the spaces next to the puzzle diagrams.

1. *Four Squares with One Less Toothpick.* Arrange thirteen toothpicks as shown in the diagram below. You are challenged to remove one toothpick from the group and then form four squares of equal size by moving only five of the remaining toothpicks.

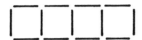

2. *Changing a Square to a Cross.* Arrange twelve toothpicks as shown in the diagram below. You are challenged to move only eight of the toothpicks to form a cross.

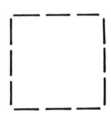 

3. *Changing Twelve Squares to Three Squares.* Twenty-four toothpicks are arranged to form nine small squares as in the diagram below. You are challenged to remove six of the toothpicks so that three squares remain.

 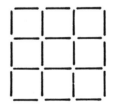

4. *Changing Eleven Toothpicks to Nine.* Eleven toothpicks are arranged as diagrammed below. Without removing any of the toothpicks from the group, you are challenged to change them to nine.

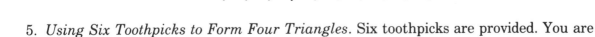

5. *Using Six Toothpicks to Form Four Triangles.* Six toothpicks are provided. You are challenged to form four triangles of equal size, using only the six toothpicks.

Have Fun with Math

More Toothpick Math

After getting together twenty-six toothpicks you'll be ready to attempt to solve the five toothpick puzzles provided on this sheet. You can show your solutions in the spaces next to the diagrams.

1. *Changing a Hexagon into Two Diamonds.* Arrange six toothpicks to form a hexagon as diagrammed below. You are challenged to rearrange two toothpicks and add one more to form two diamonds.

2. *Making a Square Larger.* Arrange four toothpicks to form a square as illustrated in the diagram below. You are challenged to give two more toothpicks a break and use all six to make a larger square.

3. *Add to the Sides of a Square and Not Change Its Value.* Twenty toothpicks are arranged to form a square, as diagrammed below. You are challenged to rearrange four toothpicks and add four more toothpicks to the figure so that the total number of toothpicks on each side is nine.

 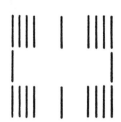 

4. *Changing the Way a House Faces.* Arrange ten toothpicks to form the outline of a house that faces left, as in the diagram below. You are challenged to rearrange only two toothpicks to make the house face right.

5. *The Grape in a Dessert Glass.* Arrange four toothpicks and a coin as shown in the diagram below. This arrangement represents a grape in a dessert glass. You are challenged to move only two toothpicks to get the grape (coin) to the outside of the glass (toothpicks) without touching the grape (coin).

Have Fun with Math

Math with Coins

Five coin puzzles are provided on this sheet. Obtain a supply of ten coins of the same size; then try to solve the puzzles. You can show your solutions in the spaces next to the diagrams.

1. *Three and One-Half Dozen.* Nine coins are arranged in a row as shown in the diagram below. You are challenged to move one coin so you will have three and one-half dozen.

2. *Making Two Rows of Four Coins Each.* Six coins are arranged in two rows as shown in the diagram below. You are challenged to move one coin to make two rows of four coins each.

3. *Rolling One Coin around Another.* Imagine that you are rolling one coin (A) around another coin of equal size (B), as shown in the diagram below. Does the moving coin make a complete revolution as it moves around the other coin, or does it make more than one complete revolution? You are challenged to answer this question before you attempt to illustrate it with the two coins.

4. *Making a Circle of Coins.* Arrange six coins of equal size as shown in the diagram below. You are challenged to slide only two coins to new positions to form a complete circle of coins.

5. *Reversing a Triangle of Coins.* Arrange ten coins to form a triangle of coins as illustrated in the diagram below. You are challenged to turn the triangle upside down by rearranging only three of the coins.

Have Fun with Math

Forming Words Related to Math

See how well you can recall some words related to math and how well you can spell these words. You are to substitute any *one* letter for another in each word listed below, without changing the sequence of the remaining letters in the word, to form a new word that can be associated with math. Write this new word in the space next to the listed word. The first one is done as an example. Time is limited to 30 minutes.

1. aid _____*add*_____
2. art _____
3. bum _____
4. case _____
5. court _____
6. cram _____
7. crime _____
8. dive _____
9. done _____
10. fine _____
11. grape _____
12. hero _____
13. hour _____
14. joint _____
15. late _____
16. lean _____
17. lime _____
18. lumber _____
19. mine _____
20. old _____

21. patio _____
22. pen _____
23. pets _____
24. plant _____
25. plug _____
26. right _____
27. rode _____
28. room _____
29. say _____
30. scalp _____
31. sever _____
32. sinus _____
33. sox _____
34. spare _____
35. steed _____
36. too _____
37. tower _____
38. traction _____
39. tube _____
40. won _____

Scores: 0–5, Asleep   6–12, Dozing   13–20, Awake
21–28, Alert   29–36, Very Alert   37–40, Quiz-Whiz

Have Fun with Math

Pun with Math

Try to find the mathematical words that respond to the following statements. The results should be "fun puns." A list of words to help you is provided at the bottom of the sheet. Time is limited to 15 minutes.

1. _____ What they did at the dinner table.
2. _____ A murderous message.
3. _____ What he did after her phone call from the airport.
4. _____ Without strength.
5. _____ The part of a tree that is underground.
6. _____ Opposite of good traction.
7. _____ The ship that Noah built.
8. _____ Condition of a mad hatter.
9. _____ What the boy friend had to do to meet his date.
10. _____ An angular disaster.
11. _____ What a mystic has.
12. _____ Condition of an angry person.
13. _____ The way poets express themselves.
14. _____ What they did to be winners.
15. _____ King of the beasts.
16. _____ When you're through adding.
17. _____ Person who isn't with it.
18. _____ Condition of a lost record.
19. _____ Made especially for ice cream.
20. _____ Not at all beautiful.

add	decimal	fraction	nine	powers	subtraction
addend	decagon	inverse	numerator	pyramid	three
angle	denominator	irrational	one	quotient	triangle
arc	diameter	kilogram	parallelogram	radius	two
centimeter	dividend	line	per cent	rectangle	week
cone	eight	mean	pi	root	weight
cube	formula	meter	plane	sphere	year
cylinder	four	minute	point	square	zero

Scores:

0–3, Non-Punner	4–6, Poor Punner	7–10, Unfair Punner
11–14, Fair Punner	15–18, Punny	19–20, Very Punny

Have Fun with Math

Some Units of Measure That Are Different

Some units of measure with which you may not be familiar are presented below. All are defined in *Webster's Collegiate Dictionary*. Select the answer you feel is correct for each question and write its letter in the space provided at the left of the problem. Time is limited to 15 minutes.

_____ 1. Still used to measure distance in some countries are the perch, the pole, or the rod. What distance in metric units is represented by a rod (or pole, or perch)?   (a) less than a meter   (b) approximately 5 dm   (c) approximately 5 m   (d) more than a km   (e) Answer is not listed.

_____ 2. The stone is a measure of weight used in England. What weight in metric units is represented by one stone?   (a) nearly 10 kg   (b) approximately 6 kg   (c) about 3 kg   (d) less than a kg   (e) Answer is not listed.

_____ 3. A friend tells you he plans to be away from home for a fortnight. How long a period of time would this be?   (a) 4 days   (b) 20 days   (c) one month   (d) 6 weeks   (e) Answer is not listed.

_____ 4. A woman lived to the age of four score and seven years. How many years did this woman live?   (a) 27 years   (b) 47 years   (c) 67 years   (d) 87 years   (e) Answer is not listed.

_____ 5. The mil is a unit used in some countries to measure the diameter of wire. What distance in metric units is represented by one mil?   (a) .025 mm   (b) .25 mm   (c) 2.5 mm   (d) .25 cm   (e) Answer is not listed.

_____ 6. Horse traders measure the height of a horse in number of hands. What distance in metric units is represented by one hand?   (a) 10.2 cm   (b) 2½ dm   (c) .45 m   (d) 1¼ m   (e) Answer is not listed.

_____ 7. Mariners measure the depth of water in number of fathoms. What depth in metric units is measured by one fathom?   (a) 2 dm   (b) ½ m   (c) about 1 m   (d) nearly 1 km   (e) Answer is not listed.

_____ 8. The Bible refers to a measure called a cubit, which is still in use in some countries. What length in metric units is represented by one cubit?   (a) 1 dm   (b) about ½ m   (c) 75 cm   (d) 30 dm   (e) Answer is not listed.

_____ 9. The speed of a ship or airplane is usually measured in number of knots. What rate in metric units is represented by one knot?   (a) less than 1 km/hr   (b) about 5 km/hr   (c) approximately 3 km/hr   (d) nearly 10 km/hr   (e) Answer is not listed.

_____ 10. A carat is a unit of weight for measuring precious stones such as diamonds, emeralds, or pearls. What weight in metric units is represented by one carat?   (a) nearly a kg   (b) about 20 g   (c) almost 2 g   (d) 200 mg   (e) Answer is not listed.

Scores: 0–1, KO's   2–3, Very Frail   4–5, Frail
              6–7, OK   8–9, Real Great   10, Terrific _____

A Logic Puzzle

Below are eight statements about four college students. Use the statements to match the names of the students with the graduating class, favorite sport, and chosen profession of each student. As you become certain of a fact, fill in that fact in the chart below the statements.

1. Dave, who doesn't care for racquetball, often plays tennis with the student who is a senior.
2. Jason expects to follow a career in education when he finishes college.
3. Freda, who is a close friend of Lisa, is completing her senior year.
4. The girl whose favorite sport is tennis plans to practice law.
5. The freshman, who does not bowl or play tennis, is not the theology student.
6. Skating is the favorite sport of the sophomore student.
7. The student whose chosen profession is medicine spends most of her free time bowling.
8. One of the four students is a junior.

Name	Class	Favorite Sport	Chosen Profession

Have Fun with Math

Another Logic Puzzle

Each of five people is a different nationality, lives on a different floor of a five-story apartment building, has a different favorite game, a different favorite drink, and a different kind of pet. Using the statements below, identify the nationality, apartment floor, favorite game, favorite drink, and kind of pet of each person. As you become certain of a fact, fill in that fact in the chart below the statements.

1. The person who owns the parrot lives on the top floor.
2. The Canadian, who lives on the middle floor, does not like the monkey.
3. The Indonesian, who doesn't like orange juice, is considered a champion chess player.
4. The bridge player sometimes pours milk for his pet.
5. The owner of the canary, who does not drink coffee, lives on the street floor.
6. The Frenchman upset friends by serving hot chocolate at his poker party.
7. The Nigerian lives on a lower floor from the Peruvian than does the Indonesian.
8. The person who owns the monkey had tea when he visited the owner of the parrot.
9. The pinochle player does not like tea.
10. The owner of the lizard, who does not play Scrabble, lives on the fourth floor.
11. Neither the Frenchman nor the Peruvian live on the second floor.
12. A bobcat is the pet of the bridge player.

Apartment Floor	Nationality	Favorite Game	Favorite Drink	Pet

Have Fun with Math

Tri-It

Tri-It is a game played by two people. The object of the game is for a player to have produced more triangles than the opponent upon the completion of a game. A game is completed when no more plays can be made. The diagrams below have 36 dots and will make 49 triangles. You can outline more game diagrams on grid paper.

After flipping a coin to see who plays first, the players take turns making plays. A play consists of drawing a single horizontal or oblique line between two adjacent dots of a game diagram. A turn consists of one play, except when a bonus play is earned. A player earns a bonus play, which must be taken, each time the player completes a triangle.

Upon completing a triangle, the player puts his or her mark, either an *X* or an *O*, inside the triangle to identify it. The player with the most triangles is the winner. A tally is made when the game is completed. To make a tally, indicate the number of *X*'s in a row at the left and the number of *O*'s at the right; then add the respective numbers for all the rows. A completed game is shown below.

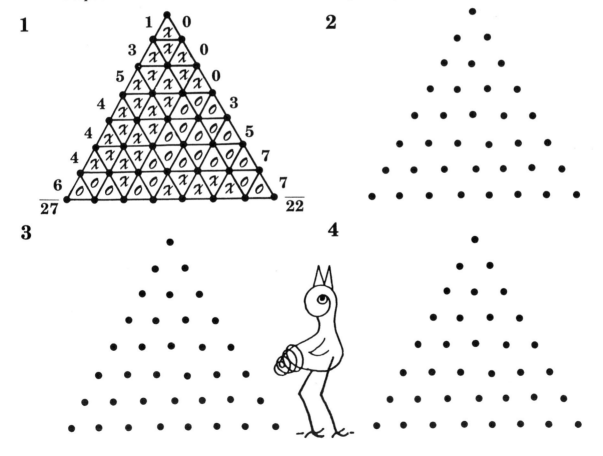

Square-It

The game of Square-It is very similar to the game of Tri-It. In Square-It, squares are completed instead of the triangles in Tri-It. A turn consists of two plays (instead of one), except when a square is completed in the first play and a bonus play is earned. In that case, the second play is the bonus play. A player earns a bonus play, which must be taken, when the player completes a square.

The diagrams below have 64 dots and will make 49 squares for a completed game. A completed game, with tally, is shown below. You can outline more game diagrams on grid paper.

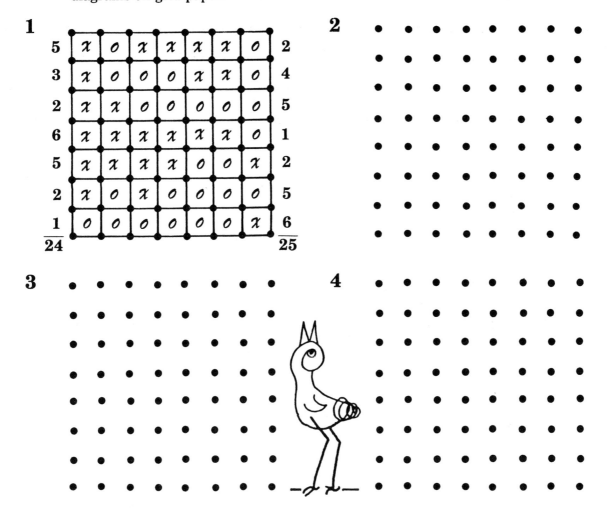

Part IX
Pre-Algebra

167

What's That Number?

Each item below describes a number. Try to identify the number and write it in the space provided to the left of the problem. Time is limited to 20 minutes.

_____ 1. This number is half as large as the product of 3 and 6.

_____ 2. Twice this number is 1 less than half of 26.

_____ 3. This number, when multiplied by 3, is equal to twice the sum of 8 and 7.

_____ 4. Three times this number is equal to the average of 8 and 16.

_____ 5. When this number is multiplied by 5, it is equal to twice the sum of 18 and 12 divided by 3.

_____ 6. Twice the product of 6 and 5 is three times as great as this number.

_____ 7. When this number is multiplied by 6, the product is 10 greater than the product of 7 and 8.

_____ 8. The average of this number and the next two consecutive numbers is equal to the difference of 35 and 25.

_____ 9. When this number is divided by 4, the quotient is $\frac{1}{3}$ as large as the sum of 16 and 11.

_____ 10. The difference of this number and 9 is twice as large as $\frac{2}{3}$ of 12.

_____ 11. Five times this number is 4 more than $\frac{3}{4}$ of 48.

_____ 12. When this number is divided by 4, the quotient is 1 less than $\frac{3}{8}$ of 16.

_____ 13. The average of this number and the next consecutive odd number is 2 more than $\frac{2}{3}$ of 15.

_____ 14. The square of this number is twice the sum of 5 and 13.

_____ 15. Twice the square of this number is $\frac{1}{2}$ the square of 10.

_____ 16. The square of 6 plus this number is equal to the square of 7.

_____ 17. The square of this number is 8 less than $\frac{1}{2}$ the square of 12.

_____ 18. This number, when multiplied by 3, is equal to 4 times the square of 3.

_____ 19. The product of this number and 10 is equal to the square of this number.

_____ 20. The sum of the square of this number and this number is 20.

Scores:

0–3, Hum Dum   4–7, Oh Hum
8–10, Hum   11–15, Hum Ho
16–18, Ho Ho   19–20, Hi Ho

Have Fun with Math

Rapid Multiplication with Some Special Pairs of Numbers

You can learn to tell at a glance that 59×61 is equal to 3,599 and that 83×77 is equal to 6,391. Notice in the first example that 59 is 1 less than 60 and 61 is 1 more than 60; in the second example, 83 is 3 more than 80 and 77 is 3 less than 80.

The product of these kinds of numbers is found by applying the following rule: Multiply the multiple of the tens digit by itself and annex two zeros; multiply the difference above and below the multiple of ten by itself; subtract the second result from the first; the difference is the desired product. (This is a rule developed from a method of doing certain special products in algebra.)

Example: 28×32 is found as follows: 3 is the multiple of 10; 3×3 is 9. Annex two zeros; 900. The difference above and below 30 is 2; 2×2 is 4. Subtract 4 from 900; $900 - 4$. The product is 896.

Example: 54×46 is found as follows: 5 is the multiple of 10; 5×5 is 25. Annex two zeros; 2,500. The difference above and below 50 is 4; 4×4 is 16. Subtract 16 from 2,500; $2,500 - 16$. The desired product is 2,484.

Example: 75×85 is found as follows: 8 is the multiple of 10; 8×8 is 64. Annex two zeros; 6,400. The difference above and below 80 is 5; 5×5 is 25. Subtract 25 from 6,400; $6,400 - 25$. The desired product is 6,375.

Try solving the following examples using the illustrated method. Write your answers in the spaces provided.

(1) $29 \times 31 =$ _____

(2) $22 \times 18 =$ _____

(3) $39 \times 41 =$ _____

(4) $52 \times 48 =$ _____

(5) $27 \times 33 =$ _____

(6) $51 \times 49 =$ _____

(7) $38 \times 42 =$ _____

(8) $73 \times 67 =$ _____

(9) $79 \times 81 =$ _____

(10) $53 \times 47 =$ _____

(11) $58 \times 62 =$ _____

(12) $24 \times 16 =$ _____

(13) $87 \times 93 =$ _____

(14) $71 \times 69 =$ _____

(15) $36 \times 44 =$ _____

(16) $82 \times 78 =$ _____

(17) $25 \times 35 =$ _____

(18) $64 \times 56 =$ _____

(19) $45 \times 55 =$ _____

(20) $43 \times 37 =$ _____

(21) $85 \times 95 =$ _____

(22) $74 \times 66 =$ _____

(23) $88 \times 92 =$ _____

(24) $109 \times 111 =$ _____

(25) $105 \times 115 =$ _____

Rapid Multiplication with Any Pair of Two-Digit Numbers

Would you like to learn how to multiply any pair of two-digit numbers mentally? If so, the following illustration shows how it is accomplished. It is very similar to the way multiplication is done in algebra.

Example: 43 × 76

```
  43
  76
2,800

  24 }
  21 }  450

  18
3,268
```

1. Find the product of the tens digits (4 × 7 = 28) and annex two zeros (2,800).

2. Cross-multiply the pairs of digits (4 × 6 = 24 and 3 × 7 = 21). Find the sum of these two products (24 + 21 = 45) and annex a zero (450).

3. Find the product of the units digits (3 × 6 = 18).

4. Find the sum of the three results (2,800 + 450 + 18 = 3,268).

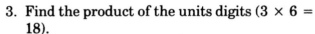

Try solving the following multiplications using the illustrated method (do not use pencil and paper).

(1) 23 × 36 = _____   (9) 56 × 94 = _____   (18) 32 × 79 = _____

(2) 17 × 52 = _____   (10) 42 × 37 = _____   (19) 71 × 29 = _____

(3) 66 × 33 = _____   (11) 28 × 34 = _____   (20) 64 × 49 = _____

(4) 64 × 38 = _____   (12) 27 × 76 = _____   (21) 39 × 61 = _____

(5) 60 × 87 = _____   (13) 34 × 68 = _____   (22) 28 × 43 = _____

(6) 51 × 49 = _____   (14) 76 × 27 = _____   (23) 38 × 84 = _____

(7) 34 × 26 = _____   (15) 23 × 81 = _____   (24) 85 × 53 = _____

(8) 27 × 44 = _____   (16) 46 × 68 = _____   (25) 47 × 52 = _____

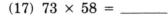

(17) 73 × 58 = _____

Have Fun with Math

Addition Number Puzzles

The number puzzles below test your addition and subtraction skills. In these puzzles it is possible to replace each question mark (?) with a digit. Do this by rewriting each item, including the correct digit(s), in the spaces below and/or to the right of each puzzle. Remember, each puzzle is an addition problem.

(1)	(2)	(3)	(4)	(5)	(6)	(7)	(8)	(9)	(10)
2	6	2	3	5	6	7	?	?	?
?	?	?	?	?	?	?	7	6	5
4	9	7	8	9	10	13	15	15	?2

(11)	(12)	(13)	(14)	(15)	(16)	(17)	(18)	(19)	(20)
?	?	?	?	8	?	7	9	?	6
9	3	8	9	?	3	?	?	7	?
?7	?0	?6	?8	?3	?1	?1	?5	?5	?5

(21)	(22)	(23)	(24)	(25)	(26)	(27)	(28)	(29)	(30)
?	9	??	?0	6	?	??	3?	?9	?7
?	?	7	?	??	1	?	8	?	7
18	?6	18	11	17	??	30	?8	37	5?

(31)	(32)	(33)	(34)	(35)	(36)	(37)	(38)	(39)	(40)
3?	8	?8	?5	2?	37	2?	?1	?5	3?
6	??	?	5	9	?	?	?	3?	?7
?3	63	36	4?	?3	?2	20	40	81	66

(41)	(42)	(43)	(44)	(45)	(46)	(47)	(48)	(49)	(50)
?2	6?	?7	???	43?	?3?	568	7?	865	?7
2?	?7	8?	497	?66	3?5	???	?8	???	9?
62	?12	?29	836	9?3	883	745	?04	?671	?95

Have Fun with Math

Number Puzzles with Addition and Subtraction

In the number puzzles below, enough clues are provided so you can replace each question mark (?) and/or letter with the correct digit. A letter that appears more than once in a puzzle stands for the same digit each time it appears in that puzzle. Show your solution by rewriting each item, including the correct digits, in the spaces to the right and/or below each puzzle.

(1)	(2)	(3)	(4)	(5)
3?8 +?37 ──── 80?	893 − ??? ──── 286	76? + 3?4 ──── ??52	?56? − 7?9 ──── 7?10	?38 6?5 24? ──── ?674

(6)	(7)	(8)	(9)	(10)
3?0?8 − 6?5? ───── ?3126	?38217 4?6253 74?096 823?71 6049?6 ────── ?12206?	?873 51? 92?47 ?8 5203 ───── ??3607	37064358 − ?????? ───────── ?7064359	9?03475 ?2 3106? ?24 82?809 ──────── ??0?1947

(11)	(12)	(13)	(14)	(15)
A + A ─── 16	A7 +3A ─── ?2	A8 −2A ─── ?2	A5 + A? ─── ?69	?36 − AB ─── AB

(16)	(17)	(18)	(19)	(20)
1AB + AB ──── ?14	1AB + BA8 ──── ??36	?A7 − BB ──── AA	16A A85 A?7 ──── ?75	3?0B B453 B6?B ──── ??779

(21)	(22)	(23)	(24)	(25)
?7?0 B?B1 8B2B ───── ?07B7	B27 BB35 ??B ───── ??301	C8 C27 C509 ───── ???C	DD DD DD ──── ??8	HOW HOT HO HO ───── ?323

Have Fun with Math

Multiplication Number Puzzles

In the number puzzles below, enough clues are provided so you can replace the question marks and/or letters with the correct digits. A letter that appears more than once in a puzzle stands for the same digit each time it appears in that puzzle. See how many puzzles you can solve. Show your solutions by rewriting each puzzle, including the correct digits, in the spaces to the right and/or below the puzzles.

(1)
?3
  ?
—
46
	(2)
	?7
	  5
	—
	8?
		(3)
		1?
		  7
		—
		?1
			(4)
			??
			  ?
			—
			57
				(5)
				?6
				  ?
				—
				3?8

(6)
5?
  ?
—
2?6
	(7)
	9?
	  ?
	—
	?65
		(8)
		6?
		  ?
		—
		56?
			(9)
			??
			  ?
			—
			7?3
				(10)
				???
				  ?
				—
				938

(11)
2?6
  ?
—
?048
	(12)
	4??
	  9
	—
	??85
		(13)
		A3A
		  A
		—
		??1A
			(14)
			AA8
			  8
			—
			???A
				(15)
				AAA
				  3
				—
				??6A

(16)
??3A
  A
—
A81A
	(17)
	AAA
	  B
	—
	?BB2
		(18)
		AAB
		  B
		—
		38AB
			(19)
			?A7B
			  B
			—
			A?37B
				(20)
				B?236
				  A
				—
				ABAAA

(21) AAB1?4 B — ?ABAA38	(22) 2? ?4 — 1?? ?8 — ??4	(23) 2? ?? — ?7 ??? — 2?1?	(24) ??9 ?? — ???3 ???7 — ???7?	(25) 82?? ??? — ????6 7???8 ????8 — ?0???8?

Have Fun with Math

Division Number Puzzles

The division number puzzles below have enough clues so you can replace the question marks and/or letters with the correct digits. A letter that appears more than once in a puzzle stands for the same digit each time it appears in that puzzle. See how many puzzles you can solve. Show your solutions by rewriting each puzzle, including the correct digits, in the spaces to the right and/or below the puzzles.

(1) $\frac{5}{7\overline{)??}}$	(2) $\frac{??}{3\overline{)9?}}$	(3) $\frac{9}{?\overline{)?2}}$	(4) $\frac{??}{6\overline{)?4}}$	(5) $\frac{?3}{7\overline{)??}}$
(6) $\frac{??}{?\overline{)85}}$ $\frac{17}{5\overline{)85}}$	(7) $\frac{83}{?\overline{)??2}}$	(8) $\frac{??}{7\overline{)?99}}$ $\frac{57}{7\overline{)399}}$	(9) $\frac{3?}{9\overline{)??2}}$	(10) $\frac{?7}{?\overline{)?68}}$
(11) $\frac{45?}{9\overline{)???2}}$ $\frac{458}{9\overline{)4122}}$	(12) $\frac{?36}{?\overline{)5??6}}$	(13) $\frac{AAA}{9\overline{)???3}}$	(14) $\frac{?AA}{A\overline{)4?7A}}$	(15) $\frac{A?A}{A\overline{)??16}}$
(16) $\frac{??3A}{A\overline{)7?1A}}$	(17) $\frac{??AA}{7\overline{)?A?8}}$	(18) $\frac{AAA}{A\overline{)3BBA}}$	(19) $\frac{AAAB}{B\overline{)3??29}}$	(20) $\frac{B32A}{A\overline{)??B2A}}$
(21) $\frac{?36AA}{B\overline{)ABBBBB}}$	(22) $\frac{?7}{??\overline{)???}}$ $\frac{?9}{2??}$ $\frac{??3}{}$	(23) $\frac{??}{7?\overline{)?5?1}}$ 78 $\frac{2??}{1??}$ $\frac{?5?}{35}$	(24) $\frac{??9}{3??\overline{)??????}}$ $\frac{12??}{????}$ $\frac{??53}{}$	(25) $\frac{2??}{???\overline{)????0}}$ 386 $\frac{???}{????}$ $\frac{1930}{????}$ $\frac{????}{8}$

More Number Puzzles

In the blocks below are number puzzles on addition, subtraction, multiplication, and division. Enough clues are provided so you can replace each question mark with a digit that will lead to puzzle solutions. Each puzzle does have a solution; see how many of them you can solve. Show your solutions by rewriting each puzzle, with the correct digits inserted, in the spaces to the right of the puzzles.

(1)	(2)
96?5 ?07 ?126 7? ?8246	??0?8 17?7 ??00? ?9 2????2

(3)	(4)
?8?6 − 94? 2?59	??54?? − ??806 5?74

(5)	(6)
??7 ??? ??85 ??96? 5?????	??9 ??? ??16 5??? 21?? ????3?

(7)	(8)
??9 ?3?)8???5 ??? 1??? ???? 3??? ????	4??? 2?)??0?3 ?? ?? ?? ??? ??? 9

Have Fun with Math

Fraction Puzzles

Enough clues are provided in the fraction puzzles below so you can replace each question mark with a digit that leads to puzzle solutions. See how many puzzles you can solve. Show your solutions by rewriting the puzzles, with missing digits inserted, in the spaces directly below the puzzles.

(1) $\frac{1}{2} = \frac{4}{?}$	(2) $\frac{1}{4} = \frac{?}{16}$	(3) $\frac{?}{6} = \frac{4}{24}$	(4) $\frac{1}{?} = \frac{6}{48}$	(5) $\frac{3}{4} = \frac{??}{24}$
(6) $\frac{5}{?} = \frac{?5}{24}$	(7) $\frac{?}{4} = \frac{18}{?4}$	(8) $\frac{7}{?} = \frac{?8}{32}$	(9) $\frac{3}{?} = \frac{1?}{40}$	(10) $\frac{2?}{?5} = \frac{?6}{75}$
(11) $\frac{?1}{2?} = \frac{4?}{96}$	(12) $\frac{7}{?0} = \frac{3?}{10?}$	(13) $\frac{5}{?2} = \frac{?5}{6?}$	(14) $\frac{7}{?6} = \frac{?5}{8?}$	(15) $\frac{?}{8} = \frac{4?}{4?}$
(16) $\frac{?}{6} + \frac{?}{6} = \frac{1}{3}$	(17) $\frac{?}{3} + \frac{?}{6} = \frac{1}{2}$	(18) $\frac{5}{?2} + \frac{1}{1?} = \frac{1}{2}$	(19) $\frac{?}{2} + \frac{?}{4} = \frac{3}{?}$	(20) $\frac{1}{6} + \frac{7}{??} = \frac{3}{?}$
(21) $\frac{?}{2} + \frac{?}{3} = \frac{5}{?}$	(22) $\frac{11}{15} - \frac{1}{?} = \frac{2}{?}$	(23) $\frac{?}{3} + \frac{1}{4} = \frac{1?}{?2}$	(24) $\frac{?}{12} + \frac{?}{16} = \frac{41}{??}$	(25) $\frac{?}{8} - \frac{?}{3} = \frac{7}{??}$

Have Fun with Math

Alphametics

Alphametics are mathematical puzzles in which letters replace digits in the arithmetical processes. The same letter is used for the same digit throughout a puzzle. Clues, along with trial and error, enable you to replace each letter with a digit to follow the arithmetical process of a puzzle correctly. Try solving the puzzles below, showing your solutions in the spaces to the right and/or below the puzzles. Some puzzles may have more than one solution; some digits may be interchangeable.

(1) AB AB AB CB	(2) BA − AB B	(3) AAAA × A AAAA	(4) AAAA × B BBBB
(5) AA AA BB BB EDCB	(6) AA AA)ABA AA AA AA	(7) BA CA BA EDC EAAA	(8) AB AB)ADC AB BC BC
(9) ONE ONE ONE ONE FOUR Use N = 7	(10) TEN TEN FORTY SIXTY Use T = 8	(11) FIVE TWO ONE EIGHT Use E = 1	(12) SEVEN − FOUR THREE Use E = 6
(13) RUM + DUM MATH Use A = 4	(14) THIS IS VERY FUNNY Use N = 9	(15) DO × IT = NOW Use O = 3	(16) √TODAY = PAY Use Y = 6

     Have Fun with Math

Mathograms

A mathogram is a mathematical puzzle in which letters that spell a word have been substituted for the digits of numbers. The object is to find the digits represented by each letter, then arrange the letters in ascending order of the digits they represent, using each letter only once, forming a word. The first puzzle has been solved for you. Study the solution carefully; then try to solve the other puzzles.

(1)

```
    B E I R       5271
    R I N U       1704
  E R N C U      21084
P L C A I N     368970
    B E I R       5271
C A C R I C U   8981784
```

R E P U B L I C A N
1 2 3 4 5 6 7 8 9 0

(2)

```
    T R Y H
    H E L I
  S Y S T I
Y S H L E L
    T R Y H
R A R S C T I
```

Hint: R = 6

1 2 3 4 5 6 7 8 9 0

(3)

```
          D R E G
  S I G ) S G S N E G
          S I G
            T N E
            N O R
          D A E G
          D A E G
```

Hint: S = 3

1 2 3 4 5 6 7 8 9 0

(4)

```
              C A S R
  V H R ) L V I A A V
          V H R
          H C L A
          H C I A
            I S A V
          H U O U
            L A
```

Hint: U = 9

1 2 3 4 5 6 7 8 9 0

Have Fun with Math

A Coded Message

You can find a message by substituting the letters arranged in the grid for the pairs of coordinates listed below. Each pair of coordinates locates a letter of the message in the grid. What is the message?

9	U	S	G	J	V	D	A	M	O	D
8	L	E	T	Q	F	L	Z	K	H	Y
7	O	M	H	G	S	U	T	C	R	E
6	F	I	B	N	B	N	K	G	L	R
5	K	T	K	E	Y	Q	P	X	J	A
4	X	W	H	I	C	R	P	E	M	I
3	A	E	Q	F	O	Y	U	C	O	B
2	W	S	D	P	J	C	N	X	J	S
1	Y	V	Q	V	B	T	P	R	Z	L
0	M	G	O	K	E	N	H	A	W	Z
	0	1	2	3	4	5	6	7	8	9

$\overline{(2,8)}$ $\overline{(2,4)}$ $\overline{(0,7)}$ $\overline{(1,2)}$ $\overline{(3,5)}$ $\quad$ $\overline{(8,0)}$ $\overline{(8,8)}$ $\overline{(2,0)}$ $\quad$ $\overline{(3,0)}$ $\overline{(6,2)}$ $\overline{(8,9)}$ $\overline{(0,2)}$

$\overline{(1,8)}$ $\overline{(4,9)}$ $\overline{(1,3)}$ $\overline{(5,4)}$ $\overline{(4,5)}$ $\overline{(6,7)}$ $\overline{(6,0)}$ $\overline{(9,4)}$ $\overline{(3,6)}$ $\overline{(7,6)}$ $\quad$ $\overline{(2,7)}$ $\overline{(6,9)}$ $\overline{(3,1)}$ $\overline{(9,7)}$

$\overline{(0,3)}$ $\quad$ $\overline{(5,8)}$ $\overline{(8,3)}$ $\overline{(1,5)}$ $\quad$ $\overline{(5,1)}$ $\overline{(4,3)}$ $\quad$ $\overline{(9,1)}$ $\overline{(7,4)}$ $\overline{(9,5)}$ $\overline{(7,1)}$ $\overline{(5,6)}$.

Have Fun with Math

Another Coded Message

You can find a message by substituting the letters arranged in the grid for the pairs of coordinates listed below. Each pair of coordinates locates a letter of the message in the grid. What is the message?

	0	1	2	3	4	5	6	7	8	9
9	P	H	Y	U	D	V	M	O	E	S
8	Y	R	S	J	L	A	E	K	N	A
7	L	E	X	T	Q	M	I	R	P	Z
6	K	D	O	X	I	H	M	F	T	E
5	C	L	X	C	F	K	U	W	A	S
4	Q	H	G	V	T	A	Y	J	M	G
3	O	P	N	L	C	N	K	B	S	P
2	R	U	B	F	O	S	B	G	E	B
1	C	N	J	U	Q	D	U	I	G	Z
0	O	V	H	R	Z	T	I	E	D	V

‾(8,3) ‾(5,4) ‾(5,0) ‾(7,1) ‾(9,9) ‾(3,2) ‾(5,8) ‾(3,5) ‾(3,7) ‾(6,7) ‾(0,3) ‾(2,3) ‾(4,6) ‾(2,8)

‾(0,6) ‾(1,1) ‾(7,9) ‾(7,5) ‾(6,0) ‾(8,8) ‾(2,4) ‾(0,8) ‾(4,2) ‾(3,1) ‾(1,9) ‾(8,5) ‾(1,0) ‾(1,7)

‾(4,9) ‾(0,0) ‾(5,3) ‾(9,6) ‾(6,4) ‾(2,6) ‾(6,1) ‾(7,7) ‾(9,2) ‾(8,2) ‾(9,5) ‾(4,4) .

Have Fun with Math

Positive and Negative Number Puzzles

In these puzzles, positive and negative numbers are placed in a grid arrangement. The sums of the rows are in the right-hand column of a puzzle; the sums of the columns are in the bottom row. A number without a sign is a positive number. A puzzle is solved by filling in the blanks with numbers that give the correct sums. In the first puzzle, only the sums are missing. Four puzzles are provided to challenge you.

1

									Sum
−8	0	3	6	−9	2	5	−8	2	
0	−2	5	−8	2	−6	9	−2	−4	
1	−5	8	−4	8	−3	−7	1	5	
−9	2	−5	7	2	4	7	0	−2	
6	2	−7	1	−5	−9	4	8	−2	
5	6	−9	−4	−5	8	−1	4	−7	
4	−7	0	−3	5	8	−3	−5	7	
−5	7	4	−7	2	−6	1	−5	9	
0	−3	6	8	−2	6	−7	1	−4	
Sum									

2

									Sum
−9		−8	7	0		3	2	−6	
−4	−7	2		1	7	0	5		5
0	5	−9	−2		3	−7	2	4	4
6	1	4	−9	7	−8	3		−1	
4	−6		−5	0		7	−3		2
−3	3	−1	3	−8		−3	2	−7	−7
−9	4	−7	−3			6	0	−2	−6
	3	5	2	−6	−6	−3	2	4	8
7		6	9	−3	−7	1	−8	0	0
Sum		−1	−7	−5		−3		−5	7	−3

3

									Sum
	1	−7	−3		−4		−5	1	5
	−5	−2	9	6	−3	0	−7	4	
	1	−8	5	−2	9	6	−3	0	5
−2	0		4		8	−5	2	−9	6
	−1	8		2	−9	6		0	−6
−2	8	4	−9	−5	1	−6	2	6	
9	−5	1	−6	2		3	7	−3	1
1	−8	5		−9	6	3	0		−7
−7	4	−1	8	−5	−2		6	5	−1
Sum	2		7	5	−2		7	−1	−3	

4

									Sum
6		4	−9	3		4	−8	2	−5
7	0	−3		−9	4	−8	1	4	
−1	−5	9	−2	5	−8		−4	7	2
	−1	−5	9	−3	8	2	−6	−3	8
−6			0	4	−8	1		9	−9
−3	6	−9	−2	5	8				
−7		5	−8	3	−1	5	9	−3	3
1	5	9	2		0	−7	3	−7	0
	−7	1	5	2	6		−4	−8	−3
Sum	6	0	5	1		2	−4	−8	1	

Have Fun with Math

Graph of *Hippocampus hudsonius*

See if you can produce a figure on the grid by connecting the points located by the coordinates provided below. Plot and connect the points by line segments in numbered order. A colored pencil will be helpful in locating the points and drawing the connecting lines. When the figure is completed, give it a better name.

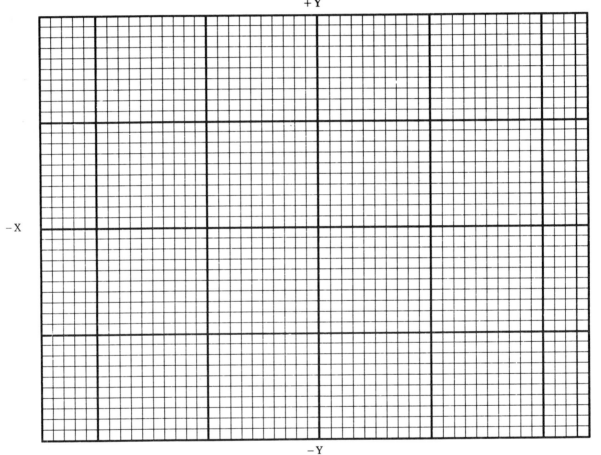

Start
1. (−8, +6)
2. (−7½, +3)
3. (−8, −2)
4. (−8, −6)
5. (−7, −9)
6. (−4, −12)
7. (0, −13)
8. (+4, −13½)
9. (+8, −13)
10. (+12, −11)
11. (+16, −8)
12. (+19, −3)
13. (+20, 0)

14. (+19, +4)
15. (+16, +5)
16. (+14, +4)
17. (+13, +3)
18. (+14, +2)
19. (+16, +2½)
20. (+17, +2)
21. (+17½, 0)
22. (+16, −2)
23. (+14, −4)
24. (+11, −5½)
25. (+8, −6)
26. (+5, −3)

27. (+3, 0)
Restart
28. (+5, −3)
29. (+6, 0)
30. (+7, +2)
31. (+4, +1½)
32. (+2, +2)
33. (+1, +3)
34. (0, +6)
35. (−2, +10)
36. (−4, +12½)
37. (−6, +13½)
38. (−12, +15)
39. (−15½, +11)

40. (−17, +9)
41. (−17, +5)
42. (−19, +1)
43. (−20, −1)
44. (−21, −2)
45. (−20, −2)
46. (−19, −3)
47. (−17, 0)
48. (−15, +2)
49. (−12, +4)
50. (−8, +6)
51. (−7, +8)
52. (−7½, +10)

Restart
53. (−11, +10)
54. (−12, +10)
55. (−13½, +9)
56. (−13½, +8)
57. (−13, +7)
58. (−12, +7)
59. (−11, +8)
60. (−11, +10)
Restart
61. (−13½, +9)
62. (−12, +9)
63. (−12, +7)
End

Have Fun with Math

Graph of a Large Cetacean

See if you can produce a figure on the grid by connecting the points located by the coordinates provided below. Plot and connect the points by line segments in numbered order. A colored pencil will be helpful in locating the points and drawing the connecting lines. When the figure is completed, give it a better name.

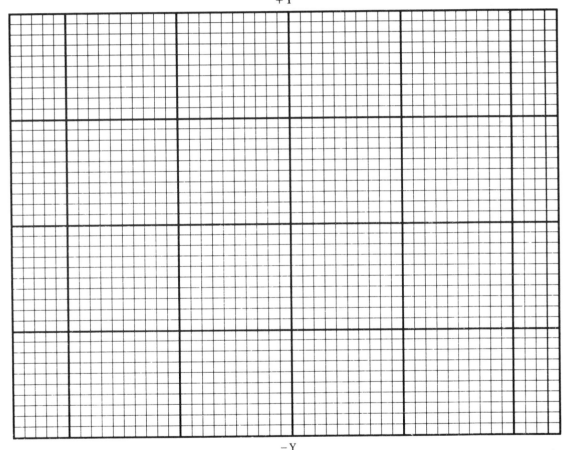

+Y

−X

+X

−Y

Start
1. (−18, +1½)
2. (−20,0)
3. (−23, −4)
4. (−22½, −5)
5. (−21½, −5)
6. (−19, −3)
7. (−16,0)
8. (−18, +1)
9. (−21½, +5)
10. (−22½, +7)
11. (−22, +8)
12. (−20, +10)
13. (−18, +11)
14. (−16, +11)
15. (−12, +10)
16. (−7, +7)
17. (−2, +5)
18. (−1, +7)

19. (+½, +9)
20. (+1½, +9)
21. (+2, +8)
22. (+2, +4½)
Restart
23. (−2, +5)
24. (+2, +4½)
25. (+5, +4½)
26. (+10, +6)
27. (+14, +10)
28. (+16, +14)
29. (+18, +17)
30. (+20, +18)
31. (+21, +18)
32. (+21½, +17)
33. (+21, +15)
34. (+19½, +13)
35. (+18, +10)
36. (+20, +10½)

37. (+21, +10½)
38. (+23, +9)
39. (+24, +7)
40. (+23, +6)
41. (+21, +7)
42. (+19, +7)
43. (+16, +5)
44. (+10, −5)
45. (+7, −10)
46. (+3, −13)
47. (0, −14)
48. (−2, −14)
49. (−5, −13)
50. (−9, −9)
51. (−11, −7½)
52. (−14, −7)
53. (−18, −6½)
Restart
54. (−15, −4)

55. (−18, −6½)
56. (−21, −8)
57. (−23, −8)
58. (−24, −7)
59. (−23½, −5)
60. (−23, −4)
61. (−23½, −5)
62. (−23, −6)
63. (−22, −6)
64. (−20, −5)
65. (−14½,0)
66. (−20, +5)
67. (−22, +8)
Restart
68. (−3, −11)
69. (0, −9)
70. (+3, −6)
71. (+4, −3)

72. (+4½, −1)
73. (+4, +½)
74. (+3, +½)
75. (−3, −5)
76. (−6, −6)
Restart
77. (−10,0)
78. (−11, +2)
79. (−12, +2)
80. (−13, +1)
81. (−13,0)
82. (−12, −1)
83. (−10,0)
Restart
84. (−12, +2)
85. (−12, +1)
86. (−13,0)
End

Have Fun with Math

Graph of *Delphinus delphis*

See if you can produce a figure on the grid by connecting the points located by the coordinates provided below. Plot and connect the points by line segments in numbered order. A colored pencil will be helpful in locating the points and drawing the connecting lines. When the figure is completed, give it a better name.

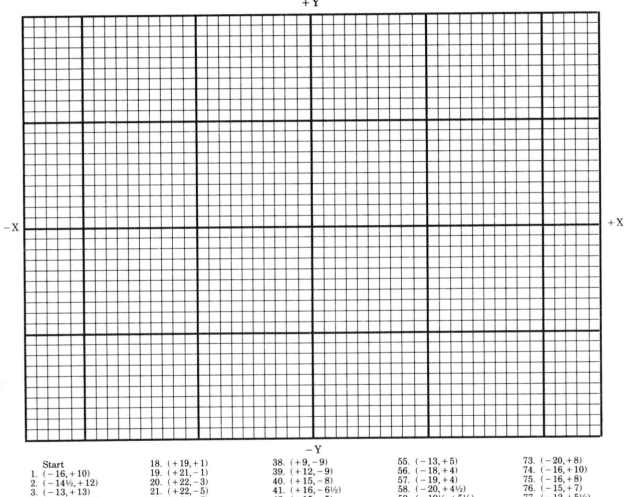

+Y

−X

+X

−Y

Start	18. (+19, +1)	38. (+9, −9)	55. (−13, +5)	73. (−20, +8)
1. (−16, +10)	19. (+21, −1)	39. (+12, −9)	56. (−18, +4)	74. (−16, +10)
2. (−14½, +12)	20. (+22, −3)	40. (+15, −8)	57. (−19, +4)	75. (−16, +8)
3. (−13, +13)	21. (+22, −5)	41. (+16, −6½)	58. (−20, +4½)	76. (−15, +7)
4. (−11, +13½)	22. (+21, −7)	42. (+15, −5)	59. (−19½, +5½)	77. (−12, +5½)
5. (−8, +13½)	23. (+19, −10)	43. (+9, −4)	60. (−19, +6)	**Restart**
6. (−5, +13)	24. (+16, −11)	44. (0, −2)	**Restart**	78. (−12, +8)
7. (−1, +12)	25. (+14, −11½)	**Restart**	61. (−12, +5½)	79. (−11, +8½)
8. (+2, +10)	26. (+12, −13)	45. (+1, 0)	62. (−13½, +5½)	80. (−10½, +8)
9. (+4, +9)	27. (+8, −15)	46. (0, −2)	63. (−17, +5)	81. (−10½, +7)
10. (+7, +9)	28. (+5, −16)	47. (−1, −3)	64. (−18½, +4¾)	82. (−11¾, +6¾)
11. (+10, +9½)	29. (+3, −16)	48. (−3, −4)	65. (−19, +5)	83. (−12, +7)
12. (+11, +9)	30. (+3, −15)	49. (−3½, −3)	66. (−18, +6)	84. (−12, +8)
13. (+11, +8)	31. (+4, −13½)	50. (−4, −1)	**Restart**	**Restart**
14. (+10, +6)	32. (+6, −12)	51. (−5, +2)	67. (−13½, +5½)	85. (−12, +8)
Restart	33. (+7, −11)	52. (−5, +4)	68. (−16, +6)	86. (−11½, +8)
15. (+6, +8)	34. (+5, −9)	**Restart**	69. (−18, +6)	87. (−11, +7½)
16. (+10, +6)	35. (+3½, −7)	53. (−4, −1)	70. (−19, +6)	88. (−11¾, +6¾)
17. (+16, +3)	36. (+5, −6½)	54. (−11, +4)	71. (−20, +7)	**End**
	37. (+7, −8)		72. (−20½, +7½)	

Have Fun with Math

Graph of *Odobenus rosmarus*

See if you can produce a figure on the grid by connecting the points located by the coordinates provided below. Plot and connect the points by line segments in numbered order. A colored pencil will be helpful in locating the points and drawing the connecting lines. When the figure is completed, give it a better name.

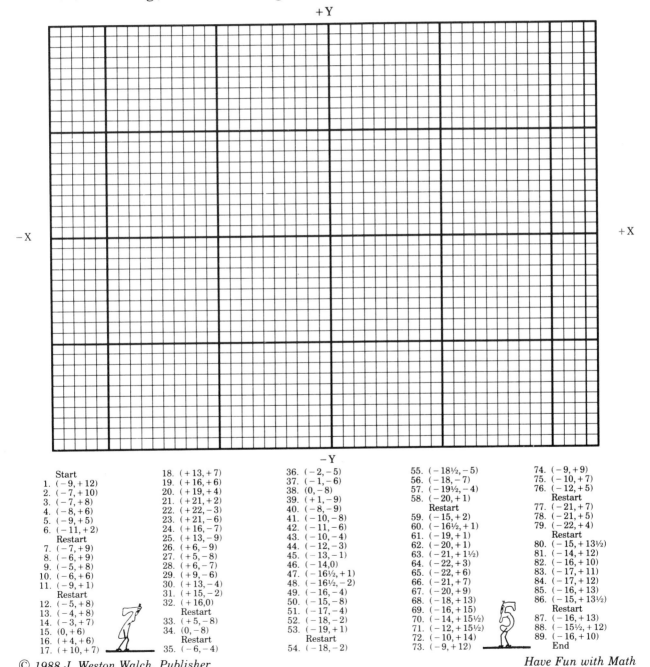

Start
1. (−9, +12)
2. (−7, +10)
3. (−7, +8)
4. (−8, +6)
5. (−9, +5)
6. (−11, +2)
Restart
7. (−7, +9)
8. (−6, +9)
9. (−5, +8)
10. (−6, +6)
11. (−9, +1)
Restart
12. (−5, +8)
13. (−4, +8)
14. (−3, +7)
15. (0, +6)
16. (+4, +6)
17. (+10, +7)

18. (+13, +7)
19. (+16, +6)
20. (+19, +4)
21. (+21, +2)
22. (+22, −3)
23. (+21, −6)
24. (+16, −7)
25. (+13, −9)
26. (+6, −9)
27. (+5, −8)
28. (+6, −7)
29. (+9, −6)
30. (+13, −4)
31. (+15, −2)
32. (+16, 0)
Restart
33. (+5, −8)
34. (0, −8)
Restart
35. (−6, −4)

36. (−2, −5)
37. (−1, −6)
38. (0, −8)
39. (+1, −9)
40. (−8, −9)
41. (−10, −8)
42. (−11, −6)
43. (−10, −4)
44. (−12, −3)
45. (−13, −1)
46. (−14, 0)
47. (−16½, +1)
48. (−16½, −2)
49. (−16, −4)
50. (−15, −8)
51. (−17, −4)
52. (−18, −2)
53. (−19, +1)
Restart
54. (−18, −2)

55. (−18½, −5)
56. (−18, −7)
57. (−19½, −4)
58. (−20, +1)
Restart
59. (−15, +2)
60. (−16½, +1)
61. (−19, +1)
62. (−20, +1)
63. (−21, +1½)
64. (−22, +3)
65. (−22, +6)
66. (−21, +7)
67. (−20, +9)
68. (−18, +13)
69. (−16, +15)
70. (−14, +15½)
71. (−12, +15½)
72. (−10, +14)
73. (−9, +12)

74. (−9, +9)
75. (−10, +7)
76. (−12, +5)
Restart
77. (−21, +7)
78. (−21, +5)
79. (−22, +4)
Restart
80. (−15, +13½)
81. (−14, +12)
82. (−16, +10)
83. (−17, +11)
84. (−17, +12)
85. (−16, +13)
86. (−15, +13½)
Restart
87. (−16, +13)
88. (−15½, +12)
89. (−16, +10)
End

Have Fun with Math

Graph of *Otaria jubata*

See if you can produce a figure on the grid by connecting the points located by the coordinates provided below. Plot and connect the points by line segments in numbered order. A colored pencil will be helpful in locating the points and drawing the connecting lines. When the figure is completed, give it a better name.

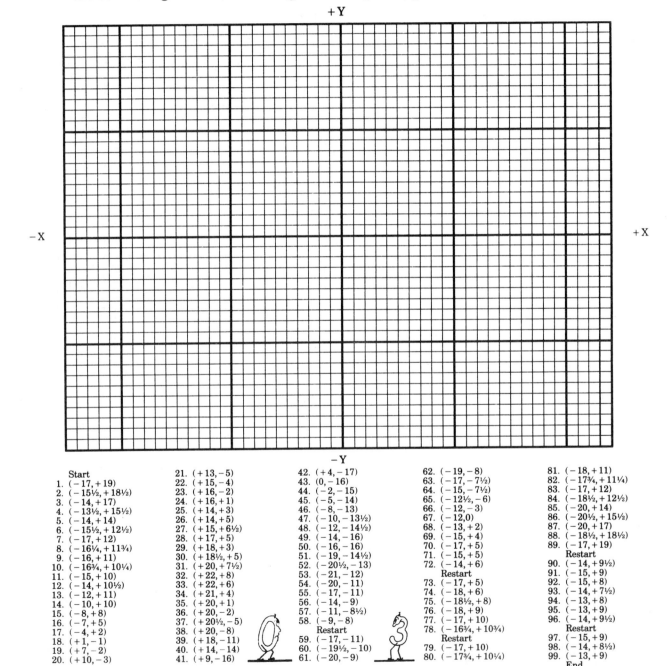

+Y

−X

+X

−Y

Start
1. (−17, +19)
2. (−15½, +18½)
3. (−14, +17)
4. (−13½, +15½)
5. (−14, +14)
6. (−15½, +12½)
7. (−17, +12)
8. (−16¼, +11¾)
9. (−16, +11)
10. (−16¾, +10¼)
11. (−15, +10)
12. (−14, +10½)
13. (−12, +11)
14. (−10, +10)
15. (−8, +8)
16. (−7, +5)
17. (−4, +2)
18. (+1, −1)
19. (+7, −2)
20. (+10, −3)

21. (+13, −5)
22. (+15, −4)
23. (+16, −2)
24. (+16, +1)
25. (+14, +3)
26. (+14, +5)
27. (+15, +6½)
28. (+17, +5)
29. (+18, +3)
30. (+18½, +5)
31. (+20, +7½)
32. (+22, +8)
33. (+22, +6)
34. (+21, +4)
35. (+20, +1)
36. (+20, −2)
37. (+20½, −5)
38. (+20, −8)
39. (+18, −11)
40. (+14, −14)
41. (+9, −16)

42. (+4, −17)
43. (0, −16)
44. (−2, −15)
45. (−5, −14)
46. (−8, −13)
47. (−10, −13½)
48. (−12, −14½)
49. (−14, −16)
50. (−16, −16)
51. (−19, −14½)
52. (−20½, −13)
53. (−21, −12)
54. (−20, −11)
55. (−17, −11)
56. (−14, −9)
57. (−11, −8½)
58. (−9, −8)
Restart
59. (−17, −11)
60. (−19½, −10)
61. (−20, −9)

62. (−19, −8)
63. (−17, −7½)
64. (−15, −7½)
65. (−12½, −6)
66. (−12, −3)
67. (−12, 0)
68. (−13, +2)
69. (−15, +4)
70. (−17, +5)
71. (−15, +5)
72. (−14, +6)
Restart
73. (−17, +5)
74. (−18, +6)
75. (−18½, +8)
76. (−18, +9)
77. (−17, +10)
78. (−16¾, +10¾)
Restart
79. (−17, +10)
80. (−17¾, +10¼)

81. (−18, +11)
82. (−17¾, +11¼)
83. (−17, +12)
84. (−18½, +12½)
85. (−20, +14)
86. (−20½, +15½)
87. (−20, +17)
88. (−18½, +18½)
89. (−17, +19)
Restart
90. (−14, +9½)
91. (−15, +9)
92. (−15, +8)
93. (−14, +7½)
94. (−13, +8)
95. (−13, +9)
96. (−14, +9½)
Restart
97. (−15, +9)
98. (−14, +8½)
99. (−13, +9)
End

Have Fun with Math

I have an
appendix!

HAVE FUN
WITH MATH

APPENDIX

ANSWERS

Part I. WHOLE NUMBERS

Page 2.

#		#	
1.	1369	13.	6139
2.	1396	14.	6193
3.	1639	15.	6319
4.	1693	16.	6391
5.	1936	17.	6913
6.	1963	18.	6931
7.	3169	19.	9136
8.	3196	20.	9163
9.	3619	21.	9316
10.	3691	22.	9361
11.	3916	23.	9613
12.	3961	24.	9631

Page 4.

Row 1: 7+7=14 | 3+9=12 | 2+6=8 | 3+2=5 | 4+5=9 | 1+2=3 | 8+8=16 | 9+2=11 | 5+1=6 | 0+9=9 | 8+6=14 | 9+6=15 | 0+7=7

Row 2: 3+1=4 | 0+8=8 | 2+5=7 | 1+1=2 | 3+6=9 | 1+8=9 | 6+3=9 | 2+0=2 | 7+4=11 | 9+8=17 | 5+6=11 | 2+3=5 | 7+0=7

Row 3: 4+9=13 | 0+3=3 | 5+8=13 | 1+6=7 | 4+7=11 | 1+3=4 | 4+0=4 | 5+2=7 | 1+0=1 | 3+3=6 | 5+9=14 | 7+6=13 | 8+0=8

Row 4: 7+1=8 | 2+9=11 | 4+6=10 | 7+8=15 | 4+4=8 | 0+1=1 | 7+2=9 | 3+7=10 | 3+4=7 | 7+5=12 | 0+2=2 | 4+3=7 | 9+0=9

Row 5: 2+1=3 | 8+4=12 | 9+5=14 | 9+4=13 | 0+4=4 | 8+9=17 | 5+4=9 | 3+0=3 | 6+2=8 | 0+5=5 | 6+5=11 | 9+3=12 | 4+1=5

Row 6: 6+1=7 | 9+7=16 | 6+8=14 | 2+4=6 | 5+3=8 | 8+1=9 | 6+6=12 | 7+9=16 | 5+5=10 | 9+1=10 | 6+9=15 | 8+7=15 | 9+9=18

Row 7: 3+5=8 | 2+8=10 | 4+8=12 | 3+8=11 | 7+3=10 | 1+7=8 | 6+4=10 | 6+0=6 | 2+7=9 | 0+0=0 | 1+4=5 | 8+2=10 | 4+2=6

Row 8: 6+7=13 | 8+5=13 | 2+2=4 | 0+6=6 | 1+9=10 | 1+5=6 | 5+7=12 | 8+3=11 | 5+0=5

Page 3.

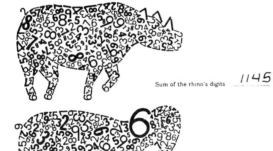

Sum of the rhino's digits: 1145

Sum of the elephant's digits: 1320

The _elephant_ is heavier by __175__

Page 5.

Common Sum: 14

7 8 2 4 5 6 3 6 5 3 7 6 3 1 4 5 8 3 5 2 4 7 0 8 3 5 6 0 1 9 7 6 7 1 8 0
1 3 0 4 6 5 8 9 5 6 6 6 3 1 4 2 1 5 6 4 1 3 7 6 2 4 1 0 7 9 7 6 4 5 2 3 5
7 1 5 8 4 3 2 9 6 5 1 3 6 4 8 3 1 2 1 6 2 4 0 3 5 8 8 7 2 5 1 5 6 1 7 3
3 2 4 5 7 3 3 2 0 5 4 7 0 4 4 3 5 2 1 2 5 8 1 8 6 3 3 1 0 4 6 5 6 5 7 2
0 7 2 4 3 5 3 6 3 6 0 4 1 7 8 2 5 4 3 6 2 2 3 5 4 0 3 8 1 6 7 5 7 1 6 5
1 3 4 0 6 2 7 3 5 4 2 7 2 8 1 3 4 5 3 4 7 9 1 5 4 2 3 7 3 3 5 4 2 0 4 0
2 7 9 4 1 4 2 8 3 7 3 2 4 5 6 8 3 1 4 6 7 9 3 4 2 5 5 6 1 2 2 4 1 3 6 1
3 5 6 7 5 1 4 3 6 6 6 7 4 2 3 5 8 4 1 6 7 4 9 2 5 0 3 4 5 7 8 2 1 3 5 8

Common Sum: 19

9 7 4 8 9 5 2 4 5 6 7 8 6 2 3 2 4 7 5 4 2 8 6 4 6 1 5 3 6 9 5 2 8 5 0 4
9 8 2 8 4 2 8 5 6 8 9 2 2 9 7 2 5 3 1 8 9 5 2 1 3 8 4 2 7 4 7 9 7 3
9 0 8 3 7 9 5 6 6 8 2 3 5 6 2 8 4 5 7 2 3 8 5 8 6 1 7 2 4 5 7 4 7 3 5
3 7 3 9 6 7 9 5 4 1 5 8 7 1 2 3 6 3 0 8 5 4 7 2 1 3 8 9 2 1 5 4 2 7 5
9 4 6 4 8 5 8 4 2 7 0 2 2 9 8 6 2 0 3 8 9 3 2 1 6 7 7 6 9 3 7 4 6 8 2 9
0 6 8 7 2 5 3 2 8 2 3 5 3 1 8 2 3 0 3 6 4 2 7 3 5 6 2 8 6 3 8 0 5 5 8 6
2 7 9 3 8 3 4 5 8 2 6 8 7 5 4 3 1 5 2 3 6 8 6 8 2 8 9 8 3 7 9 6 7 4 7 8
3 7 4 5 4 9 5 7 1 4 2 6 8 6 7 2 1 3 8 2 2 5 1 8 3 9 1 4 8 7 2 6 7 3 4 5

4    5 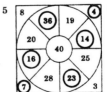   6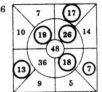

Page 6.

1 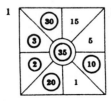   2   3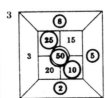

There may be other correct number combinations.

Page 7.

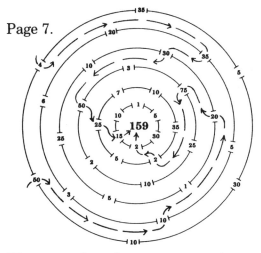

There may be other correct number combinations.

Page 8.

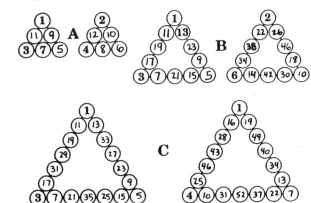

Page 9.

A

11	12	13	14
15	16	17	18
19	20	21	22
23	24	25	26

26	12	13	23
15	21	20	18
19	17	16	22
14	24	25	11

B

1	3	5	7
9	11	13	15
17	19	21	23
25	27	29	31

31	3	5	25
9	21	19	15
17	13	11	23
7	27	29	1

C

32	4	6	26
10	22	20	16
18	14	12	24
8	28	30	2

D

48	6	9	39
15	33	30	24
27	21	18	36
12	42	45	3

E

64	8	12	52
20	44	40	32
36	28	24	48
16	56	60	4

F

80	10	15	65
25	55	50	40
45	35	30	60
20	70	75	5

Page 10.

14	7	12
9	11	13
10	15	8

68	35	2	59	26
11	53	20	62	44
29	71	38	5	47
32	14	56	23	65
50	17	74	41	8

53	38	23	8	49	34	19
12	46	31	16	50	42	27
20	54	39	24	9	43	35
28	13	47	32	17	51	36
29	21	55	40	25	10	44
37	22	14	48	33	18	52
45	30	15	56	41	26	11

Page 11.

(1) 158	(2) 653	(3) 174	(4) 372
158) 1 851 1009) 2 9001 10010) 3 01001 11011	653) 1 356 1009) 2 9001 10010) 3 01001 11011	174) 1 471 645) 2 546 1191) 3 1911 3102) 4 2013 5115	372) 1 273 645) 2 546 1191) 3 1911 3102) 4 2013 5115

(5) 782	(6) 998	
782) 1 287 1069) 2 9601 10670) 3 07601 18271) 4 17281 35552) 5 25553 61105) 6 50116 111221) 7 122111 233332	998) 1 899 1897) 2 7981 9878) 3 8789 18667) 4 76681 95348) 5 84359 179707) 6 707971 887678) 7 876788 1764466) 8 6644671 8409137) 9 7319048 15728185) 10 58182751	73910936) 11 63901937 137812673) 12 377218731 516031504) 13 406130615 922162219) 14 912261229 1834423448) 15 8443244381 10277667829) 16 92876677201 103154345030) 17 030543451301 133697796331

Page 12.

1

17	3	13
7	11	15
9	19	5

2

8	1	6
3	5	7
4	9	2

3

21	7	17
11	15	19
13	23	9

4

27	6	21
12	18	24
15	30	9

5

19	5	6	16
8	14	13	11
12	10	9	15
7	17	18	4

6

48	6	9	39
15	33	30	24
27	21	18	36
12	42	45	3

7

52	10	13	43
19	37	34	28
31	25	22	40
16	46	49	7

8

29	18	7	26	15
10	24	13	27	21
16	30	19	8	22
17	11	25	14	28
23	12	31	20	9

9

71	38	5	62	29
14	56	23	65	47
32	74	41	8	50
35	17	59	26	68
53	20	77	44	11

Page 13.

×	5	8	0	6	1	3	2	7	9	4
3	15	24	0	18	3	9	6	21	27	12
6	30	48	0	36	6	18	12	42	54	24
0	0	0	0	0	0	0	0	0	0	0
8	40	64	0	48	8	24	16	56	72	32
4	20	32	0	24	4	12	8	28	36	16
5	25	40	0	30	5	15	10	35	45	20
9	45	72	0	54	9	27	18	63	81	36
2	10	16	0	12	2	6	4	14	18	8
1	5	8	0	6	1	3	2	7	9	4
7	35	56	0	42	7	21	14	49	63	28

Page 14.

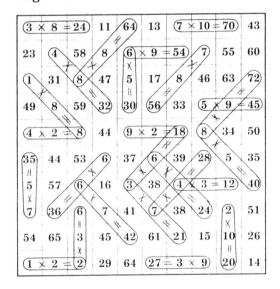

Page 15.

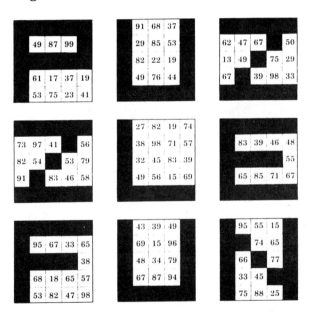

Page 16.

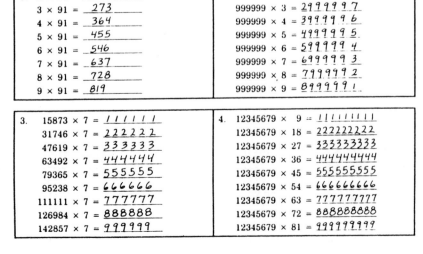

1.
$2 \times 91 = 182$
$3 \times 91 = 273$
$4 \times 91 = 364$
$5 \times 91 = 455$
$6 \times 91 = 546$
$7 \times 91 = 637$
$8 \times 91 = 728$
$9 \times 91 = 819$

2.
$999999 \times 2 = 1999998$
$999999 \times 3 = 2999997$
$999999 \times 4 = 3999996$
$999999 \times 5 = 4999995$
$999999 \times 6 = 5999994$
$999999 \times 7 = 6999993$
$999999 \times 8 = 7999992$
$999999 \times 9 = 8999991$

3.
$15873 \times 7 = 111111$
$31746 \times 7 = 222222$
$47619 \times 7 = 333333$
$63492 \times 7 = 444444$
$79365 \times 7 = 555555$
$95238 \times 7 = 666666$
$111111 \times 7 = 777777$
$126984 \times 7 = 888888$
$142857 \times 7 = 999999$

4.
$12345679 \times 9 = 111111111$
$12345679 \times 18 = 222222222$
$12345679 \times 27 = 333333333$
$12345679 \times 36 = 444444444$
$12345679 \times 45 = 555555555$
$12345679 \times 54 = 666666666$
$12345679 \times 63 = 777777777$
$12345679 \times 72 = 888888888$
$12345679 \times 81 = 999999999$

5.
$987654321 \times 9 = 8888888889$
$987654321 \times 18 = 17777777778$
$987654321 \times 27 = 26666666667$
$987654321 \times 36 = 35555555556$
$987654321 \times 45 = 44444444445$
$987654321 \times 54 = 53333333334$
$987654321 \times 63 = 62222222223$
$987654321 \times 72 = 711111112$
$987654321 \times 81 = 80000000001$

Page 17.

1.

$1 \times 8 + 1 = 9$
$12 \times 8 + 2 = 98$
$123 \times 8 + 3 = 987$
$1234 \times 8 + 4 = 9876$
$12345 \times 8 + 5 = 98765$
$123456 \times 8 + 6 = 987654$
$1234567 \times 8 + 7 = 9876543$
$12345678 \times 8 + 8 = 98765432$
$123456789 \times 8 + 9 = 987654321$

2.

$9 \times 1 + 2 = 11$
$9 \times 12 + 3 = 111$
$9 \times 123 + 4 = 1111$
$9 \times 1234 + 5 = 11111$
$9 \times 12345 + 6 = 111111$
$9 \times 123456 + 7 = 1111111$
$9 \times 1234567 + 8 = 11111111$
$9 \times 12345678 + 9 = 111111111$
$9 \times 123456789 + 10 = 1111111111$

5.

$1 + 1 + 1 = 3$ and $3 \times 37 = 111$
$2 + 2 + 2 = 6$ and $6 \times 37 = 222$
$3 + 3 + 3 = 9$ and $9 \times 37 = 333$
$4 + 4 + 4 = 12$ and $12 \times 37 = 444$
$5+5+5 = 15$ and $15 \times 37 = 555$
$6+6+6 = 18$ and $18 \times 37 = 666$
$7+7+7 = 21$ and $21 \times 37 = 777$
$8+8+8 = 24$ and $24 \times 37 = 888$
$9+9+9 = 27$ and $27 \times 37 = 999$

3.

$9 \times 1 - 1 = 8$
$9 \times 12 - 1 = 107$
$9 \times 123 - 1 = 1106$
$9 \times 1234 - 1 = 11105$
$9 \times 12345 - 1 = 111104$
$9 \times 123456 - 1 = 1111103$
$9 \times 1234567 - 1 = 11111102$
$9 \times 12345678 - 1 = 111111101$
$9 \times 123456789 - 1 = 1111111100$

4.

$(3-1) \times (3+1) = 3 \times 3 - 1 = 8$
$(4-1) \times (4+1) = 4 \times 4 - 1 = 15$
$(5-1) \times (5+1) = 5 \times 5 - 1 = 24$
$(6-1) \times (6+1) = 6 \times 6 - 1 = 35$
$(7-1) \times (7+1) = 7 \times 7 - 1 = 48$
$(8-1) \times (8+1) = 8 \times 8 - 1 = 63$
$(9-1) \times (9+1) = 9 \times 9 - 1 = 80$
$(15-1) \times (15+1) = 15 \times 15 - 1 = 224$
$(50-1) \times (50+1) = 50 \times 50 - 1 = 2249$

Page 18.

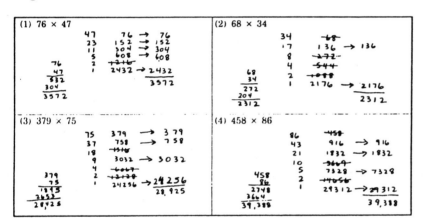

Page 19.

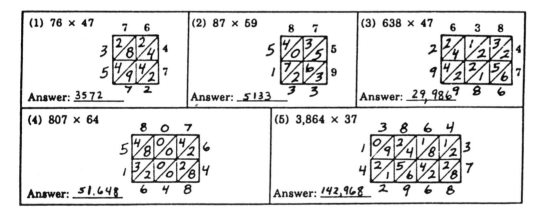

(1) 76×47 — Answer: 3572

(2) 87×59 — Answer: 5133

(3) 638×47 — Answer: 29,986

(4) 807×64 — Answer: 51,648

(5) $3,864 \times 37$ — Answer: 142,968

Page 20.

1

2	25	20
100	10	1
5	4	50

2

128	1	32
4	16	64
8	256	2

3

150	12	15
3	30	300
60	75	6

4

10	500	25
125	50	20
100	5	250

5

96	3	384
192	48	12
6	768	24

6

243	1	2187
729	81	9
3	6561	27

Page 21.

6 4)24	8 7)56	5 5)25	1 5)5	8 9)72	1 1)1	3 9)27	0 8)0	3 7)21
9 5)45	7 9)63	2 3)6	0 1)0	2 6)12	6 8)48	4 7)28	1 4)4	6 1)6
2 8)16	8 6)48	5 2)10	1 7)7	7 4)28	4 6)24	4 9)36	0 6)0	7 2)14
3 3)9	5 8)40	7 7)49	2 1)2	2 5)10	2 7)14	4 5)20	1 9)9	6 5)30
4 8)32	1 6)6	6 2)12	0 7)0	2 4)8	4 3)12	3 2)6	9 7)63	5 3)15
7 8)56	8 4)32	8 5)40	3 8)24	7 5)35	9 9)81	4 4)16	3 4)12	3 5)15
3 6)18	6 7)42	8 3)24	1 3)3	9 3)27	6 6)36	9 2)18	0 4)0	5 1)5
8 2)16	1 8)8	9 1)9	2 2)4	0 3)0	5 7)35	3 2)6	9 8)72	8 1)8
2 9)18	5 9)45	5 6)30	4 1)4	6 9)54	7 1)7	4 2)8	0 5)0	9 6)54
9 4)36	1 2)2	0 2)0	7 3)21	8 8)64	3 1)3	5 4)20	7 6)42	6 3)18

Page 22.

Col. I(3)	Col. II(4)	Col. III(5)	Col. IV(6)	Col. V(8)	Col. VI(9)	Col. VII(12)
5,234	7,912	7,024	2,388	875	657	12,308
9,108	52,168	40,355	6,083	5,716	1,971	312
783	247,686	25,284	8,564	15,036	514,865	4,137
7,345	8,643	5,552	297	25,127	5,781	7,128
47,881	211	350	2,795	14,223	42,569	928
812	114	927	40,812	453	384	84
74,842	14,892	3,125	63,624	7,216	7,295	2,132
7,356	7,546	84,262	522	92,576	27,633	62,736
1,257	723	1,487	2,375	1,492	1,548	17,216
382	5,628	600	724	1,152	837	719

Page 23.

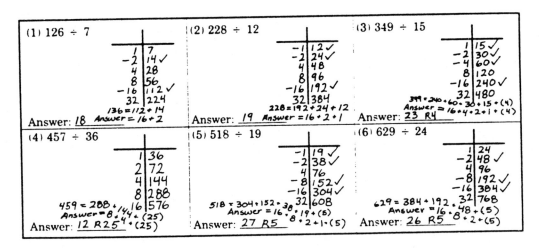

Page 24.

1
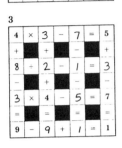

3	×	2	÷	2	=	3
×		×		×		+
3	+	4	–	2	=	5
		÷		×		–
5	+	1	–	2	=	4
4	+	8	–	8	=	4

2
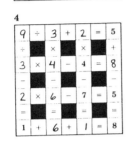

1	×	6	÷	2	=	3
+		÷		+		×
9	+	2	–	8	=	3
		+				–
5	+	3	–	2	=	6
5	+	6	–	8	=	3

3

4	×	3	–	7	=	5
+		+				+
8	÷	2	–	1	=	3
–		+				÷
3	×	4	–	5	=	7
=		=		=		=
9	–	9	+	1	=	1

4

9	÷	3	+	2	=	5
÷		×		×		+
3	×	4	–	4	=	8
		–				–
2	×	6	–	7	=	5
=		=		=		=
1	+	6	+	1	=	8

Page 25.

1
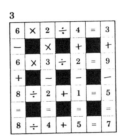

3	×	3	–	2	=	7
×		×		×		–
3	×	2	–	3	=	3
–				÷		+
2	×	3	÷	6	=	1
=		=		=		=
7	–	3	+	1	=	5

2
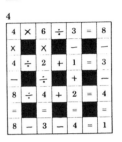

9	÷	3	–	2	=	1
÷		+		×		×
3	×	6	–	9	=	9
+		–		÷		–
2	+	7	–	6	=	3
=		=		=		=
5	–	2	+	3	=	6

3

6	×	2	÷	4	=	3
–		×		+		+
6	×	3	÷	2	=	9
+		–		–		–
8	÷	2	+	1	=	5
=		=		=		=
8	÷	4	+	5	=	7

4

4	×	6	÷	3	=	8
×		×		–		–
4	÷	2	+	1	=	3
–		÷		+		–
8	÷	4	+	2	=	4
=		=		=		=
8	–	3	–	4	=	1

Page 26.

1. 14,313
2. 1 less than 4 is 3; 2 less than 3 is 1; 3 is **2** more than 1.
3. The product of 8 and 7 is 56; 7 less than 8 is **1**.
4. 96 divided by 6 equals 16; 96 times 6 is **576**.
5. **0**; the product of any number and 0 is 0.
6. **1**
7. Twice 30 plus 3 is 63; twice 3 plus 30 is 36; 63 minus 36 is **27**.
8. 2 + 3 + 4 + 5 + 6 + 7 + 8 + 9 = **44**
9. He had the **11** that did not die.
10. If the bottle cost $1.05 and the stopper cost $.05, then the bottle would cost $1.00 more than the stopper. The stopper costs **5¢**.

Page 27.

1. 5	2. 5	3. 5	4. 0	■	5. 7	6. 6
7. 9	5	9	■	8. 7	3	6
■	9. 9	■	10. 8	5	■	11. 7
12. 6	8	■	13. 8	■	14. 4	2
15. 3	■	16. 4	8	■	17. 1	■
18. 5	19. 3	6	■	20. 2	0	21. 7
22. 7	7	■	23. 4	8	9	6

Page 28.

Sum

	1. 387	2. 51	3. 75	4. 315	828
	5. 123	6. 267	7. 243	8. 195	828
	9. 219	10. 171	11. 147	12. 291	828
	13. 99	14. 339	15. 363	16. 27	828
Sum	828	828	828	828	828

Part II. FRACTIONS

Page 30.

1 ²⁄₄ = ¹⁄₂	**2** ⁴⁄₈ = ¹⁄₂	**1** ⁷⁄₂₁ = ¹⁄₃	**3** ¹²⁄₄ = ?	**1** ⁷⁄₃₅ = ¹⁄₅
1 ⁵⁄₅ = ?	**6** ²⁄₁₂ = ¹⁄₆	**3** ⁶⁄₂ = ?	**2** ²³⁄₄₆ = ¹⁄₂	**8** ¹⁶⁄₂ = ?
5 ⁴⁄₂₀ = ¹⁄₅	**2** ⁷⁄₆ = 1¹⁄₆	**7** ⁶⁄₄₂ = ¹⁄₇	**1** ¹³⁄₈ = ?⁵⁄₈	**1** ³²⁄₉₆ = ¹⁄₃
9 ²⁵⁄₁₆ = 1⁹⁄₁₆	**3** ²⁷⁄₈₁ = ¹⁄₃	**1** ¹⁹⁄₁₂ = ?⁷⁄₁₂	**4** ⁸⁄₁₀ = ⁴⁄₅	**10** ¹³⁄₁₀ = 1³⁄₁₀
4 ⁹⁄₁₂ = ³⁄₄	**1** ⁶⁄₄ = 1¹⁄₂	**5** ¹⁰⁄₁₂ = ⁵⁄₆	**1** ¹²⁄₉ = 1¹⁄₃	**3** ²¹⁄₂₈ = ³⁄₄
4 ²⁸⁄₁₆ = 1³⁄₄	**3** ¹²⁄₁₆ = ³⁄₄	**2** ¹⁸⁄₁₂ = 1¹⁄₂	**4** ¹⁸⁄₂₄ = ³⁄₄	**5** ⁶⁵⁄₃₂ = 1⁵⁄₈
9 ²⁰⁄₃₆ = ⁵⁄₉	**2** ⁷⁄₃ = ?¹⁄₃	**8** ⁵⁶⁄₆₄ = ⁷⁄₈	**1** ¹³⁄₄ = 3¹⁄₄	**2** ⁵⁸⁄₈₇ = ²⁄₃
3 ²²⁄₇ = ?¹⁄₇	**7** ⁵²⁄₉₁ = ⁴⁄₇	**5** ³²⁄₉ = 3⁵⁄₉	**7** ⁹¹⁄₁₀₄ = ⁷⁄₈	**5** ⁶⁵⁄₁₂ = ?⁵⁄₁₂
16 ¹³⁵⁄₁₄₄ = 15⁄?	**7** ¹¹⁵⁄₁₆ = ?³⁄₁₆	**4** ⁸⁰⁄₁₀₀ = ⁴⁄₅	**2** ¹⁰⁄₄ = 2¹⁄₂	**19** ³⁶⁰⁄₄₅₆ = 15⁄?
5 ³⁴⁄₈ = ?²⁄₃	**5** ⁴⁰⁵⁄₅₆₇ = ⁵⁄₇	**4** ⁴⁵⁄₂₀ = 2¹⁄₄	**11** ²⁵⁶⁄₃₅₂ = 8⁄?	**1** ⁵⁰⁄₁₂ = 4¹⁄₆

Page 31.

3 2²⁄₃ = ?	**5** ¹⁄₃ = ⁵⁄₁₅	**7** 6¹⁄₇ = ?	**7** ¹⁄₄ = ⁷⁄₂₈	**7** 6¹⁶⁄₁₆ = ?
6 ¹⁄₈ = ⁶⁄₄₈	**10** 8⁶⁄₃ = ?	**6** ¹⁄₁₂ = ⁶⁄₇₂	**10** 8¹⁸⁄₉ = ?	**7** ¹⁄₆ = ⁷⁄₄₂
12 6³⁰⁄₅ = ?	**7** ¹⁄₁₀ = ⁷⁄₇₀	**2** 5⁶⁄₉ = 5²⁄₃	**10** ⁵⁄₆ = ¹⁰⁄₁₂	**4** 4⁵⁄₂₀ = 4¹⁄₄
8 ²⁄₃ = ⁸⁄₁₂	**6** 6³⁵⁄₄₂ = 6⁵⁄₆	**28** ⁷⁄₈ = ²⁸⁄₃₂	**2** 7⁸⁄₁₂ = 7²⁄₃	**9** ³⁄₁₆ = ⁹⁄₄₈
15 2¹⁶⁄₃₀ = 2⁸⁄?	**34** ¹⁷⁄₃₂ = ⁷⁄₆₄	**8** 5²⁵⁄₄₀ = 5⁵⁄₈	**40** ⁵⁄₉ = ⁷⁄₇₂	**4** 6⁹⁄₅ = 7⁴⁄₅
21 ⁵⁄₇ = 15⁄?	**10** 8⁵⁄₂ = ?¹⁄₂	**24** ³⁄₈ = ⁹⁄?	**5** 3¹³⁄₈ = 4⁵⁄₈	**25** ⁵⁄₉ = ⁷⁄₄₅
6 5¹⁄₆ = ?¹⁄₆	**36** ⁷⁄₁₂ = 21⁄?	**9** 2¹⁹⁄₁₀ = 3⁹⁄₁₀	**24** ³⁄₄ = 18⁄?	**8** 6²⁹⁄₁₂ = ?⁵⁄₁₂
54 ⁹⁄₁₆ = ⁷⁄₉₆	**7** 5¹⁰⁄₄ = ?¹⁄₂	**64** ¹¹⁄₁₆ = 44⁄?	**3** 6⁸⁄₆ = 7¹⁄?	**75** ¹⁵⁄₁₆ = ⁷⁄₈₀
3 7³?⁄₁₂ = 9?⁄?	**100** ⁹⁄₁₀ = 90⁄?	**2** 5¹⁵⁄₁₀ = 6¹⁄₂	**60** ³⁄₅ = ⁷⁄₁₀₀	**1** 1¹⁰⁄₈ = 2¹⁄₄
100 ⁴⁄₂₅ = 16⁄?	**2** 4¹⁵⁄₆ = 6¹⁄₂	**85** ¹⁷⁄₂₀ = ⁷⁄₁₀₀	**5** 2²⁶⁄₁₆ = 3⁷⁄₈	**34** ¹⁷⁄₅₀ = ⁷⁄₁₀₀

Page 32.

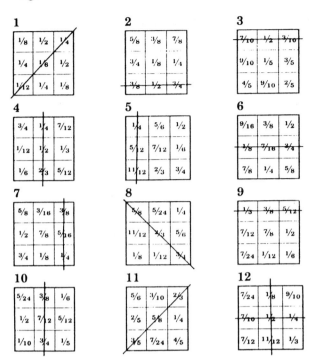

1

1/8	1/2	1/4
1/4		1/2
1/12	1/4	1/8

2

5/8	3/8	7/8
3/4	1/8	1/4
3/8	1/2	3/4

3

7/10	1/2	3/10
9/10	1/5	3/5
4/5	9/10	2/5

4

3/4	1/4	7/12
1/12	1/2	1/3
1/6	2/3	5/12

5

1/4	5/6	1/2
5/12	7/12	1/6
11/12	2/3	3/4

6

9/16	3/8	1/2
1/8	7/16	3/4
7/8	1/4	5/8

7

5/8	3/16	3/8
1/2	7/8	5/16
3/4	1/8	1/4

8

3/8	5/24	1/4
11/12	2/3	5/6
1/8	1/12	3/4

9

1/3	3/8	5/12
7/12	7/8	1/2
7/24	1/12	1/6

10

5/24	3/8	1/6
1/2	7/12	5/12
1/10	3/4	1/5

11

5/6	3/10	2/3
2/5	5/8	1/4
3/5	7/24	4/5

12

7/24	1/8	9/10
7/10	1/2	1/4
7/12	11/12	1/3

Page 33.

	1/6	3/4	1/3	2/3	1/2	5/6	1/4	5/12	1/12	7/12
3/4	11/12	1 1/2	1 1/12	1 5/12	1 1/4	1 7/12	1	1 1/6	5/6	1 1/3
1/3	1/2	1 1/12	2/3	1	5/6	1 1/6	7/12	3/4	5/12	11/12
7/12	3/4	1 1/3	11/12	1 1/4	1 1/12	1 5/12	5/6	1	2/3	1 1/6
1/4	5/12	1	7/12	11/12	3/4	1 1/12	1/2	2/3	1/3	5/6
1/12	1/4	5/6	5/12	3/4	7/12	11/12	1/3	1/2	1/6	2/3
1/6	1/3	11/12	1/2	5/6	2/3	1	5/12	7/12	1/4	3/4
2/3	5/6	1 5/12	1	1 1/3	1 1/6	1 1/2	11/12	1 1/12	3/4	1 1/4
5/6	1	1 7/12	1 1/6	1 1/2	1 1/3	1 2/3	1 1/12	1 1/4	11/12	1 5/12
1/2	2/3	1 1/4	5/6	1 1/6	1	1 1/3	3/4	11/12	7/12	1 1/12
11/12	1 1/12	1 2/3	1 1/4	1 7/12	1 5/12	1 3/4	1 1/6	1 1/3	1	1 1/2

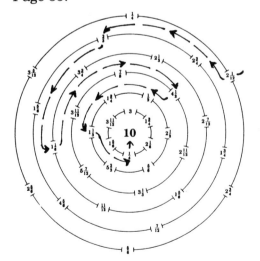

Page 34.

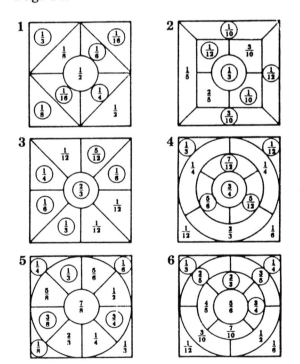

There may be other correct number combinations.

Page 35.

There may be other correct number combinations.

Page 36.

1

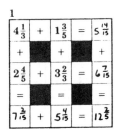

4⅓ + 1⅗ = 5 14/15		
+	+	+
2⅘ + 3⅔ = 6 7/15		
=	=	=
7 2/15 + 5 4/15 = 12⅖		

2

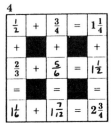

9½ − 6⅔ = 2⅚		
−	−	−
6¾ − 4⅚ = 1 11/12		
=	=	=
2¾ − 1⅚ = 11/12		

3

5⅚ − 3½ = 2⅓		
+	+	+
4¾ − 2⅔ = 2 1/12		
=	=	=
10 7/12 − 6⅙ = 4 5/12		

4

½ + ¾ = 1¼		
+	+	+
⅔ + ⅚ = 1½		
=	=	=
1⅙ + 1 7/12 = 2¾		

5

2⅚ − 1½ = 1⅓		
−	−	−
1⅓ − 1¼ = 5/12		
=	=	=
1⅙ − ¼ = 11/12		

6

5¾ + 3⅙ = 8 11/12		
−	−	−
3⅔ + 1½ = 5⅙		
=	=	=
2 1/12 + 1⅔ = 3¾		

Page 37.

4⅘	2⅗	4
3	3⅖	4⅕
3⅓	5	2⅘

17	9¾	½	14¾	6½
2¾	13¼	5	15⅕	11
7¼	17¾	9½	1¼	11¾
8	3½	14	5¾	16¼
12⅕	4¼	18½	10¼	2

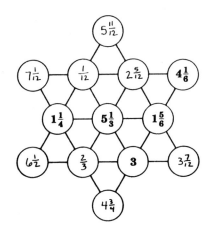

10⅗	7⅗	4⅗	1⅗	9⅘	6⅗	3⅗
2⅗	9⅗	6⅕	3⅗	10	8⅔	5⅖
4	10⅘	7⅘	4⅘	1⅗	8⅗	7
5⅓	2⅗	9⅗	6⅖	3⅗	10⅓	7⅕
5⅘	4⅓	11	8	5	2	8⅘
7⅗	4⅗	2⅘	9⅗	6⅗	3⅗	10⅗
9	6	3	11⅕	8⅖	5⅗	2⅗

Page 39.

(star diagram)
Outer/inner circles: 5 11/12; 7 1/12, 1/12, 2 5/12, 4⅙; 1¼, 5⅓, 1⅚; 6½, ⅔, 3, 3 7/12; 4¾

Page 38.

1

2	¼	1½
¾	1¼	1¾
1	2¼	½

2

5⅔	1	4⅓
2⅓	3⅔	5
3	6⅓	1⅔

3

3½	1⅙	2⅚
1⅚	2⅓	3⅙
2⅙	3⅚	1½

4

5⅗	1⅕	4⅕
2⅗	3⅗	4⅘
3	6	1⅘

5

6⅓	1⅔	2	5⅓
2⅔	4⅓	4⅓	3⅔
4	3⅓	3	5
2⅓	5⅔	6	1⅓

6

12	1½	2¼	9¾
3¾	8¼	7½	6
6¾	5¼	4½	9
3	10½	11¼	¾

7

10⅖	2	2⅗	8⅗
3⅘	7⅖	6⅘	5⅗
6⅕	5	4⅖	8
3⅗	9⅕	9⅘	1⅖

8

3	1⅝	¼	2⅝	1¼
⅝	2⅜	1	2¾	2
1⅜	3⅛	1¾	⅜	2⅛
1½	¾	2½	1⅛	2⅞
2¼	⅞	3¼	1⅞	½

9

14⅖	7⅘	1⅕	12⅗	6
3	11⅖	4⅘	13⅕	9⅗
6⅗	15	8⅖	1⅘	10⅕
7⅕	3⅗	12	5⅖	13⅘
10⅘	4⅕	15⅗	9	2⅖

Page 40.

×	$\frac{2}{5}$	$\frac{1}{4}$	$\frac{2}{3}$	$\frac{5}{6}$	$\frac{1}{5}$	$\frac{3}{4}$	$\frac{1}{3}$	$\frac{4}{5}$	$\frac{1}{2}$	$\frac{5}{12}$
$\frac{3}{4}$	$\frac{3}{10}$	$\frac{3}{16}$	$\frac{1}{2}$	$\frac{5}{8}$	$\frac{3}{20}$	$\frac{9}{16}$	$\frac{1}{4}$	$\frac{3}{5}$	$\frac{3}{8}$	$\frac{5}{16}$
$\frac{1}{5}$	$\frac{2}{25}$	$\frac{1}{20}$	$\frac{2}{15}$	$\frac{1}{6}$	$\frac{1}{25}$	$\frac{3}{20}$	$\frac{1}{15}$	$\frac{4}{25}$	$\frac{1}{10}$	$\frac{1}{12}$
$\frac{1}{6}$	$\frac{1}{15}$	$\frac{1}{24}$	$\frac{1}{9}$	$\frac{5}{36}$	$\frac{1}{30}$	$\frac{1}{8}$	$\frac{1}{18}$	$\frac{2}{15}$	$\frac{1}{12}$	$\frac{5}{72}$
$\frac{11}{12}$	$\frac{11}{30}$	$\frac{11}{48}$	$\frac{11}{18}$	$\frac{55}{72}$	$\frac{11}{60}$	$\frac{11}{16}$	$\frac{11}{36}$	$\frac{11}{15}$	$\frac{11}{24}$	$\frac{55}{144}$
$\frac{1}{2}$	$\frac{1}{5}$	$\frac{1}{8}$	$\frac{1}{3}$	$\frac{5}{12}$	$\frac{1}{10}$	$\frac{3}{8}$	$\frac{1}{6}$	$\frac{2}{5}$	$\frac{1}{4}$	$\frac{5}{24}$
$\frac{7}{12}$	$\frac{7}{30}$	$\frac{7}{48}$	$\frac{7}{18}$	$\frac{35}{72}$	$\frac{7}{60}$	$\frac{7}{16}$	$\frac{7}{36}$	$\frac{7}{15}$	$\frac{7}{24}$	$\frac{35}{144}$
$\frac{4}{5}$	$\frac{8}{25}$	$\frac{1}{5}$	$\frac{8}{15}$	$\frac{2}{3}$	$\frac{4}{25}$	$\frac{3}{5}$	$\frac{4}{15}$	$\frac{16}{25}$	$\frac{2}{5}$	$\frac{1}{3}$
$\frac{1}{12}$	$\frac{1}{30}$	$\frac{1}{48}$	$\frac{1}{18}$	$\frac{5}{72}$	$\frac{1}{60}$	$\frac{1}{16}$	$\frac{1}{36}$	$\frac{1}{15}$	$\frac{1}{24}$	$\frac{5}{144}$
$\frac{2}{3}$	$\frac{4}{15}$	$\frac{1}{6}$	$\frac{4}{9}$	$\frac{5}{9}$	$\frac{2}{15}$	$\frac{1}{2}$	$\frac{2}{9}$	$\frac{8}{15}$	$\frac{1}{3}$	$\frac{5}{18}$
$\frac{1}{4}$	$\frac{1}{10}$	$\frac{1}{16}$	$\frac{1}{6}$	$\frac{5}{24}$	$\frac{1}{20}$	$\frac{3}{16}$	$\frac{1}{12}$	$\frac{1}{5}$	$\frac{1}{8}$	$\frac{5}{48}$

Page 42.

÷	$\frac{3}{4}$	$\frac{3}{5}$	$\frac{2}{3}$	$\frac{1}{6}$	$\frac{1}{3}$	$\frac{1}{5}$	$\frac{5}{6}$	$\frac{1}{4}$	$\frac{1}{2}$	$\frac{4}{5}$
$\frac{3}{5}$	$\frac{4}{5}$	1	$\frac{9}{10}$	$3\frac{3}{5}$	$1\frac{4}{5}$	3	$\frac{18}{25}$	$2\frac{2}{5}$	$1\frac{1}{5}$	$\frac{3}{4}$
$\frac{1}{3}$	$\frac{4}{9}$	$\frac{5}{9}$	$\frac{1}{2}$	2	1	$1\frac{2}{3}$	$\frac{2}{5}$	$1\frac{1}{3}$	$\frac{2}{3}$	$\frac{5}{12}$
$\frac{1}{2}$	$\frac{2}{3}$	$\frac{5}{6}$	$\frac{3}{4}$	3	$1\frac{1}{2}$	$2\frac{1}{2}$	$\frac{3}{5}$	2	1	$\frac{5}{8}$
$\frac{1}{5}$	$\frac{4}{15}$	$\frac{1}{3}$	$\frac{3}{10}$	$1\frac{1}{5}$	$\frac{3}{5}$	1	$\frac{6}{25}$	$\frac{4}{5}$	$\frac{2}{5}$	$\frac{1}{4}$
$\frac{2}{3}$	$\frac{8}{9}$	$1\frac{1}{9}$	1	4	2	$3\frac{1}{3}$	$\frac{4}{5}$	$2\frac{2}{3}$	$1\frac{1}{3}$	$\frac{5}{6}$
$\frac{4}{5}$	$1\frac{1}{15}$	$1\frac{1}{3}$	$1\frac{1}{5}$	$4\frac{4}{5}$	$2\frac{2}{5}$	4	$\frac{24}{25}$	$3\frac{1}{5}$	$1\frac{3}{5}$	1
$\frac{5}{6}$	$1\frac{1}{9}$	$1\frac{7}{18}$	$1\frac{1}{4}$	5	$2\frac{1}{2}$	$4\frac{1}{6}$	1	$3\frac{1}{3}$	$1\frac{2}{3}$	$1\frac{1}{24}$
$\frac{1}{4}$	$\frac{1}{3}$	$\frac{5}{12}$	$\frac{3}{8}$	$1\frac{1}{2}$	$\frac{3}{4}$	$1\frac{1}{4}$	$\frac{3}{10}$	1	$\frac{1}{2}$	$\frac{5}{16}$
$\frac{1}{6}$	$\frac{2}{9}$	$\frac{5}{18}$	$\frac{1}{4}$	1	$\frac{1}{2}$	$\frac{5}{6}$	$\frac{1}{5}$	$\frac{2}{3}$	$\frac{1}{3}$	$\frac{5}{24}$
$\frac{2}{5}$	$\frac{8}{15}$	$\frac{2}{3}$	$\frac{3}{5}$	$2\frac{2}{5}$	$1\frac{1}{3}$	2	$\frac{12}{25}$	$1\frac{3}{5}$	$\frac{4}{5}$	$\frac{1}{2}$

Page 41.

(1)

$$\frac{1}{2} + \frac{1}{3} = \frac{3+2}{2\times3} = \frac{5}{6}$$
$$\frac{1}{3} + \frac{1}{4} = \frac{4+3}{3\times4} = \frac{7}{12}$$
$$\frac{1}{4} + \frac{1}{5} = \frac{5+4}{4\times5} = \frac{9}{20}$$
$$\frac{1}{5} + \frac{1}{6} = \frac{6+5}{6\times5} = 11/30$$
$$\frac{1}{6} + \frac{1}{7} = \frac{7+6}{6\times7} = 13/42$$
$$\frac{1}{8} + \frac{1}{9} = \frac{9+8}{8\times9} = 17/72$$
$$\frac{1}{10} + \frac{1}{11} = \frac{11+10}{10\times11} = 21/110$$
$$\frac{1}{12} + \frac{1}{13} = \frac{13+12}{12\times13} = 25/156$$

$$\frac{1}{2} + \frac{1}{2} = \frac{2+2}{2\times2} = 1$$
$$\frac{1}{2} + \frac{1}{4} = \frac{4+2}{2\times4} = \frac{3}{4}$$
$$\frac{1}{3} + \frac{1}{6} = \frac{6+3}{3\times6} = \frac{1}{2}$$
$$\frac{1}{3} + \frac{1}{8} = \frac{8+3}{3\times8} = 11/24$$
$$\frac{1}{4} + \frac{1}{8} = \frac{8+4}{4\times8} = 3/8$$
$$\frac{1}{8} + \frac{1}{10} = \frac{10+8}{8\times10} = 9/40$$
$$\frac{1}{12} + \frac{1}{15} = \frac{15+12}{12\times15} = 3/20$$
$$\frac{1}{15} + \frac{1}{20} = \frac{20+15}{15\times20} = 7/60$$

(2)

$$\frac{1}{1\times2} = \frac{1\times1}{1\times2} = \frac{1}{2}$$
$$\frac{1}{1\times2} + \frac{1}{2\times3} = \frac{2\times2}{2\times3} = \frac{2}{3}$$
$$\frac{1}{1\times2} + \frac{1}{2\times3} + \frac{1}{3\times4} = \frac{3\times3}{3\times4} = 3/4$$
$$\frac{1}{1\times2} + \frac{1}{2\times3} + \frac{1}{3\times4} + \frac{1}{4\times5} = \frac{4\times4}{4\times5} = 4/5$$
$$\frac{1}{1\times2} + \frac{1}{2\times3} + \frac{1}{3\times4} + \frac{1}{4\times5} + \frac{1}{5\times6} = \frac{5\times5}{5\times6} = 5/6$$
$$\frac{1}{1\times2} + \frac{1}{2\times3} + \frac{1}{3\times4} + \frac{1}{4\times5} + \frac{1}{5\times6} + \frac{1}{6\times7} = \frac{6\times6}{6\times7} = 6/7$$
$$\frac{1}{1\times2} + \frac{1}{2\times3} + \frac{1}{3\times4} + \frac{1}{4\times5} + \frac{1}{5\times6} + \frac{1}{6\times7} + \frac{1}{7\times8} = \frac{7\times7}{7\times8} = 7/8$$
$$\frac{1}{1\times2} + \frac{1}{2\times3} + \frac{1}{3\times4} + \frac{1}{4\times5} + \frac{1}{5\times6} + \frac{1}{6\times7} + \frac{1}{7\times8} + \frac{1}{8\times9} = \frac{8\times8}{8\times9} = 8/9$$

Page 43.

1 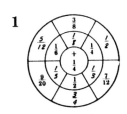 **2**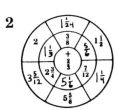

3 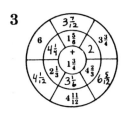 **4**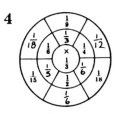

5 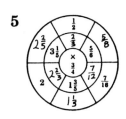 **6**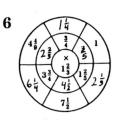

Page 44.

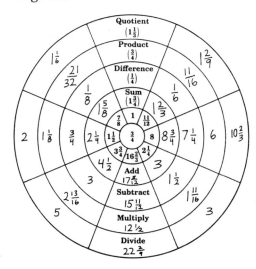

Page 45.

1

$1\frac{1}{2}$	×	$1\frac{1}{3}$	=	2
×	■	×	■	×
$1\frac{2}{3}$	×	$1\frac{1}{5}$	=	2
=	■	=	■	=
$2\frac{1}{2}$	×	$1\frac{3}{5}$	=	4

2

$1\frac{1}{4}$	÷	$1\frac{1}{2}$	=	$\frac{5}{6}$
÷	■	÷	■	÷
$3\frac{1}{3}$	÷	$1\frac{1}{4}$	=	$2\frac{2}{3}$
=	■	=	■	=
$\frac{3}{8}$	÷	$1\frac{1}{5}$	=	$\frac{5}{16}$

3

$1\frac{1}{3}$	÷	$2\frac{2}{3}$	=	$\frac{1}{2}$
÷	■	×	■	÷
$3\frac{1}{5}$	×	$1\frac{1}{4}$	=	4
=	■	=	■	=
$\frac{5}{12}$	÷	$3\frac{1}{3}$	=	$\frac{1}{8}$

4

$2\frac{4}{5}$	×	$1\frac{1}{4}$	=	$3\frac{1}{2}$
×	■	×	■	×
$3\frac{1}{3}$	×	$3\frac{3}{5}$	=	12
=	■	=	■	=
$9\frac{1}{3}$	×	$4\frac{1}{2}$	=	42

5

$2\frac{2}{3}$	÷	$5\frac{1}{3}$	=	$\frac{1}{2}$
÷	■	÷	■	÷
$3\frac{1}{5}$	÷	$2\frac{2}{5}$	=	$1\frac{1}{3}$
=	■	=	■	=
$\frac{5}{6}$	÷	$2\frac{2}{9}$	=	$\frac{3}{8}$

6

$2\frac{1}{2}$	×	$1\frac{3}{5}$	=	4
×	■	÷	■	×
$4\frac{2}{5}$	÷	$3\frac{1}{5}$	=	$1\frac{3}{8}$
=	■	=	■	=
11	×	$\frac{1}{2}$	=	$5\frac{1}{2}$

Page 46.

1

5	$\frac{2}{5}$	$\frac{1}{2}$
$\frac{1}{10}$	1	10
2	$2\frac{1}{2}$	$\frac{1}{5}$

2

$\frac{1}{2}$	$6\frac{1}{4}$	5
25	$2\frac{1}{2}$	$\frac{1}{4}$
$1\frac{1}{4}$	1	$12\frac{1}{2}$

3

$3\frac{1}{5}$	$\frac{1}{10}$	$12\frac{4}{5}$
$6\frac{2}{5}$	$1\frac{3}{5}$	$\frac{2}{5}$
$\frac{1}{5}$	$25\frac{3}{5}$	$\frac{4}{5}$

4

$6\frac{1}{4}$	$\frac{1}{2}$	$\frac{5}{8}$
$\frac{1}{8}$	$1\frac{1}{4}$	$12\frac{1}{2}$
$2\frac{1}{2}$	$3\frac{1}{8}$	$\frac{1}{4}$

5

$1\frac{3}{5}$	$\frac{4}{5}$	$25\frac{3}{5}$
$51\frac{1}{5}$	$3\frac{1}{5}$	$\frac{1}{5}$
$\frac{2}{5}$	$12\frac{4}{5}$	$6\frac{2}{5}$

6

$6\frac{2}{3}$	$\frac{1}{3}$	$16\frac{2}{3}$
$8\frac{1}{3}$	$3\frac{1}{3}$	$1\frac{1}{3}$
$\frac{2}{3}$	$33\frac{1}{3}$	$1\frac{2}{3}$

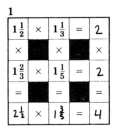
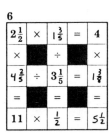

Page 47.

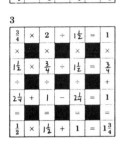

1

3	÷	1	−	$\frac{1}{2}$	=	$2\frac{1}{2}$
×		+		+		×
1	+	1	+	$\frac{1}{2}$	=	$2\frac{1}{2}$
−		+		+		÷
$\frac{1}{2}$	+	$\frac{1}{2}$	+	$1\frac{1}{2}$	=	$2\frac{1}{2}$
=		=		=		=
$2\frac{1}{2}$	+	$2\frac{1}{2}$	−	$2\frac{1}{2}$	=	$2\frac{1}{2}$

2

2	×	$1\frac{1}{3}$	÷	1	=	$2\frac{2}{3}$
×		÷		×		+
1	×	$\frac{2}{3}$	÷	$\frac{2}{3}$	=	1
÷		−		+		−
3	×	$\frac{2}{3}$	÷	$\frac{2}{3}$	=	3
=		=		=		=
$\frac{2}{3}$	+	$1\frac{1}{3}$	−	$1\frac{1}{3}$	=	$\frac{2}{3}$

3

$\frac{3}{4}$	×	2	÷	$1\frac{1}{2}$	=	1
×		×		×		×
$1\frac{1}{2}$	×	$\frac{3}{4}$	÷	$1\frac{1}{2}$	=	$\frac{3}{4}$
÷		÷		÷		+
$2\frac{1}{4}$	+	1	−	$2\frac{1}{4}$	=	1
=		=		=		=
$\frac{1}{2}$	×	$1\frac{1}{2}$	+	1	=	$1\frac{3}{4}$

4

$1\frac{1}{5}$	×	$\frac{2}{5}$	÷	$\frac{4}{5}$	=	$\frac{3}{5}$
+		+		÷		+
$\frac{1}{5}$	÷	$\frac{1}{5}$	+	$\frac{2}{5}$	=	$1\frac{2}{5}$
+		−		+		−
$1\frac{3}{5}$	+	$\frac{1}{5}$	−	$\frac{1}{5}$	=	$1\frac{3}{5}$
=		=		=		=
3	−	$\frac{2}{5}$	−	$2\frac{1}{5}$	=	$\frac{2}{5}$

Page 48.

1

$\frac{1}{2}$	×	3	÷	1	=	$1\frac{1}{2}$
×		÷		×		+
4	×	$1\frac{1}{2}$	÷	2	−	3
+		+		−		−
2	×	$1\frac{1}{2}$	−	$\frac{1}{2}$	=	$2\frac{1}{2}$
=		=		=		=
4	−	$3\frac{1}{2}$	+	$1\frac{1}{2}$	=	2

2

3	×	$\frac{2}{3}$	÷	3	=	$\frac{2}{3}$
×		×		+		+
$\frac{2}{3}$	×	2	+	$\frac{1}{3}$	=	$1\frac{2}{3}$
÷		+		−		+
2	+	$1\frac{1}{3}$	−	$2\frac{2}{3}$	=	$\frac{2}{3}$
=		=		=		=
1	+	$2\frac{2}{3}$	−	$\frac{2}{3}$	=	3

3

$2\frac{1}{4}$	×	$\frac{1}{2}$	÷	$\frac{3}{4}$	=	$1\frac{1}{2}$
÷		×		+		+
$\frac{3}{4}$	×	$1\frac{1}{2}$	÷	$2\frac{1}{4}$	=	$\frac{1}{2}$
÷		÷		−		+
$\frac{3}{4}$	+	$\frac{1}{4}$	+	$\frac{1}{2}$	=	$1\frac{1}{2}$
=		=		=		=
4	−	3	+	$2\frac{1}{2}$	=	$3\frac{1}{2}$

4

2	÷	$\frac{2}{5}$	×	$1\frac{1}{5}$	=	6
×		+		×		−
$1\frac{4}{5}$	÷	$1\frac{1}{5}$	×	2	=	3
−		+		÷		−
$2\frac{1}{5}$	−	$1\frac{3}{5}$	+	$\frac{4}{5}$	=	$1\frac{2}{5}$
=		=		=		=
$1\frac{2}{5}$	+	$3\frac{1}{5}$	−	3	=	$1\frac{3}{5}$

Page 49.

1. b; $\frac{1}{4} \times 8 = 2$; $2 \div 12 = \frac{1}{6}$
2. c; $\frac{1}{2} \times 3 = 1\frac{1}{2}$; $1\frac{1}{2} \div 4 = \frac{3}{8}$
3. c; $\frac{1}{2} \times 10 = 5$; $5 - 3 = 2$; $2 \div 5 = \frac{2}{5}$
4. d; $3 + 2 = 5$; $5 \div 6 = \frac{5}{6}$
5. a; $\frac{2}{3} \times 6 = 4$; $\frac{4}{5} \times 10 = 8$; $4 \div 8 = \frac{1}{2}$
6. e; $3 - \frac{1}{3} = 2\frac{2}{3}$; $4 + \frac{1}{4} = 4\frac{1}{2}$; $4\frac{1}{2} - 2\frac{2}{3} = 1\frac{5}{6}$
7. d; $15 \div \frac{1}{5} = 75$; $75 + 5 = 80$
8. a; 3 kg is $\frac{1}{4}$ the weight of the melon; the melon weighs 12 kg.
9. b; $\frac{1}{5}$ of the cabbage weighs $\frac{4}{5}$ kg; $\frac{5}{5}$ of the cabbage weighs 4 kg.
10. e; $\frac{1}{4} + \frac{1}{6} + \frac{1}{6} + \frac{1}{12} + \frac{1}{3}$ = one whole; there is nothing left for school supplies.

Page 50.

Y O U C A N H A V E F U N W I T H M A T H.

25	21
15	14
21	23
3	9
1	20
14	8
8	13
1	1
22	20
5	8
6	

Page 51.

1. 1	2. 2			3. 2	4. 1	
5. 2	4			6. 1	2	
	7. 3	8. 7			9. 6	10. 4
		11. 2	12. 1	13. 6		
14. 7	15. 2			16. 4	17. 8	
	18. 1	19. 8			20. 8	21. 7
	22. 2	1			23. 2	4

Page 52.

1. 13¢; one quarter (25¢) plus one cent (1¢) equals 26¢; $\frac{1}{2}$ of 26¢ is 13¢.
2. 10; half of 10 multiplied by 10 is 50.
3. Neither; the sum of $\frac{1}{3}$ and $\frac{1}{4}$ is $\frac{7}{12}$.
4. None; a centimeter is divided into ten millimeters.
5. None; those birds not killed flew away.
6. Pop it; it has to be popcorn!
7. $2\frac{1}{2}$ hours; you take one pill to start with, then one every half hour.
8. One whole (1; this and that) is what part of one and a half wholes ($1\frac{1}{2}$; this and that and half of this and that); $1:1\frac{1}{2} = \frac{2}{3}$.
9. The $\frac{1}{2}$ kg of \$10 gold pieces; $\frac{1}{2}$ kg of gold is worth more than $\frac{1}{4}$ kg of gold.
10. Mrs. Smith gave her children the inside part of the oranges; she made orange juice from the oranges and gave equal amounts to her two children.

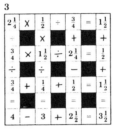

Page 53.

				Sum
1. 9	2. $\frac{5}{6}$	3. $1\frac{5}{12}$	4. $7\frac{1}{4}$	$19\frac{1}{2}$
5. $2\frac{7}{12}$	6. $6\frac{1}{12}$	7. $5\frac{1}{2}$	8. $4\frac{1}{3}$	$18\frac{1}{2}$
9. $4\frac{11}{12}$	10. $3\frac{3}{4}$	11. $3\frac{1}{6}$	12. $6\frac{2}{3}$	$18\frac{1}{2}$
13. 2	14. $7\frac{5}{6}$	15. $8\frac{5}{12}$	16. $\frac{1}{4}$	$18\frac{1}{2}$
Sum $18\frac{1}{2}$	$18\frac{1}{2}$	$18\frac{1}{2}$	$18\frac{1}{2}$	$18\frac{1}{2}$

Page 54.

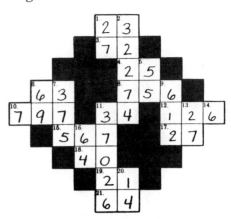

Part III. DECIMALS

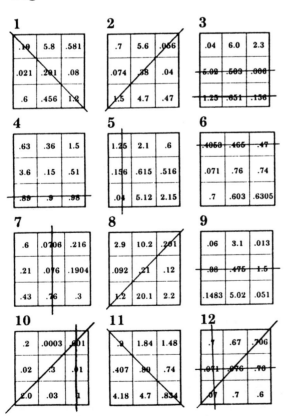

Page 56.

1

.19	5.8	.581
.021	.291	.08
.6	.456	1.2

2

.7	5.6	.056
.074	.38	.04
1.5	4.7	.47

3

.04	6.0	2.3
5.02	.503	.006
1.23	.651	.156

4

.63	.36	1.5
3.6	.15	.51
.89	.9	.98

5

1.25	2.1	.6
.156	.615	.516
.04	5.12	2.15

6

.4053	.465	.47
.071	.76	.74
.7	.603	.6305

7

.6	.0706	.216
.21	.076	.1904
.43	.76	.3

8

2.9	10.2	.201
.092	.21	.12
1.2	20.1	2.2

9

.06	3.1	.013
.08	.475	1.5
.1483	5.02	.051

10

.2	.0003	.001
.02	.3	.01
2.0	.03	1

11

.9	1.84	1.48
.407	.80	.74
4.18	4.7	.834

12

.7	.67	.706
.071	.076	.76
.07	.7	.6

Page 57.

1. .5; .6; .7
2. .9; .11; .13
3. .6; .5; .4
4. 3.5; 4.3; 5.1
5. 7.8; 7.1; 6.3
6. 7.2; 6.5; 5.8
7. 5.8; 5.3; 4.8
8. .37; .69; 1.33
9. 6.0; 7.3; 8.6
10. 1.6; 2.2; 2.9
11. .32; .44; .58
12. 3.2; 6.4; 12.8
13. 3.0; 4.1; 5.4
14. 17.0; 13.8; 7.4
15. 7.5; 6.4; 5.1
16. 7.6; 10.6; 14.1
17. 17.0; 13.8; 7.4
18. 3.125; 1.5625; .78125
19. .00005; .000006; .0000007
20. .00013; .000016; .0000019

Page 58.

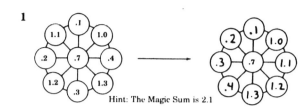

Hint: The Magic Sum is 2.1

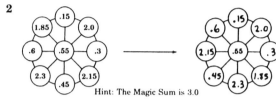

Hint: The Magic Sum is 3.0

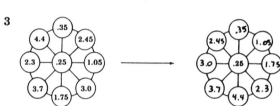

Page 59.

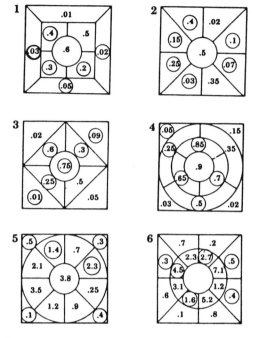

There may be other number combinations.

Page 60.

1. <	14. >
2. >	15. <
3. >	16. >
4. =	17. >
5. =	18. =
6. <	19. >
7. =	20. <
8. <	21. <
9. =	22. =
10. <	23. >
11. >	24. =
12. <	25. >
13. =	

Page 61.

1

1.9	+	.09	=	1.99
+		+		+
.08	+	2.3	=	2.38
=		=		=
1.98	+	2.39	=	4.37

2

7.4	−	4.596	=	2.804
−				−
5.024	−	3.9	=	1.124
=		=		=
2.376	−	.696	=	1.68

3

25.6	−	5.24	=	20.36
+		+		+
1.64	−	.05	=	1.59
=		=		=
27.24	−	5.29	=	21.95

4

1.357	+	4.8	=	6.157
+		+		+
.043	+	3.09	=	3.133
=		=		=
1.4	+	7.89	=	9.29

5

8.9	−	5.09	=	3.81
−		−		−
6.085	−	3.705	=	2.38
=		=		=
2.815	−	1.385	=	1.43

6

5.4	+	2.94	=	8.34
−		−		−
1.902	+	.038	=	1.94
=		=		=
3.498	+	2.902	=	6.4

Page 62.

1

2.01	.26	1.56
78	1.3	1.12
1.04	2.34	.52

2

2.1	2.45	.7
.35	1.75	3.15
2.8	1.05	1.4

3

1.36	3.06	.68
1.02	1.7	2.38
2.72	.34	2.04

4

.82	.96	.26
.12	.68	1.24
1.1	.4	.54

5

4.35	2.6	4.0	.15
.85	3.3	1.9	5.05
.5	3.65	2.15	4.7
5.4	1.55	2.95	1.2

6

1.55	3.8	2.0	6.95
6.05	2.9	4.7	.65
6.5	2.45	4.25	1.1
.2	5.15	3.35	5.6

7

1.9	.15	.275	1.525
.525	1.275	1.15	.9
1.025	.775	.65	1.4
.4	1.65	1.775	.025

8

2.84	.56	1.28	1.4	2.12
1.52	2.24	2.96	.68	.8
.2	.92	1.64	2.36	3.08
2.48	2.6	.32	1.04	1.76
1.16	1.88	2.0	2.72	.44

9

2.95	5.05	5.4	7.5	.85
6.8	7.15	.5	2.6	4.7
.15	2.25	4.35	6.45	8.55
4.0	6.1	8.2	1.55	1.9
7.85	1.2	3.3	3.65	5.75

Page 63.

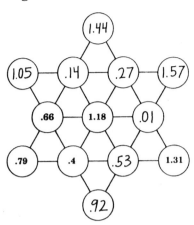

Page 64.

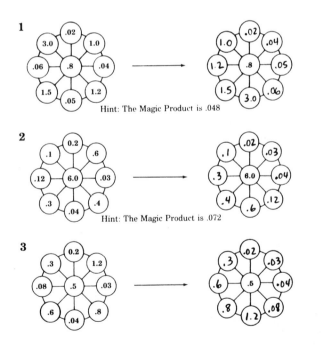

1 Hint: The Magic Product is .048

2 Hint: The Magic Product is .072

3

Page 65.

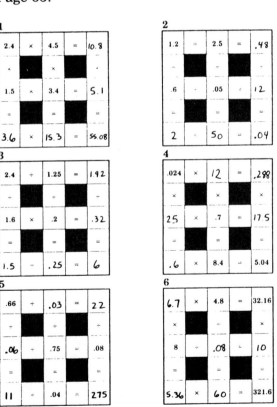

Page 66.

1

1.0	1.25	.1
.05	.5	5.0
2.5	.2	.25

2

.4	12.8	.1
.2	.8	3.2
6.4	.05	1.6

3

12.5	.25	5.0
1.0	2.5	6.25
1.25	25	.5

4

.3	15	.75
3.75	1.5	.6
3.0	.15	7.5

5

6.4	.2	.4
.05	.8	12.8
1.6	3.2	.1

6

2.7	656.1	.3
.9	8.1	72.9
218.7	.1	24.3

Page 67.

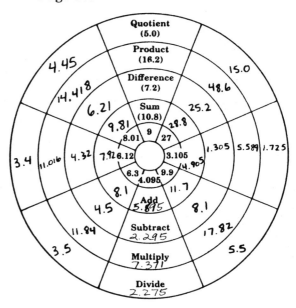

Page 68.

1

1	÷	.2	×	1.2	=	6
×	■	+	■	×		−
3.6	÷	1.2	×	.4	=	1.2
÷	■	+	■	÷		=
2.4	−	1	+	.6	=	2
=	■	=	■	=		=
1.2	+	2.4	−	.8	=	2.8

2

1.2	×	.6	÷	.4	=	1.8
−	■	+	■	÷		+
.4	÷	.2	+	.2	=	2.2
+	■	+	■	+		+
.8	+	.4	−	.2	=	1
=	■	=	■	=		=
1.6	+	1.2	+	2.2	=	5

3

.25	×	3	÷	.5	=	1.5
×	■	÷	■	+		+
4	×	.75	÷	2	=	1.5
+	■	−	■	−		+
2	×	1.5	−	1.5	=	1.5
=	■	=	■	=		=
3	+	2.5	−	1	=	4.5

4

4.5	×	2	÷	1.5	=	6
÷	■	×	■	−		−
1.5	+	.5	+	1	=	3
−	■	÷	■	+		+
.5	÷	.25	+	.5	=	2.5
=	■	=	■	=		=
2.5	+	4	+	1	=	5.5

Page 69.

1

3	÷	1.5	−	1.5	=	.5
×	■	+	■	+		×
.5	+	1	+	.5	=	2
+	■	−	■	+		+
.5	+	.5	+	1.5	=	2.5
=	■	=	■	=		=
2	+	2	−	.5	=	3.5

2

1.2	×	.4	÷	.8	=	.6
+	■	÷	■	÷		+
.2	÷	.2	+	.4	=	1.4
+	■	×	■	+		−
1.6	−	.2	+	.2	=	1.6
=	■	=	■	=		=
3	−	.4	−	2.2	=	.4

3

1	÷	.4	×	1.2	=	3
+	■	+	■	×		−
1.8	÷	.6	×	1	=	3
+	■	−	■	÷		+
2.4	+	.6	+	.6	=	3.6
=	■	=	■	=		=
5.2	+	.4	−	2	=	3.6

4

2.5	÷	.5	×	.2	=	1
×	■	×	■	×		+
.2	×	3	×	5	=	3
+	■	÷	■	×		−
.5	×	1.5	÷	.5	=	1.5
=	■	=	■	=		=
1	+	1	+	.5	=	2.5

Page 70.

1.	.001	**.1**	**1/10**	1/100
2.	**1/20**	5.0	1/2	**.05**
3.	**.25**	1/2	**1/4**	.52
4.	2½	**.4**	.25	**2/5**
5.	**.6**	3/4	.65	**3/5**
6.	7½	**.75**	**3/4**	.075
7.	**3.2**	8/25	**3 1/5**	.165
8.	.027	**2 7/10**	27/100	**2.7**
9.	.19	**1 9/10**	**1.9**	9 1/10
10.	**7.5**	3/4	.075	**7½**
11.	6.25	**.625**	6½	**5/8**
12.	**7/8**	8.75	**.875**	3/4
13.	**5 4/5**	**5.8**	.58	5/8
14.	.625	1/32	**.0625**	**1/16**
15.	**4.3**	.43	43/1000	**4 3/10**
16.	5/8	**6 3/8**	**6.375**	.6375
17.	**.125**	1/16	**1/8**	8
18.	1/6	**.08 1/3**	.625	**1/12**
19.	**.16 2/3**	**1/6**	.66 2/3	1/3
20.	.875	**5/6**	**.83 1/3**	2/3
21.	.032	3 1/5	**.32**	**8/25**
22.	1/30	**1/3**	3 1/3	**.33 1/3**
23.	**.66 2/3**	1 2/3	6.6	**2/3**
24.	**3/200**	.0015	**.015**	3/20
25.	26½	**2 5/8**	**2.625**	26.25

Page 71.

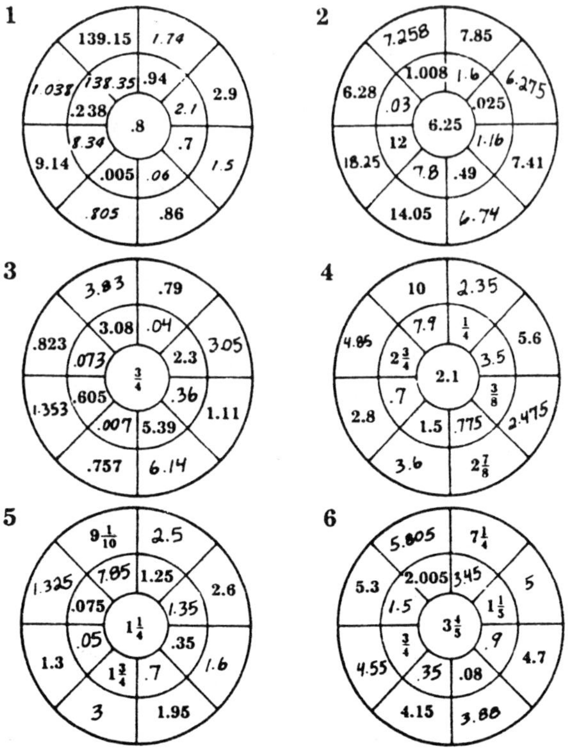

Page 72.

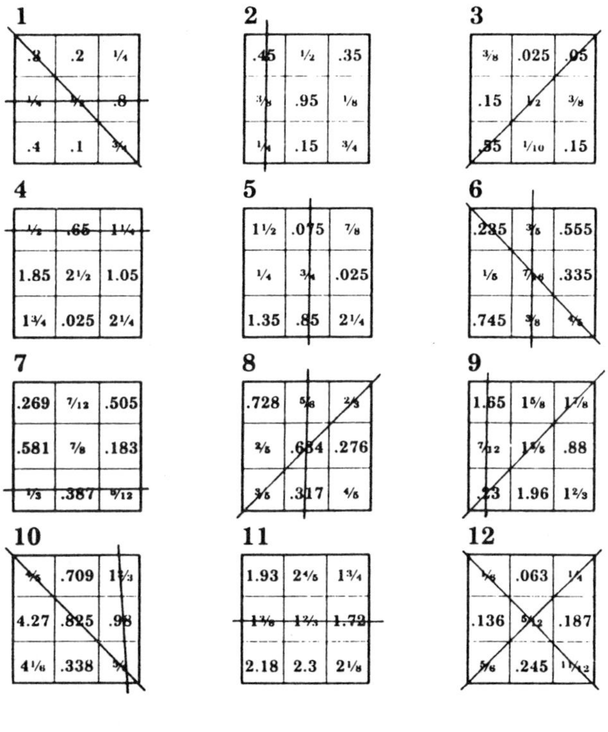

Page 73.

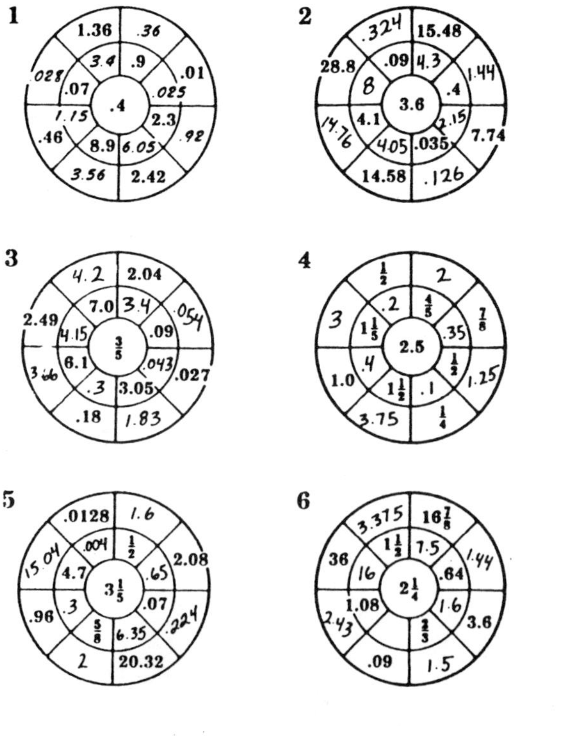

Page 74.

5/6 = .833333̄   7/12 = .583333̄   2/15 = .133333̄
8/27 = .296296̄   5/37 = .135135̄   23/33 = .696969̄

1/9 = .111111̄   1/99 = .010101̄
2/9 = .222222̄   2/99 = .020202̄
3/9 = .333333̄   5/99 = .050505̄
4/9 = .444444̄   8/99 = .080808̄
5/9 = .555555̄   10/99 = .101010̄
6/9 = .666666̄   16/99 = .161616̄
7/9 = .777777̄   56/99 = .565656̄
8/9 = .888888̄   75/99 = .757575̄

1/11 = .090909̄   1/999 = .001001̄
2/11 = .181818̄   2/999 = .002002̄
3/11 = .272727̄   5/999 = .005005̄
4/11 = .363636̄   8/999 = .008008̄
5/11 = .454545̄   16/999 = .016016̄
6/11 = .545454̄   56/999 = .056056̄
7/11 = .636363̄   75/999 = .075075̄
8/11 = .727272̄   90/999 = .090090̄
9/11 = .818181̄   175/999 = .175175̄
10/11 = .909090̄   587/999 = .587587̄

Page 75.

1. $8.09
2. $1.05
3. $4.28 ($2.90 + $.43 + $.45 + $.50)
4. $1,498; you get 1¢ in stamps for each dollar spent.
5. 10 quarters, 5 dimes, and 3 nickels.
6. $9.05
7. One $10 bill, one $5 bill, two dimes, and one penny.
8. 12 quarters, 1 dime, and 1 nickel.
9. $5.64
10. She gives you two quarters; you give her a nickel.

Page 76.

Sum

1.	2.	3.	4.	
14	1.4	2.3	11.3	29
5.	6.	7.	8.	
4.1	9.5	8.6	6.8	29
9.	10.	11.	12.	
7.7	5.9	5	10.4	29
13.	14.	15.	16.	
3.2	12.2	13.1	.5	29

Sum

| 29 | 29 | 29 | 29 | 29 |

Page 77.

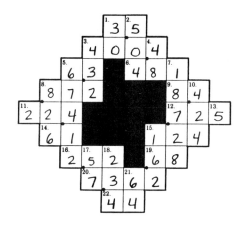

Page 78.

1. d; 7 is 4 more than 3; 7/8 = .875
2. b; .4 of 2 = .8; .8 ÷ 4 = .2
3. a; 1.2 ÷ .75 = 1.6
4. e; .6 × 15 = 9; 9 − 3 = 6; 6/12 = .5
5. c; .5 of 6 = 3; 3/5 = .6
6. d; 15 ÷ .3 = 50; 50 + 15 = 65
7. c; 6 − .3 = 5.7; 3 + .6 = 3.6; 5.7 − 3.6 = 2.1
8. b; .5 + 20 = 20.5; 20.5 ÷ .5 = 41
9. e; ½ × .4 = .2; ¼ × .5 = .125; .2 + .125 = .325
10. a; .6 × 4 = 2.4; .4 × 5 = 2; 2.4 ÷ 2 = 1.2

Page 79.

<u>M A T H</u> <u>I S</u> <u>A</u> <u>T O O L</u> <u>O F</u> <u>W I S D O M</u>.
13   12
1   15
20   6
8   23
9   9
19   19
1   4
20   15
15   13
15

Page 80.

(1) 1	(2) 2	(3) 5	■	(4) 8	(5) 9	■
(6) 1	7	8	(7) 3	■	(8) 2	(9) 4
(10) 2	6	■	(11) 1	(12) 3	3	6
■	■	(13) 2	5	2	■	■
(14) 6	(15) 3	4	9	■	(16) 8	(17) 7
(18) 4	4	■	(19) 2	(20) 4	7	5
■	(21) 2	(22) 4	■	(23) 3	3	6

Part IV. PERCENT

Page 82.

1.	~~1/20~~	1/2	50%	~~15%~~	.5
2.	~~2 1/2%~~	.25	~~40%~~	1/4	25%
3.	12 1/2%	.125	1/8	~~.8~~	~~8%~~
4.	.33 1/3	~~30%~~	33 1/3%	~~3/100~~	1/3
5.	1/6	~~12%~~	.16 2/3	~~1/12~~	16 2/3%
6.	.66 2/3	~~5/6~~	66 2/3%	2/3	~~56%~~
7.	75%	3/4	~~8 1/2%~~	.75	~~3/40~~
8.	5/8	~~66 2/3%~~	.625	~~7/12~~	62 1/2%
9.	83 1/3%	~~.67 1/2~~	~~7/8~~	.83 1/3	5/6%
10.	.875	~~83 1/2%~~	7/8	~~5/6~~	87 1/2%
11.	1/10	~~.001~~	10%	.1	~~1%~~
12.	.4	~~4%~~	~~.4%~~	40%	2/5
13.	~~700%~~	7/10	~~.07~~	70%	.7
14.	1/2%	~~1/25~~	1/200	~~5%~~	.005
15.	.16	~~1/6~~	16%	4/25	~~1.6%~~
16.	120%	1 1/5	~~12%~~	~~.012~~	1.2
17.	~~5.3%~~	53%	.53	53/100	~~.0053~~
18.	.055	11/200	~~55%~~	5 1/2%	~~.555~~
19.	~~.065~~	65%	~~6 1/4%~~	.65	13/20
20.	~~.062~~	.62	31/50	62%	~~6 1/5~~
21.	~~5 5/9~~	55 5/9%	5/9	~~59%~~	.55 5/9
22.	~~17.5~~	1 3/4	175%	1.75	~~17 1/2%~~
23.	~~3/50~~	.006	~~.6~~	3/500	.6%
24.	1 3/5	160%	~~16.0~~	~~16%~~	1.6
25.	~~275%~~	.275	11/40	27 1/2%	~~11/25~~

Page 83.

1

3/4	20%	3/5
.95	50%	.8
.45	1/3	70%

2

~~.2~~	~~1/4~~	~~28%~~
1/3	1/10	.3
12%	.35	16%

3

1/2	10%	3/4
15%	.12	20%
.3	1/8	.27

4

48%	.36	2/3
~~1/6~~	~~.2~~	~~24%~~
3/8	28%	.87

5

9/10	70%	80%
78%	.62	3/4
.875	2/3	.7

6

[illegible]	60%	13/20
57%	.7	7/12
.615	2/5	75%

7

6%	.37	1/3
.875	2/3	90%
~~1/12~~	~~10%~~	~~.15~~

8

1/2%	1/2	.05
.01	.4	12%
1/10	70%	.045

9

14/25	38%	3/5
.52	.6	35%
65%	11/20	.58

10

~~1 3/4~~	~~170%~~	~~1.6~~
42%	.12	5/12
~~.56~~	~~2/5~~	~~62%~~

11

.005	.2%	3/20
3/500	.4%	.01
.7%	.005	1/5

12

.8	1/15	22%
60%	[illegible]	.85
1/3	.05	20%

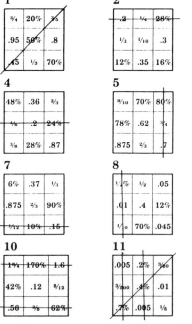

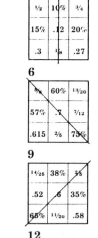

Page 84.

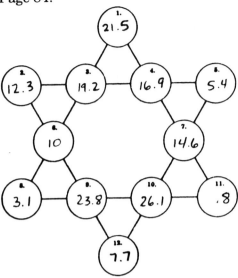

Page 85.

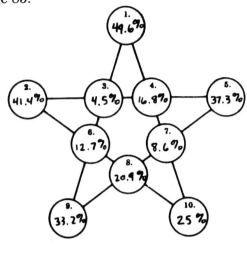

Page 86.

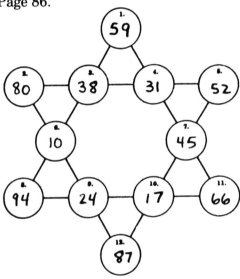

Page 87.

No.	Percent	Base	Percentage
1.	18%	46	8·28
2.	50%	12	6
3.	36%	50	18
4.	6%	24	1.44
5.	25%	24	6
6.	87½%	8	7
7.	3%	5,000	150
8.	83⅓%	54	45
9.	6%	200	12
10.	83⅓%	582	485
11.	120%	90	108
12.	100%	38	38
13.	40%	31.5	12.6
14.	60%	935	561
15.	4½%	624	28.08
16.	60¾%	940	571.05
17.	5%	$34.00	$1.70
18.	2½%	80	2
19.	187½%	112	210
20.	33⅓%	10½	3½
21.	.5%	1600	8
22.	52%	25	13
23.	6%	$14.50	$.87
24.	¾%	54	.405
25.	180%	10	18

Page 88.

				Sum
1. .8	2. 19	3. 17.7	4. 4.7	42.2
5. 15.1	6. 7.3	7. 8.6	8. 11.2	42.2
9. 9.9	10. 12.5	11. 13.8	12. 6	42.2
13. 16.4	14. 3.4	15. 2.1	16. 20.3	42.2
Sum 42.2	42.2	42.2	42.2	42.2

Page 89.

1. c; if 6 is 50% more than the number, then it is 150% of the number; 6 is 150% of 4.
2. d; if 8 is 60% less than the number, then it is 40% of the number; 40% of 20 is 8.
3. b; 25 is 15 more than 10; 15 is 150% of 10.
4. a; 1½ more than anything is 150% of it.
5. c; 12 is 120% of 10; 10 is 50% of 20.
6. e; 50% more than 40% is 60%; 12 is 60% of 20.
7. b; 50% of 16 is 8; 8 is 20% less than 10; 10 is half of 20.
8. d; 25% of 20 is 5; 15 is 10 more than 5; 10 is 200% of 5.
9. a; a decline from 20 to 10 is a drop of 10; 10 is 50% of 20.
10. e; a gain from 10 to 40 is an increase of 30; 30 is 300% of 10.

Page 90.

Page 91.

WORK IS A COMPANION OF SUCCESS.

23	9
15	15
18	14
11	15
9	6
19	19
1	21
3	3
15	3
13	5
16	19
1	19
14	

Page 92.

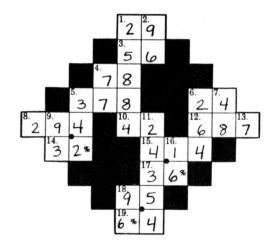

Part V. POWERS AND ROOTS

Page 94.

(1)

$1^2 = 0 \times 8 + 1 = \underline{1}$
$3^2 = 1 \times 8 + 1 = \underline{9}$
$5^2 = 3 \times 8 + 1 = \underline{25}$
$7^2 = 6 \times 8 + 1 = \underline{49}$
$9^2 = 10 \times 8 + 1 = \underline{81}$
$11^2 = 15 \times \underline{8+1} = \underline{121}$
$13^2 = 21 \times \underline{8+1} = \underline{169}$
$15^2 = 28 \times \underline{8+1} = \underline{225}$
$17^2 = \underline{36} \times \underline{8+1} = \underline{289}$
$19^2 = \underline{45, 8+1 = 361}$

(2)

$1 = \underline{1^2}$
$1 + 3 = \underline{2^2}$
$1 + 3 + 5 = \underline{3^2}$
$1 + 3 + 5 + 7 = \underline{4^2}$
$1 + 3 + 5 + 7 + 9 = \underline{5^2}$
$1 + 3 + 5 + 7 + 9 + 11 = \underline{6^2}$
$1 + 3 + 5 + 7 + 9 + 11 + 13 = \underline{7^2}$
$1 + 3 + 5 + 7 + 9 + 11 + 13 + 15 = \underline{8}$
$1 + 3 + 5 + 7 + 9 + 11 + 13 + 15 + 17 = \underline{9^2}$
$1 + 3 + 5 + 7 + 9 + 11 + 13 + 15 + 17 + 19 = \underline{10^2}$

(5)

$1^2 = \underline{1}$
$11^2 = \underline{121}$
$111^2 = \underline{12321}$
$1111^2 = \underline{1234321}$
$11111^2 = \underline{123454321}$
$111111^2 = \underline{12345654321}$
$1111111^2 = \underline{1234567654321}$
$11111111^2 = \underline{123456787654321}$
$111111111^2 = \underline{12345678987654321}$

(3)

$2^2 - 1^2 = 4 - 1 = \underline{3}$
$3^2 - 2^2 = 9 - 4 = \underline{5}$
$4^2 - 3^2 = 16 - 9 = \underline{7}$
$5^2 - 4^2 = 25 - 16 = \underline{9}$
$6^2 - 5^2 = 36 - 25 = \underline{11}$
$7^2 - 6^2 = 49 - 36 = \underline{13}$
$3^2 - 7^2 = 64 - 49 = \underline{15}$
$9^2 - 8^2 = 81 - 64 = \underline{17}$
$10^2 - 9^2 = 100 - 81 = \underline{19}$
$11^2 - 10^2 = \underline{121 - 100 = 21}$

(4)

$(3 \times 1) + 1 = 4 = \underline{2}^2$
$(4 \times 2) + 1 = 9 = \underline{3}^2$
$(5 \times 3) + 1 = 16 = \underline{4}^2$
$(6 \times 4) + 1 = 25 = \underline{5}^2$
$(7 \times 5) + 1 = 36 = \underline{6}^2$
$(8 \times 6) + 1 = \underline{49} = \underline{7}^2$
$(10 \times 8) + 1 = \underline{81} = \underline{9}^2$
$(14 \times 12) + 1 = \underline{169} = \underline{13}^2$
$(20 \times 22) + 1 = \underline{441} = \underline{21}^2$
$(34 \times 36) + 1 = \underline{1225} = \underline{35}^2$

Page 95.

$1 \times 3 = (2 - 1) \times (2 + 1) = 2 \times 2 - 1 = 2^2 - 1 = \underline{3}$
$2 \times 4 = (3 - 1) \times (3 + 1) = 3 \times 3 - 1 = 3^2 - 1 = \underline{8}$
$3 \times 5 = (4 - 1) \times (4 + 1) = 4 \times 4 - 1 = 4^2 - 1 = \underline{15}$
$4 \times 6 = (5 - 1) \times (5 + 1) = 5 \times 5 - 1 = 5^2 - 1 = \underline{24}$
$5 \times 7 = (6 - 1) \times (6 + 1) = 6 \times 6 - 1 = \underline{6^2 - 1 = 36 - 1 = 35}$
$6 \times 8 = (7 - 1) \times (7 + 1) = 7 \times 7 - 1 = \underline{7^2 - 1 = 49 - 1 = 48}$
$7 \times 9 = (8 - 1) \times (8 + 1) = 8 \times 8 - 1 = \underline{8^2 - 1 = 64 - 1 = 63}$
$8 \times 10 = (9 - 1) \times (9 + 1) = 9 \times 9 - 1 = \underline{9^2 - 1 = 81 - 1 = 80}$
$14 \times 16 = (15 - 1) \times (15 + 1) = \underline{15 \times 15 - 1 = 15^2 - 1 = 225 - 1 = 224}$
$19 \times 21 = (20 - 1) \times (20 + 1) = \underline{20 \times 20 - 1 = 20^2 - 1 = 400 - 1 = 399}$
$49 \times 51 = (50 - 1) \times (50 + 1) = \underline{50 \times 50 - 1 = 50^2 - 1 = 2500 - 1 = 2499}$
$99 \times 101 = (100 - 1) \times (100 + 1) = \underline{100 \times 100 - 1 = 100^2 - 1 = 10000 - 1 = 9999}$

$8 \times 12 = (10 - 2) \times (10 + 2) = 100 - 4 = \underline{96}$
$13 \times 17 = (15 - 2) \times (15 + 2) = 225 - 4 = \underline{221}$
$18 \times 22 = (20 - 2) \times (20 + 2) = 400 - 4 = \underline{396}$
$24 \times 26 = (25 - 1) \times (25 + 1) = 625 - 1 = \underline{624}$
$23 \times 27 = (25 - 2) \times (25 + 2) = 625 - 4 = \underline{621}$
$7 \times 13 = (10 - 3) \times (10 + 3) = 100 - 9 = \underline{91}$
$12 \times 18 = (15 - 3) \times (15 + 3) = \underline{225 - 9 = 216}$
$22 \times 28 = (25 - 3) \times (25 + 3) = \underline{625 - 9 = 616}$
$46 \times 54 = (50 - 4) \times (50 + 4) = \underline{2500 - 16 = 2484}$

$1\ 1/2 \times 2\ 1/2 = 2 \times 2 - 1/4 = \underline{3.75}$
$2\ 1/2 \times 3\ 1/2 = 3 \times 3 - 1/4 = \underline{8.75}$
$3\ 1/2 \times 4\ 1/2 = 4 \times 4 - 1/4 = \underline{15.75}$
$4\ 1/2 \times 5\ 1/2 = 5 \times 5 - 1/4 = \underline{24.75}$
$5\ 1/2 \times 6\ 1/2 = \underline{6 \times 6 - 1/4 = 35.75}$
$7\ 1/2 \times 8\ 1/2 = \underline{8 \times 8 - 1/4 = 63.75}$
$9\ 1/2 \times 10\ 1/2 = \underline{10 \times 10 - 1/4 = 99.75}$
$14\ 1/2 \times 15\ 1/2 = \underline{15 \times 15 - 1/4 = 224.75}$
$19\ 1/2 \times 20\ 1/2 = \underline{20 \times 20 - 1/4 = 399.75}$

Examples to Solve:

1. $29 \times 31 = \underline{899}$
2. $39 \times 41 = \underline{1599}$
3. $59 \times 61 = \underline{3599}$
4. $28 \times 32 = \underline{896}$
5. $79 \times 81 = \underline{6399}$
6. $38 \times 42 = \underline{1596}$
7. $48 \times 52 = \underline{2496}$
8. $58 \times 62 = \underline{3596}$
9. $78 \times 82 = \underline{6396}$
10. $27 \times 33 = \underline{891}$
11. $37 \times 43 = \underline{1591}$
12. $57 \times 63 = \underline{3591}$
13. $26 \times 34 = \underline{884}$
14. $36 \times 44 = \underline{1584}$
15. $25 \times 35 = \underline{875}$
16. $75 \times 85 = \underline{6375}$
17. $6\ 1/2 \times 7\ 1/2 = \underline{48.75}$
18. $8\ 1/2 \times 9\ 1/2 = \underline{80.75}$
19. $14\ 1/2 \times 15\ 1/2 = \underline{224.75}$
20. $24\ 1/2 \times 25\ 1/2 = \underline{624.75}$

Page 96.

Square Root	Number	Squared	Cubed	4th Power	5th Power
1.000	1	1	1	1	1
1.414	2	4	8	16	32
1.732	3	9	27	81	243
2	4	16	64	256	1,024
2.236	5	25	125	625	3125
2.449	6	36	216	1296	7776
2.646	7	49	343	2401	16,807
2,828	8	64	512	4,096	32,768
3	9	81	729	6561	59,049
3.162	10	100	1,000	10,000	100,000

Number	Squared
11	121
12	144
13	169
14	196
15	225
16	256
17	289
18	324
19	361
20	400
21	441
22	484
23	529
24	576
25	625

a. 8
b. 2
c. 16
d. 2
e. 27
f. 3
g. $5 \times 5 \times 5 \times 5 = 625$
h. $\sqrt[3]{6 \times 6 \times 6} = 6$
i. $7 \times 7 \times 7 = 343$
j. $\sqrt[4]{6 \times 6 \times 6 \times 6} = 6$
k. $\sqrt{18 \times 18} = 18$
l. $\frac{1}{2} \times \frac{1}{2} \times \frac{1}{2} = \frac{1}{8}$
m. $\sqrt[3]{\frac{1}{2} \times \frac{1}{2} \times \frac{1}{2}} = \frac{1}{2}$

Page 97.

1. 3.606
2. 8.718
3. 12.610
4. 4.219
5. 26.038
6. 3.142
7. 92.725
8. 7.399
9. 144.655
10. 21.879

Page 98.

1. 13
2. 17
3. 25
4. 29
5. 37
6. 41
7. 45
8. 60
9. 56
10. 63
11. 48
12. 36
13. 65
14. 24
15. 85
16. 80
17. 91
18. 57
19. 149
20. 252
21. 305
22. 288
23. 353
24. 135

25. 653

Page 99.

1. $2 \times 2 \times 2 \times 3 = 24$
2. $2 \times 2 \times 7 = 28$
3. $2 \times 2 \times 2 \times 2 \times 2 = 32$
4. $5 \times 7 = 35$
5. $2 \times 3 \times 7 = 42$
6. $3 \times 3 \times 5 = 45$
7. $5 \times 11 = 55$
8. $2 \times 2 \times 2 \times 7 = 56$
9. $3 \times 3 \times 7 = 63$
10. $5 \times 13 = 65$
11. $2 \times 3 \times 11 = 66$
12. $2 \times 2 \times 2 \times 3 \times 3 = 72$
13. $2 \times 3 \times 13 = 78$
14. $2 \times 2 \times 3 \times 7 = 84$
15. $3 \times 5 \times 7 = 105$
16. $3 \times 5 \times 11 = 165$
17. $5 \times 5 \times 7 = 175$
18. $3 \times 3 \times 5 \times 5 = 225$
19. $2 \times 2 \times 3 \times 3 \times 7 = 252$
20. $3 \times 3 \times 5 \times 7 = 315$

Page 100.

1. 7.94
2. $6\sqrt{2} = 8.48$
3. $5\sqrt{3} = 8.66$
4. $4\sqrt{5} = 8.94$
5. $4\sqrt{6} = 9.80$
6. $6\sqrt{6} = 14.69$
7. $5\sqrt{10} = 15.81$
8. $6\sqrt{7} = 15.88$
9. $10\sqrt{5} = 22.36$
10. $8\sqrt{10} = 25.30$
11. $15\sqrt{3} = 25.98$
12. $21\sqrt{2} = 29.69$
13. $10\sqrt{10} = 31.62$
14. $15\sqrt{7} = 39.69$
15. $21\sqrt{5} = 46.96$
16. $21\sqrt{6} = 51.43$
17. $30\sqrt{3} = 51.96$
18. $42\sqrt{2} = 59.40$
19. $40\sqrt{3} = 69.28$
20. $100\sqrt{2} = 141.42$

Page 101.

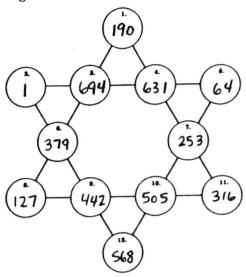

Page 102.

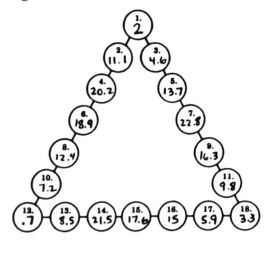

Page 103.

	Sum

1. 22.5	2. 5.5	3. 3.8	4. 27.6	59.4
5. 14	6. 17.4	7. 19.1	8. 8.9	59.4
9. 20.8	10. 10.6	11. 12.3	12. 15.7	59.4
13. 2.1	14. 25.9	15. 24.2	16. 7.2	59.4
Sum 59.4	59.4	59.4	59.4	59.4

Page 104.

Page 105.

TECHNOLOGY TREADS A
ROAD PAVED WITH MATH.

20	18
5	15
3	1
8	4
14	16
15	1
12	22
15	5
7	4
25	23
20	9
18	20
5	8
1	13
4	1
19	20
1	8

Page 106.

Part VI. METRIC MEASURE

Page 108.

1. 2.5	12. 11.3
2. 5.0	13. 2.0
3. 1.0	14. 4.8
4. 6.5	15. 12.5
5. 10.0	16. 1.5
6. 3.5	17. 2.7
7. 4.5	18. 6.0
8. .8	19. 3.0
9. 3.3	20. 4.4
10. 5.7	Sum 94.2
11. 3.2	

Page 110.

1. c; 68 millimeters, or 2.7 inches.
2. d; 28 centimeters, or 11 inches.
3. a; 19 centimeters, or 7.5 inches.
4. c; 35 millimeters, or 1.4 inches.
5. d; 46 centimeters, or 18 inches.
6. b; 2 meters, or 6.6 feet.
7. b; 38 decimeters, or 12.5 feet.
8. d; 22 centimeters, or 8.6 inches.
9. c; 4,800 kilometers, or 3,000 miles.
10. a; 112 kilometers, or 70 miles.

Page 109.

1

5	5	50
hm	m	cm
50	.05	5
dm	hm	dam
500	50	.5
mm	dm	m

2

.05	500	5
hm	mm	cm
50	5	½
cm	dm	m
5	½	50
km	dam	mm

3

20	2	.2
mm	cm	dam
2	.02	.002
dm	m	km
.002	20	2
hm	dm	cm

4

6	½	60
dm	m	cm
.06	.6	6
km	dam	m
600	60	⅗
mm	dm	hm

5

250	.25	25
dm	km	dm
25	2.5	¼
cm	hm	dam
.25	25	250
hm	m	cm

6

1,200	120	1,200
cm	dam	dm
12,000	1.2	12
mm	hm	m
12	120	1.2
dam	m	km

7

300	.3	3
dm	hm	km
3	30	30
dam	cm	m
.3	300	3
km	m	hm

8

20	200	20
dam	dm	hm
200	2,000	2,000
cm	m	mm
2	20	200
km	dm	m

9

11	.011	110
cm	dam	mm
11	110	1,100
dam	dm	cm
1,100	11	.11
m	hm	km

10

.05	500	5
km	cm	dam
50	5	5,000
m	hm	cm
½	5,000	5
hm	mm	km

11

.2	2	20
cm	dm	mm
2	.002	.2
km	m	hm
.02	.2	2
hm	dam	mm

12

20	.02	.2
dam	hm	km
.002	200	2
km	cm	m
2,000	20	2
mm	dm	hm

Page 111.

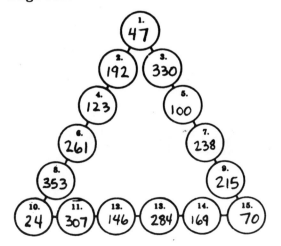

Page 112.

1. 1 m^2	11. 4.5 m^2
2. 1 m^2	12. 70,000 dm^2
3. 2 m^2	13. 80,000 m^2
4. 4 m^2	14. 80 a
5. 35,000 mm^2	15. 500 dm^2
6. 300 dm^2	16. 1 km^2
7. 12.4 m^2	17. 3.5 ha
8. 900 cm^2	18. 5 ha
9. 10 dm^2	19. 3 km^2
10. 9,500 mm^2	20. 250 ha

Page 113.

1. b; 11 square decimeters, or 170 square inches (13 inches square).
2. a; 50 square centimeters, or 7.8 square inches.
3. d; 70 square decimeters, or 7.6 square feet (33 inches square).
4. d; 6 square decimeters, or 93.5 square inches (8½ inches by 11 inches).
5. c; 29 square centimeters, or 4.5 square inches (2.4 inches in diameter).
6. a; 272 square decimeters, or 29.3 square feet (4.5 feet by 6.5 feet).
7. d; 465 square meters, or 5,000 square feet (100 feet by 50 feet).
8. c; 14 square decimeters, or 217 square inches.
9. b; 50 acres, or 54,000 square feet (360 feet by 150 feet).
10. b; 3,120 square kilometers, or 1,204 square miles.

Page 114.

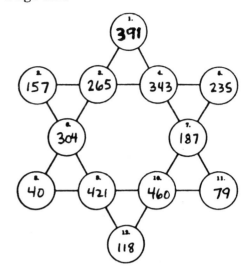

Page 115.

1. G		11. B	
2. L		12. D	
3. P		13. O	
4. C		14. F	
5. S		15. I	
6. J		16. K	
7. A		17. M	
8. N		18. H	
9. Q		19. E	
10. T		20. R	

Page 116.

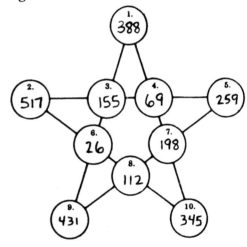

Page 117.

1. 130 cl	1,300 ml	13 dl	.013 hl	~~1.3 dal~~
2. ~~.9 l~~	3,000 ml	30 dl	.03 hl	300 cl
3. .01 dal	10 cl	100 ml	~~.001 kl~~	1 dl
4. 7 ml	~~.00007 cl~~	.07 dl	.007 l	.0007 dal
5. 200 dal	2,000 l	~~20,000 hl~~	2 kl	200,000 cl
6. .04 kl	400 dl	4 dal	~~.4 l~~	4,000 cl
7. 250 dl	.025 kl	25 l	.25 hl	~~2,500 ml~~
8. 65 cl	.65 l	~~6,500 ml~~	.0065 hl	6.5 dl
9. ~~.006 dl~~	.96 dal	960 cl	.0096 kl	9.6 l
10. .022 kl	~~220 dal~~	22 l	2,200 cl	.22 hl
11. 4.2 kl	420 dal	~~420,000 ml~~	42,000 dl	42 hl
12. 1.8 dal	~~18,000 cl~~	1,800 cl	18 l	.018 kl
13. 270 dl	27,000 ml	.027 kl	~~2.7 hl~~	2,700 cl
14. 8.8 dl	.088 dal	.0088 hl	.88 l	~~.0088 kl~~
15. ~~126 dl~~	.126 dal	1,260 ml	.00126 kl	.0126 hl
16. .00078 kl	780 ml	~~.078 hl~~	7.8 dl	.78 l
17. 5 dm³	~~50 cl~~	5 l	5,000 ml	.005 kl
18. ~~.00067 kl of H₂O~~	.067 l of H₂O	.0067 dal of H₂O	67 ml of H₂O	67 g (grams)
19. 800 g (grams)	.8 l of H₂O	800 ml of H₂O	.0008 kl of H₂O	~~80 dl of H₂O~~
20. 210 cl of H₂O	.0021 kl of H₂O	2.1 kg	~~21 l of H₂O~~	2,100 ml of H₂O

Page 118.

1. c; 237 milliliters, or ½ pint.
2. d; 75 liters, or 20 gallons.
3. a; 15 milliliters, or ½ fluid ounce.
4. b; 355 milliliters, or 12 fluid ounces.
5. b; 296 milliliters, or 10 fluid ounces.
6. d; 12 milliliters, or .36 fluid ounce.
7. d; 190 liters, or 50 gallons.
8. b; 114 deciliters, or 3 gallons.
9. c; 38 deciliters, or 1 gallon.
10. a; 464 kiloliters, or 123,000 gallons.

Page 119.

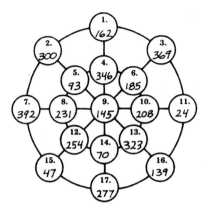

Page 120.

1. .14 g
2. .09 dg
3. 25 cg
4. 9 dg
5. .0031 hg
6. .8 cg
7. .02 hg
8. 5 kg
9. 99 g
10. 30 cg
11. .004 kg
12. 4,400 mg
13. 5 g
14. 7,000 mg
15. 300,000 dg
16. 520 cg
17. 8.5 g
18. 36,000 mg
19. 1.7 g
20. 1.2 hg

Page 121.

1. d; 7 grams, or ¼ ounce.
2. b; 65 kilograms, or 143 pounds.
3. c; 6 decigrams, or .02 ounce.
4. a; 34 hectograms, or 7½ pounds.
5. a; 23 dekagrams, or ½ pound.
6. c; 1,300 kilograms, or 1.4 short tons.
7. c; 68 dekagrams, or 1½ pounds.
8. d; 71 grams, or 2½ ounces.
9. b; 9 hectograms, or 2 pounds (1 quart).
10. a; 34 dekagrams, or 12 ounces.

Page 122.

				Sum
1. 469	2. 61	3. 90	4. 380	1000
5. 148	6. 324	7. 293	8. 235	1000
9. 264	10. 206	11. 179	12. 351	1000
13. 119	14. 409	15. 438	16. 34	1000
Sum 1000	1000	1000	1000	

Page 123.

1. c; 38° Celsius, or 100.4° Fahrenheit.
2. b; 100° Celsius, or 212° Fahrenheit.
3. a; 0° Celsius, or 32° Fahrenheit.
4. d; −40° Celsius, or −40° Fahrenheit.
5. c; 180° Celsius, or 356° Fahrenheit.
6. d; 37° Celsius, or 98.6° Fahrenheit.
7. b; 20° Celsius, or 68° Fahrenheit.
8. a; 1,085° Celsius, or 1,985° Fahrenheit.
9. a; 40° Celsius, or 104° Fahrenheit.
10. c; 26° Celsius, or 78.8° Fahrenheit.

Page 124.

1. 4	2. 7	3. 5			4. 3	5. 2
6. 6	2	5		7. 8	3	7
	8. 2	2	9. 3	9		
			10. 6			
	11. 7	4	12. 8	13. 5		
14. 4	15. 3	5		16. 6	2	17. 7
18. 5%	6%			19. 9	2	5

Page 125.

<u>MEASURE</u> <u>IS</u> <u>THE</u> <u>VO ICE</u> <u>OF</u> <u>PROGRESS</u>.

13	22
5	15
1	9
19	3
21	5
18	15
5	6
9	16
19	18
20	15
8	7
5	18
	5
	19
	19

Page 126.

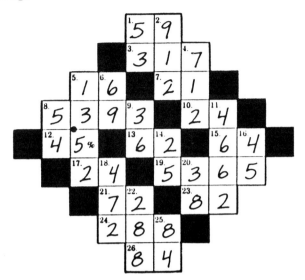

Part VII. PERIMETERS, AREAS, AND VOLUMES

Page 128.

1. 297 cm^2	5. 13.5 cm^2	9. 243 cm^2	13. 283.5 cm^2
2. 153 cm^2	6. 9 cm^2	10. 162 cm^2	14. -254.34 cm^2
3. 864 cm^2	7. 99 cm^2	11. 90 cm^2	Total Area
4. 54 cm^2	8. 13.5 cm^2	12. 108 cm^2	2,135.16 cm^2

Page 129.

1. P = 24 cm A = 24 cm^2	4. P = 32 cm A = 64 cm^2	7. P = 27 cm A = 42 cm^2
2. P = 30 cm A = 28 cm^2	5. P = 30 cm A = 54 cm^2	8. P = 25 cm A = 50 cm^2
3. P = 30 cm A = 40 cm^2	6. P = 22 cm A = 24 cm^2	9. P = 24 cm A = 42 cm^2

Page 130.

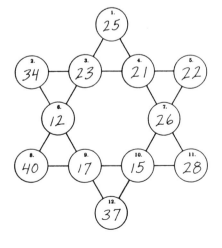

Page 131.

Volumes and Lateral Areas
1. $V = 6 \times 6 \times 6 = 216 \text{ cm}^3$
   $A = 6(6 \times 6) = 216 \text{ cm}^2$
2. $V = 4 \times 8 \times 5 = 160 \text{ cm}^3$
   $A = 2(4 \times 5) + 2(4 \times 8) + 2(5 \times 8) = 184 \text{ cm}^2$
3. $V = 3 \times 3 \times 3.14 \times 7 = 198 \text{ cm}^3$
   $A = (6 \times 3.14 \times 7) + 2(3 \times 3 \times 3.14) = 188 \text{ cm}^2$
4. $V = \frac{1}{3} \times 4 \times 4 \times 3.14 \times 9 = 151 \text{ cm}^3$
   $A = (\frac{1}{2} \times 3.14 \times 8 \times 9.85) + (4 \times 4 \times 3.14) = 174 \text{ cm}^2$
5. $V = \frac{1}{3} \times 8 \times 7 \times 7 = 131 \text{ cm}^3$
   $A = (\frac{1}{2} \times 8.73 \times 7 \times 4) + (7 \times 7) = 171 \text{ cm}^2$
6. $V = \frac{4}{3} \times 3.14 \times 4 \times 4 \times 4 = 268 \text{ cm}^3$
   $A = 4 \times 3.14 \times 4 \times 4 = 201 \text{ cm}^2$

Page 132.

a. Volume = 113 cm³
b. Volume = 9,420 cm³
c. Volume = 21,195 cm³
d. Volume = 54,000 cm³
e. Volume = 216,000 cm³
f. Volume = 37,680 cm³
g. Volume = 12,000 cm³
Total Volume = 350,408 cm³

Page 133.

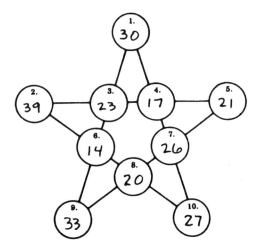

Page 134.

1. 2	2. 4		3. 2	4. 2	5. 5
6. 4	8		7. 6	6	5
8. 1	3	9. 9	1		
		10. 4	0	11. 6	12. 9
13. 3	14. 8	4		15. 5	8
16. 5	6	5		17. 6	5

Page 135.

<u>N</u><u>O</u> <u>ONE</u> <u>HATES</u> <u>A</u> <u>J</u><u>O</u><u>B</u> <u>WELL</u> <u>D</u><u>O</u><u>NE</u>.

40	36
41	41
41	28
40	49
31	31
34	38
27	38
46	30
31	41
45	40
27	31

Page 136.

		1. 4	2. 4			
	3. 1	2	3	8	4.	
5. 2	4	3		6. 4	7. 2	
8. 2	4			9. 2	0	10. 2
11. 7	6	12. 5			13. 1	3
	14. 6	4		15. 4	16. 1	5
	17. 9	18. 2	1	6		
		19. 9	4			

Part VIII. MISCELLANEOUS MATERIALS

Page 138.

Per the instructions of item 15 of the test, only items 1 and 2 are to be completed.

Page 139.

No answers are necessary.

Page 140.

```
O A H N V W P G I D X V D I V I D E A E
K W D I F F E R E N C E I C U R B T D Q
A E U D X I J A J Q C D V G B E O F Y U
M P R O V A L M W B P N I C M Z D O F O
D N U M E R A T O R H K S G O A J I T T
B X U K Y L Y J Q A X S O D M F R C G I
E S D E N O M I N A T O R I A E L I Y E
M U L T I P L I C A N D C Z W F T H Z N
B E C L T Z M R N O P E R C E N T E K T
V S Q U A R E U I M D C H R Q R K S R B
M D N U N W E H J U F I T V Y I E J S F
D K H C O Q M T L L T G V K S R O Q U M
Q P L P E R C E N T A G E I A T Y Z B U
L I T E R A U P X I T D U S D M F P T L
O R N W R I Q S V P O G D S V E N T R T
J W F T U X E H S L R Y L E A Z Z A I
G X B G F R A C T I O N V Q N O A D H P
E U F P D I J T R E K P W H C D Y N E L
S U Z A G C S F B R C I K B J M D X N Y
H P R O D U C T L M B W M I N U E N D G
```

Page 143.

1. 252
2. 667
3. 4485
4. 2958
5. 3186
6. 6970
7. 4556
8. 1287
9. 7392
10. 272
11. 2254
12. 2021
13. 1890
14. 8736
15. 2968
16. 7298
17. 5475
18. 4026
19. 2958
20. 1404
21. 8924
22. 728
23. 5624
24. 5775
25. 9207

Page 141.

1. 5616
2. 224
3. 5621
4. 9009
5. 3016
6. 9024
7. 5624
8. 2021
9. 7221
10. 2016
11. 4209
12. 2024
13. 616
14. 221
15. 2009
16. 1224
17. 3009
18. 609
19. 4216
20. 3016
21. 1221
22. 7209
23. 1216
24. 9021
25. 7224

Page 142.

1. 1625
2. 3825
3. 3325
4. 4125
5. 1625
6. 2125
7. 3375
8. 9375
9. 2275
10. 2975
11. 1925
12. 4675
13. 8075
14. 6375
15. 6175
16. 4725
17. 23,575
18. 1875
19. 2475
20. 7125
21. 4875
22. 5225
23. 2625
24. 4725
25. 19,125

Page 144.

1. $\frac{2+3}{2\times 3}=\frac{5}{6}$
2. $\frac{3+4}{3\times 4}=\frac{7}{12}$
3. $\frac{4+5}{4\times 5}=\frac{9}{20}$
4. $\frac{2+6}{2\times 6}=\frac{2}{3}$
5. $\frac{2+5}{2\times 5}=\frac{7}{10}$
6. $\frac{2+8}{2\times 8}=\frac{5}{8}$
7. $\frac{5+6}{5\times 6}=\frac{11}{30}$
8. $\frac{5+8}{5\times 8}=\frac{13}{40}$
9. $\frac{4+12}{4\times 12}=\frac{1}{3}$
10. $\frac{8+12}{8\times 12}=\frac{5}{24}$
11. $6\frac{1}{4}$
12. $12\frac{1}{4}$
13. $30\frac{1}{4}$
14. $42\frac{1}{4}$
15. $72\frac{1}{4}$
16. $156\frac{1}{4}$
17. $240\frac{1}{4}$
18. $420\frac{1}{4}$
19. $650\frac{1}{4}$
20. $2550\frac{1}{4}$

Page 145.

1. 3600
2. 3168
3. 256
4. 4896
5. 5125
6. 7600
7. $\frac{9}{20}$
8. $1\frac{1}{8}$
9. 69
10. 4.945
11. 5.03
12. 870,000
13. 9.5
14. 96
15. 180
16. 35
17. 25%
18. .0144
19. 420.25
20. 110

Page 146.

1. a; 11 months have 30 days or more.
2. c; the steer is just as heavy standing on four legs as standing on three legs.
3. d; 10 divided by ½ is 20; 20 plus 3 is 23.
4. e; 2 pairs of something is 4; 4 sets of twins would be eight children.
5. e; 3 eggs in boiling water would cook in the same time as 1 egg.
6. d; there are no marbles in an empty jar.
7. b; 1 pill at the beginning of the hour, 1 pill in half an hour, and 1 pill at the end of the hour; 3 pills in one hour.
8. b; a person is only born once; one birth day.
9. b; a dozen of anything is 12 of them.
10. c; a square plot with 16 equally spaced posts would have 5 posts on a side.

Page 147

1. The clock would not run at all without winding it.
2. A person walks halfway into a park; after that the person would be walking out of the park.
3. Four cows in a row.
4. Fifteen cents.
5. 6
6. Because it would be a foot.
7. A hole.
8. ~~8~~
9. A hole in the ground.
10. 1

Page 148.

1. One of the coins *is* a dime; the other is a quarter.
2. The eight that did not escape.
3. 6 + 7 + 8 = 21; 21 − 15 = 6
4. Yes; a house can't jump.
5. Meat.
6. Put 5 pieces of candy in one cup and 3 pieces in another; then put one cup containing pieces of candy in the third cup.
7. There is no such thing as half a hole.
8. The horse can graze over any area it wants to, unless the rope is tied to something in addition to the horse.
9. Most probably 5 more cats; when a cat catches (and eats a mouse), it probably won't do any more mouse catching for awhile.
10. Remove the *s* from *seven*.

Page 149.

1. a; ½ of 10 = 5; 5 × 10 = 50
2. e; it takes 8 half-meter cubic blocks to make a one-meter cubic block.
3. a; 60 ÷ 5 = 12; 60 × 5 = 300
4. a; if a turkey weighs 6 kg plus ⅓ its weight, then ⅔ of its weight must be 6 kg; 3/3 of its weight would be 9 kg.
5. e; if a clock strikes from hour 1 to hour 12 twice during the day, plus 24 half-hour strikes, it would strike 48 times.
6. b; 3 × 2 = 6; 6 − 3 = 3 (the original number)
7. c; there are 20 half-decimeters in a meter; there would be 400 square half-decimeters in a square meter.
8. c; it would take 2 cuts to saw a log into 3 pieces, or 6 minutes per cut; it would take 5 cuts to saw a similar log into 6 pieces; at 6 minutes per cut, it would take 30 minutes.
9. d; **ely** would remain uncovered.
10. d; there would be 6 posts on each side of the square lot, a total of 20 posts.

Page 150.

1. c; $1,000,000,000 ÷ 200,000,000 = $5
2. d; 500 (number of hundreds of dollars)
   × $7.50/$100 = $3,750.00
3. b; 30 minutes × 200 liters × 30 days (one month)
   × $.40/1000 liters = $72.00
4. e; assuming a person normally walks at the rate of
   9 minutes per kilometer, it would take 45 minutes to
   walk 5 kilometers.
5. d; assuming you could get 4 glasses per liter, it
   would take 50 liters to provide 200 glasses of lemonade for 100 people.
6. a; a half dollar, a dime, and a penny.
7. c; 30 days (1 month) × 100 watts × 24 hours × 6¢
   per kwh = $4.32
8. b; the average person can hold 150 nickels.
9. e; 150,000,000 km ÷ 12,500 km (diameter of earth)
   = 12,000
10. a; 6 m/hr. × 8 hr./day × 30 days (one month) @
    $6.00/100 = $86.40

Page 151.

1. a; there is no dirt in a hole.
2. d; 45 − 6 = 39; 45 + 6 = 51
3. e; if all but 4 of each dozen are good, then 4 of each
   dozen must be bad; 4 × 3 = 12 bad oranges.
4. b; putting all the haystacks together would make
   one large haystack.
5. d; all of the months have 28 or more days.
6. c; the dog weighs 8¾ kg, with or without the box.
7. e; we must assume that each salesman sells at the
   rate of 1 car in 5 days.
8. b; there are 5 sons, 1 daughter, and 2 parents.
9. a; Jill's height is the same, on or off the box.
10. c; since there is no year 0, the Senator lived 34 A.D.
    years; 35 + 34 = 69.

Page 153.

Designs will vary.

Page 152.

1. d; the basket would be half full one minute before it
   was full.
2. c; 8 years ago the combined ages would be 40 years
   (8 years less for each of 5 family members − 5 × 8)
   less than now; 88 − 40 = 48.
3. c; he would reach the desired spot on the 9th step,
   before falling back a half-step.
4. a; each number is increased by the square of the
   next consecutive number: $1 + 1^2; 2 + 2^2; 6 + 3^2; 15$
   $+ 4^2; 31 + 5^2; 56 + 6^2 = 92$.
5. e; it would take 3 cuts of 1 minute each to cut the
   pole into 4 pieces; 3 minutes to do the job.
6. e; since April has 30 days, April 30 would be the last
   day of the month, and since April 15 falls on a
   Wednesday, April 30 would fall on a Thursday.
7. b; since 20 posts 4 meters apart are necessary to
   fence the square plot, the plot would be 20 meters
   on a side (4 posts between each set of corner posts),
   or 400 m² in area.
8. a; they would both be off again together two weeks
   from the Friday after this Thursday.
9. e; since the first kilometer is driven at the rate of 30
   km/hr., it would be impossible to go fast enough on
   a second kilometer to average 60 km/hr.
10. b; she would be away 9 days after the day she
    planned to leave and before the day she planned to
    return.

Page 154. Examples of solutions

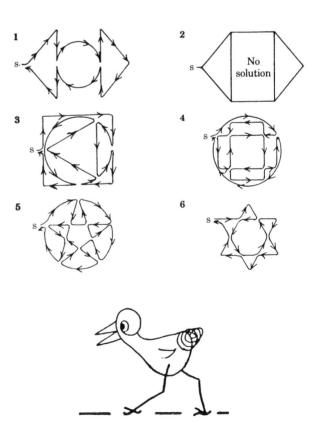

Page 155. Examples of solutions

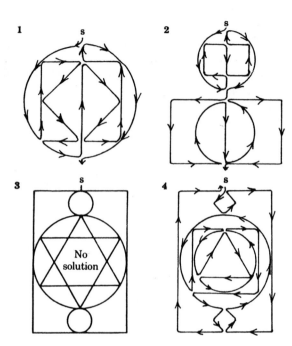

Page 157.

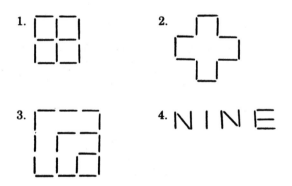

1.

2.

3.

4. N I N E

5.

Make a triangular pyramid.

Page 156.

1. 36	6. 3
2. 2	7. 0
3. 4	8. 4
4. 3	9. 1
5. 5	10. 2

Page 158.

1. Move these → Add this

2. Broken toothpicks

3. ||| ||| ||| ||| ||| ||| ||| |||

4. Before   After

Rearrange toothpicks 1 and 2.

5.

Move the horizontal toothpick a half length to the right; move the top left toothpick to the bottom right.

Page 159.

1. OOO OOOOOO

   Three and ½ Dozen

2.

   Place coin at right on top of coin to the left.

3.

When coin A has rolled halfway around coin B, it will have made a complete revolution on its axis; it will have made two revolutions by the time it has rolled completely around coin B.

4.   Move center coin in middle row and left-most coin in bottom row to new locations as shown.

Page 159 (*continued*).

5. Before   After

Page 160.

1. add
2. arc
3. sum
4. base
5. count
6. gram
7. prime
8. five
9. cone
10. line
11. graph
12. zero
13. four
14. point
15. rate
16. mean
17. time
18. number
19. nine
20. odd
21. ratio
22. ten
23. sets
24. plane
25. plus
26. eight
27. mode
28. root
29. ray
30. scale
31. seven
32. minus
33. six
34. space
35. speed
36. two
37. power
38. fraction
39. cube
40. ton

Page 161.

1. eight
2. kilogram
3. meter
4. week
5. root
6. subtraction
7. arc
8. irrational
9. weight
10. rectangle
11. powers
12. mean
13. inverse
14. one
15. line
16. addend
17. square
18. decagon
19. cone
20. plane

Page 162.

1. c; the perch, pole, and rod are all an equal measure of 5½ yards (16½ feet), or approximately 5 meters.
2. b; a stone is 14 pounds, or approximately 6 kilograms.
3. e; a fortnight is a period of 14 days; two weeks.
4. d; a score is 20.
5. a; a mil is ¹⁄₁₀₀₀ of an inch, or about .025 millimeter.
6. a; a hand is a length of 4 inches, or 10.2 centimeters.
7. e; a fathom is a length of 6 feet, or 1.83 meters.
8. b; a cubit is a length of 18 inches, or about ½ meter.
9. e; the rate of 1 knot is 1 nautical mile per hour, or 1.85 kilometers per hour.
10. d; a carat is a weight of 200 milligrams, or 3.086 grains troy.

Page 163.

A solution to the logic problem:

Dave's favorite sport is not racquetball (1); not tennis, because tennis is the favorite sport of a girl (4); and not bowling, because bowling is also the favorite sport of a girl (7); so Dave's favorite sport is skating. Since the girls' favorite sports are bowling and tennis (4,7), Jason's favorite sport is racquetball. Freda's favorite sport is tennis (1,3), so Lisa's favorite sport is bowling.

The education student is Jason (2). The student whose chosen profession is medicine is Lisa (7). Since Freda is the girl whose favorite sport is tennis, her chosen profession is law (4). By elimination, Dave is the theology student.

Freda is the senior student (3). Since skating is the favorite sport of the sophomore student (6), the sophomore student is Dave. Since the freshman student doesn't bowl or play tennis (5) (Freda's and Lisa's favorite sports, respectively), and Dave's favorite sport is skating, the freshman student's favorite sport is racquetball; this is Jason's favorite sport; thus Jason is the freshman student, so Lisa must be the junior student (8).

Summary: Dave, sophomore, skating, theology; Freda, senior, tennis, law; Jason, freshman, racquetball, education; and Lisa, junior, bowling, medicine.

Name	Class	Favorite Sport	Chosen Profession
Dave	Sophomore	Skating	Theology
Freda	Senior	Tennis	Law
Jason	Freshman	Racquetball	Education
Lisa	Junior	Bowling	Medicine

Page 164.

A solution to the logic problem:

The Canadian lives on the third floor (2). Since neither the Frenchman nor the Peruvian lives on the second floor (11), and since the Nigerian lives on a lower floor from the Peruvian than does the Indonesian (7), the Nigerian lives on the second floor, the Indonesian lives on the fourth floor, and the Peruvian lives on the fifth floor. This leaves the Frenchman on the first floor.

The owner of the parrot lives on the fifth floor (1), and this is the Peruvian; the owner of the canary lives on the first floor (5), and this is the Frenchman; the owner of the lizard lives on the fourth floor (10), and this is the Indonesian. Since the Canadian does not like the monkey (2), the Canadian's pet is the bobcat. By elimination, the Nigerian's pet is the monkey.

The favorite drink of the Frenchman (1st floor, canary) is hot chocolate (6); the favorite drink of the Canadian (3rd floor, bobcat) is milk (4); the favorite drink of the Peruvian (5th floor, parrot) is tea (8). Since the Indonesian (4th floor, lizard) does not like orange juice (3), his favorite drink must be coffee. By elimination, the Nigerian's favorite drink is orange juice.

The bridge player is the Canadian (3rd floor, bobcat, milk) (4,12); the poker player is the Frenchman (1st floor, canary, hot chocolate) (6); the chess player is the Indonesian (4th floor, lizard, coffee) (3). The pinochle player does not like tea (9), so the pinochle player must be the Nigerian (2nd floor, monkey, orange juice). By elimination, the Scrabble player is the Peruvian (5th floor, parrot, tea).

Summary: First floor, Frenchman, poker, hot chocolate, canary; second floor, Nigerian, pinochle, orange juice, monkey; third floor, Canadian, bridge, milk, bobcat; fourth floor, Indonesian, chess, coffee, lizard; and fifth floor, Peruvian, Scrabble, tea, parrot.

Apartment Floor	Nationality	Favorite Game	Favorite Drink	Pet
First Floor	Frenchman	Poker	Hot Chocolate	Canary
Second Floor	Nigerian	Pinochle	Orange Juice	Monkey
Third Floor	Canadian	Bridge	Milk	Bobcat
Forth Floor	Indonesian	Chess	Coffee	Lizard
Fifth Floor	Peruvian	Scrabble	Tea	Parrot

Pages 165 and 166.

No answers are necessary.

Part IX. PRE-ALGEBRA

Page 168.

1. 9	11. 8
2. 6	12. 20
3. 10	13. 11
4. 4	14. 6
5. 4	15. 5
6. 20	16. 13
7. 11	17. 8
8. 9	18. 12
9. 36	19. 10
10. 25	20. 4

Page 169.

1. 899	9. 6399	18. 3584
2. 396	10. 2491	19. 2475
3. 1599	11. 3596	20. 1591
4. 2496	12. 384	21. 8075
5. 891	13. 8091	22. 4884
6. 2499	14. 4899	23. 8096
7. 1596	15. 1584	24. 12,099
8. 4891	16. 6396	25. 12,075
	17. 875	

Page 170.

1. 828	9. 5264	18. 2528
2. 884	10. 1554	19. 2059
3. 2178	11. 952	20. 3136
4. 2432	12. 2052	21. 2379
5. 5220	13. 2312	22. 1204
6. 2499	14. 2052	23. 3192
7. 884	15. 1863	24. 4505
8. 1188	16. 3128	25. 2444
	17. 4234	

Page 171.

#	Problem → Answer	#	Problem → Answer
(1)	2 + 2 = 4	(2)	6 + 3 = 9
(3)	2 + 5 = 7	(4)	3 + 5 = 8
(5)	5 + 4 = 9	(6)	6 + 4 = 10
(7)	7 + 6 = 13	(8)	8 + 7 = 15
(9)	9 + 6 = 15	(10)	7 + 5 = 12
(11)	8 + 9 = 17	(12)	7 + 3 = 10
(13)	8 + 8 = 16	(14)	9 + 9 = 18
(15)	8 + 5 = 13	(16)	8 + 3 = 11
(17)	7 + 4 = 11	(18)	9 + 6 = 15
(19)	8 + 7 = 15	(20)	6 + 9 = 15
(21)	9 + 9 = 18	(22)	9 + 7 = 16
(23)	11 + 7 = 18	(24)	10 + 1 = 11
(25)	6 + 11 = 17	(26)	9 + 1 = 10
(27)	27 + 3 = 30	(28)	30 + 8 = 38
(29)	29 + 8 = 37	(30)	47 + 7 = 54
(31)	37 + 6 = 43	(32)	8 + 55 = 63
(33)	28 + 8 = 36	(34)	35 + 5 = 40
(35)	24 + 9 = 33	(36)	37 + 5 = 42
(37)	20 + 0 = 20	(38)	31 + 9 = 40
(39)	45 + 36 = 81	(40)	39 + 27 = 66
(41)	42 + 20 = 62	(42)	65 + 47 = 112
(43)	47 + 82 = 129	(44)	339 + 497 = 836
(45)	437 + 466 = 903	(46)	538 + 345 = 883
(47)	568 + 177 = 745	(48)	76 + 28 = 104
(49)	865 + 806 = 1671	(50)	97 + 98 = 195

Page 172.

(1) 368 + 437 = 805

(2) 893 − 607 = 286

(3) 768 + 384 = 1152

(4) 8569 − 759 = 7810

(5) 738 + 695 + 241 = 1674

(6) 30078 − 6952 = 23,126

(7) 538217 + 406253 + 749096 + 823571 + 604926 = 3,122,063

(8) 4873 + 516 + 92947 + 68 + 5203 = 103,607

(9) 37064358 − 9999999 = 27,064,359

(10) 9203475 + 72 + 31067 + 524 + 826809 = 10,061,947

(11) A + A = 16 → 8 + 8 = 16

(12) A7 + 3A = ?2 → 57 + 35 = 92

(13) A8 − 2A = ?2 → 68 − 26 = 42

(14) A5 + A? = ?69 → 85 + 84 = 169

(15) ?36 − AB = AB → 136 − 68 = 68

(16) 1AB + AB = ?14 → 157 + 57 = 214

(17) 1AB + BA8 = ??36 → 168 + 868 = 1036

(18) ?A7 − BB = AA → 187 − 99 = 88

(19) 16A + A85 + A?7 = ?75 → 163 + 395 + 327 = 875

(20) 3?0B + B453 + B6?B = ??779 → 3708 + 8453 + 8618 = 20,779

(21) ??0 + B?B1 + 8B2B = ?07B7 → 5780 + 6361 + 8626 = 20,767

(22) B27 + BB35 + ??B = ??301 → 927 + 9935 + 439 = 11,301

(23) C8 + C27 + C509 = ???C → 48 + 427 + 4509 = 4984

(24) DD + DD + DD = ?8 → 66 + 66 + 66 = 198

(25) HOW + HOT + HO + HO = ?323 → 602 + 601 + 60 + 60 = 1323

Page 173.

(1) ?3 23 / ? 2 / 46 46	(2) ?7 17 / 5 5 / 8? 85	(3) 1? 13 / 7 7 / ?1 91	(4) ?? 19 / ? 3 / 57 57	(5) ?6 46 / ? 8 / 3?8 368
(6) 5? 54 / ? 4 / 2?6 216	(7) 9? 93 / ? 5 / ?65 465	(8) 6? 63 / ? 9 / 56? 567	(9) ?? 87 / ? 9 / 7?3 783	(10) ??? 134 / ? 7 / 938 938
(11) 2?6 256 / ? 8 / ?048 2048	(12) 4?? 465 / 9 9 / ?785 4185	(13) A3A 636 / A 6 / ??1A 3816	(14) AAB 448 / 8 8 / ???A 3584	(15) AAA 555 / 3 3 / ??6A 1665
(16) ??3A 1136 / A 6 / A81A 6816	(17) AAA 888 / B 9 / ?BB2 7992	(18) AAB 775 / B 5 / 38AB 3875	(19) ?A7B 4275 / B 5 / A737B 21,375	(20) B?236 10236 / A 8 / ABAAA 81,888
(21) AAB1?4 997134 / B 7 / ?ABAA38 6,979,938	(22) 2? 26 / ?4 34 / 1?? 104 / ?8 78 / ??4 884	(23) 2? 29 / ?? 73 / ?? 87 / ??? 203 / 2?1? 2117	(24) ??9 229 / ?? 37 / ???3 1603 / ?? 687 / ???? 8473	(25) 82?? 8202 / ??? 493 / ???6 24606 / ???8 73818 / ???8 32808 / ?0???8? 4,043,586

Page 174.

(1) 5/35 = 5 / 7?? 7	(2) 32 / 3/96 / 3?9? ??	(3) 9 / 8/72 / ?/72 ??	(4) 14 / 6/84 / 6/?4 ??	(5) 13 / 7/91 / 7/?? ?3
(6) 17 / 5/85 / ?/85 ??	(7) 83 / 4/332 / 7/?? ??	(8) 57 / 7/399 / 7/?99 ??	(9) 38 / 9/342 / 9/?? 3?	(10) 67 / 4/268 / 7/268 ??
(11) 458 / 9/4122 / 9/??? 45?	(12) 936 / 6/5616 / 7/5?6 ?36	(13) 777 / 9/6993 / 9/??3 AAA	(14) 855 / 5/4275 / A14?7A 7AA	(15) 404 / 4/1616 / A1??16 A?A
(16) 1236 / 6/7416 / A/7?1A ??3A	(17) 1344 / 7/9408 / 7?7A?8 7?AA	(18) 666 / 6/3996 / A/3BBA AAA	(19) 4447 / 7/31129 / B/3??29 AAAB	(20) 6325 / 5/31625 / A/7??B2A B32A
(21) 23611 / 8/188888 / B/ABBBBB ?36AA	(22) 17 / 3?/663 / 39 / 273 / 273 / ?? ?????? / ?9 / 2?? / ??3	(23) 32 / 78/2531 / 234 / 191 / 156 / 35 / ?? ??/75?1 / 2?? / 1?? / 25? / 35	(24) 229 / 3?/?????? / ??9 / 12?? / ??53 / 409 / 317/129653 / 1268 / 2853 / 2853	(25) 257 / 386/99210 / 772 / 2201 / 1930 / 2710 / 2702 / 8 / ??? ??/?????0 / ??? / 1930 / ??? / 8

Page 175.

(1)		(2)	
96?5 ?07 ?126 7? ――― ?8246	9635 407 8126 78 ――― 18,246	??0?8 17?? ??00? ?9 ――― 2?????	99098 1797 99008 99 ――― 200,002
(3)		(4)	
?8?6 − 94? ――― 2?59	3806 − 947 ――― 2859	??54?? − ??806 ――― 5?74	105480 − 99806 ――― 5674
(5)		(6)	
??7 ??? ??85 ??96? ――― 5?????	637 805 3185 50960 ――― 512,785	??9 ??? ??16 5??? 21?? ――― ????3?	729 384 2916 5832 2187 ――― 279,936
(7)		(8)	
??9 ?3?)8???5 ??? 1??? ???? 3??? ????	249 335)83415 670 1641 1340 3015 3015	4??? 2?)??0?3 ?? ?? ?? ??? ??? 9	4308 23)99093 92 70 69 193 184 9

Page 176.

(1) $\frac{1}{2} = \frac{4}{?}$	(2) $\frac{1}{4} = \frac{?}{16}$	(3) $\frac{?}{6} = \frac{4}{24}$	(4) $\frac{1}{?} = \frac{6}{48}$	(5) $\frac{3}{4} = \frac{??}{24}$
$\frac{1}{2} = \frac{4}{8}$	$\frac{1}{4} = \frac{4}{16}$	$\frac{1}{6} = \frac{4}{24}$	$\frac{1}{8} = \frac{6}{48}$	$\frac{3}{4} = \frac{18}{24}$
(6) $\frac{5}{?} = \frac{?5}{24}$	(7) $\frac{?}{4} = \frac{18}{?4}$	(8) $\frac{7}{?} = \frac{?8}{32}$	(9) $\frac{3}{?} = \frac{1?}{40}$	(10) $\frac{2?}{25} = \frac{?6}{75}$
$\frac{5}{8} = \frac{15}{24}$	$\frac{3}{4} = \frac{18}{24}$	$\frac{7}{8} = \frac{28}{32}$	$\frac{3}{8} = \frac{15}{40}$	$\frac{22}{25} = \frac{66}{75}$
(11) $\frac{?1}{2?} = \frac{4?}{96}$	(12) $\frac{7}{20} = \frac{3?}{10?}$	(13) $\frac{5}{?2} = \frac{?5}{6?}$	(14) $\frac{7}{?6} = \frac{?5}{8?}$	(15) $\frac{?}{8} = \frac{4?}{4?}$
$\frac{11}{24} = \frac{44}{96}$	$\frac{7}{20} = \frac{35}{100}$	$\frac{5}{12} = \frac{25}{60}$	$\frac{7}{16} = \frac{35}{80}$	$\frac{7}{8} = \frac{42}{48}$
(16) $\frac{?}{6} + \frac{?}{6} = \frac{1}{3}$	(17) $\frac{?}{3} + \frac{?}{6} = \frac{1}{2}$	(18) $\frac{5}{?2} + \frac{1}{1?} = \frac{1}{2}$	(19) $\frac{?}{2} + \frac{?}{4} = \frac{3}{?}$	(20) $\frac{1}{6} + \frac{?}{??} = \frac{3}{?}$
$\frac{1}{6} + \frac{1}{6} = \frac{1}{3}$	$\frac{1}{3} + \frac{1}{6} = \frac{1}{2}$	$\frac{5}{12} + \frac{1}{12} = \frac{1}{2}$	$\frac{1}{2} + \frac{1}{4} = \frac{3}{4}$	$\frac{1}{6} + \frac{7}{12} = \frac{3}{4}$
(21) $\frac{?}{2} + \frac{?}{3} = \frac{5}{?}$	(22) $\frac{11}{15} - \frac{1}{?} = \frac{2}{?}$	(23) $\frac{?}{3} + \frac{1}{4} = \frac{1?}{?2}$	(24) $\frac{?}{12} + \frac{?}{16} = \frac{41}{??}$	(25) $\frac{?}{8} - \frac{?}{3} = \frac{7}{??}$
$\frac{1}{2} + \frac{1}{3} = \frac{5}{6}$	$\frac{11}{15} - \frac{1}{3} = \frac{2}{5}$	$\frac{2}{3} + \frac{1}{4} = \frac{11}{12}$	$\frac{5}{12} + \frac{7}{16} = \frac{41}{48}$	$\frac{5}{8} - \frac{1}{3} = \frac{7}{24}$

Page 177.

(1) AB 25 15 AB 25 or 15 AB 25 15 CB 75 45	(2) BA 98 −AB −89 B 9	(3) AAAA 1111 × A ×1 AAAA 1111	(4) AAAA 1111 × B ×2 BBBB 2222 or ×3 thru 9
(5) AA 33 AA 33 BB 99 BB 99 EDCB 1089	(6) AA AA)AABA → 11)1121 11 AA 11 AA 11 AA 11	(7) BA 51 CA 61 BA 51 EDC 306 EAAA 3111	(8) AB AB)ABADC → 13)169 13 AB 13 BC 39 BC 39
(9) ONE 671 ONE 671 ONE 671 ONE 671 FOUR 2684 Use N = 7	(10) TEN 850 TEN 850 FORTY 29786 SIXTY 31486 Use T = 8	(11) FIVE 9071 TWO 846 ONE 621 EIGHT 10538 Use E = 1	(12) SEVEN 36061 − FOUR −7495 THREE 28566 Use E = 6
(13) RUM 651 + DUM +751 MATH 1402 Use A = 4	(14) THIS 6835 IS 35 VERY 4127 FUNNY 10997 Use N = 9	(15) DO × IT = NOW 13 × 49 = 637 Use O = 3	(16) √TODAY = PAY √30976 = 176 Use Y = 6

Page 178.

(1) BEIR 5271 RINU 1704 ERNCU 21084 PLCAIN 368970 BEIR 5271 CACRICU 8981784 R E P U B L I C A N 1 2 3 4 5 6 7 8 9 0	(2) TRYH 4621 HELI 1507 SYSTI 32347 YSHLEL 231050 TRYH 4621 RARSCTI 6963847 Hint: R = 6 H Y S T E R I C A L 1 2 3 4 5 6 7 8 9 0
(3) DREG → 1025 SIG)SGSNEG → 345)353625 SIG 345 TNE 862 NOR 690 DAEG 1725 DAEG 1725 Hint: S = 3 D E S I G N A T O R 1 2 3 4 5 6 7 8 9 0	(4) CASB → 1507 VHR)LVIAAV → 427)643554 VHR 427 HCLA 2165 HCIA 2135 ISAV 3054 HUOU 2989 LA 65 Hint U = 9 C H I V A L R O U S 1 2 3 4 5 6 7 8 9 0

Page 179.

T H O S E — W H O — K N O W
(2,8) (2,4) (0,7) (1,2) (3,5) — (8,0) (8,8) (2,0) — (3,0) (6,2) (8,9) (0,2)

E V E R Y T H I N G — H A V E
(1,8) (4,9) (1,3) (5,4) (4,5) (6,7) (6,0) (9,4) (3,6) (7,6) — (2,7) (6,9) (3,1) (9,7)

A — L O T — T O — L E A R N
(0,3) — (5,8) (8,3) (1,5) — (5,1) (4,3) — (9,1) (7,4) (9,5) (7,1) (5,6).

Page 180.

S A T I S F A C T I O N — I S
(8,3) (5,4) (5,0) (7,1) (9,9) (3,2) (5,8) (3,5) (3,7) (6,7) (0,3) (2,3) — (4,6) (2,8)

K N O W I N G — Y O U — H A V E
(0,6) (1,1) (7,9) (7,5) (6,0) (8,8) (2,4) — (0,8) (4,2) (3,1) — (1,9) (8,5) (1,0) (1,7)

D O N E — Y O U R — B E S T
(4,9) (0,0) (5,3) (9,6) — (6,4) (2,6) (6,1) (7,7) — (9,2) (8,2) (9,5) (4,4).

Page 181.

1

									Sum
-8	0	3	6	-9	2	5	-8	2	(-7)
0	-2	5	-8	2	-6	9	-2	-4	(-6)
1	-5	8	-4	8	-3	-7	1	5	(4)
-9	2	-5	7	2	4	7	0	-2	(6)
6	2	-7	1	-5	-9	4	8	-2	(-2)
5	6	-9	-4	-5	8	-1	4	-7	(-3)
4	-7	0	-3	5	8	-3	-5	7	(6)
-5	7	4	-7	2	-6	1	-5	9	(0)
0	-3	6	8	-2	6	-7	1	-4	(5)
Sum (-6)	(0)	(5)	(-4)	(-2)	(4)	(8)	(-6)	(4)	3

2

									Sum
9	(1)	-8	7	0	(5)	3	2	-6	(-5)
-4	-7	2	(-7)	1	7	0	5	(8)	5
0	5	-9	-2	(8)	3	-7	2	4	4
6	1	4	-9	7	-8	3	(-7)	-1	(-4)
4	-6	(1)	-5	0	(-3)	7	-3	(7)	2
-3	3	-1	3	-8	(7)	-3	2	-7	-7
-9	4	-7	-3	(6)	(-1)	6	0	-2	-6
(7)	3	5	2	-6	-6	-3	2	4	8
7	(-5)	6	9	-3	-7	1	-8	0	0
Sum (-1)	-1	-7	-5	(5)	-3	(7)	-5	7	-3

3

									Sum
(5)	1	-7	-3	(8)	-4	(9)	-5	1	5
(5)	-5	-2	9	6	-3	0	-7	4	(7)
(3)	1	-8	5	-2	9	6	-3	0	5
-2	0	(7)	4	(1)	8	-5	2	-9	6
(-4)	-1	8	(-5)	2	-9	6	(-3)	0	-6
-2	8	4	-9	-5	1	-6	2	6	(-1)
9	-5	1	-6	2	(-7)	3	7	-3	1
1	-8	5	(2)	-9	6	3	0	(-7)	-7
-7	4	-1	8	-5	-2	(-9)	6	5	-1
Sum 2	(-5)	7	5	-2	(-1)	7	-1	-3	(9)

4

									Sum
6	(0)	4	-9	3	(-7)	4	-8	2	-5
7	0	-3	(6)	-9	4	-8	1	4	(2)
-1	-5	9	2	5	-8	(1)	-4	7	2
(7)	-1	-5	9	-3	8	2	-6	-3	8
-6	(2)	(-6)	0	4	-8	1	(-5)	9	-9
-3	6	-9	-2	5	8	(-2)	(6)	(0)	(9)
-7	(0)	5	-8	3	-1	5	9	-3	3
1	5	9	2	(-6)	0	-7	3	-7	0
(2)	-7	1	5	2	6	(0)	-4	-8	-3
Sum 6	0	5	1	(4)	2	-4	-8		(7)

Page 182.

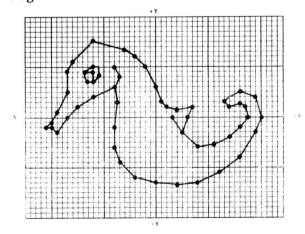

Page 183.

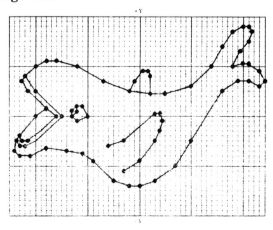

Page 184.

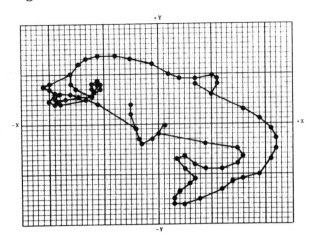

Page 185.

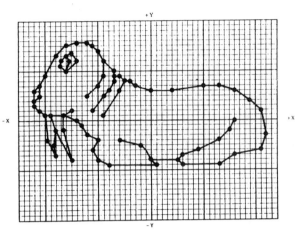

Page 186.

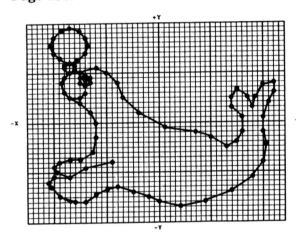

BIBLIOGRAPHY

The purpose of this bibliography is to provide selected reference books for secondary school students and teachers having an interest in recreational mathematics. These books were in print at the time of this writing. Shipping addresses of publishers are included for the benefit of those wishing to make inquiries or place orders. A brief description by the writer is included with each reference.

1. Barr, Stephen. *Mathematical Brain Benders: Second Miscellany of Puzzles.* Dover Publications, Inc., 31 East 2nd Street, Mineola, NY 11501, 1982. 224p. Paper.
   A collection of paradoxes, word problems, and number games with wit and humor.

2. Benson, William H. and Jacoby, Oswald. *New Recreations with Magic Squares.* Dover Publications, Inc., 31 East 2nd Street, Mineola, NY 11501, 1976. 192p. Paper.
   A complete book on the magic and mystery of the many kinds of magic squares. Well illustrated.

3. Benson, William H. and Jacoby, Oswald. *Magic Cubes: New Recreations.* Dover Publications, Inc., 31 East 2nd Street, Mineola, NY 11501, 1982. 96p. Paper.
   This is a book that tells how to construct three-dimensional mind bogglers. Well illustrated. No advanced mathematics needed.

4. Bezuszka, Stanley, et al. *Designs from Mathematical Patterns.* Creative Publications, P.O. Box 10328, Palo Alto, California 94303, 1978. 200p. Paper.
   The application of mathematics to design with patterns that are a blend of arithmetic and geometry. Needed materials are easily obtained. Limited reproduction permission granted.

5. Brandes, Louis Grant. *Fun with Logic.* J. Weston Walch, Publisher, P.O. Box 658, Portland, Maine 04104, 1983. 226p. Paper.
   A motivation puzzle book, with over 300 puzzles and problems, for the purpose of boosting thinking skills. Contents include fun quizzes, logic games, coin and toothpick puzzles, riddles, tricks, and a variety of other logic problems that vary from simple to complex. Many humorous drawings. Solutions and diagrams are provided, along with extra problem solving tips and directions for making puzzles.

6. Brooke, Maxey. *One Hundred Fifty Puzzles in Crypt-Arithmetic.* Dover Publications, Inc., 30 East 2nd Street, Mineola, NY 11501, 1972. 72p. Paper.
   Letters of the alphabet are substituted for digits which must be solved by number relationships. No background other than knowledge of arithmetic is needed.

7. Brooke, Maxey. *Tricks, Games, and Puzzles with Matches*. Dover Publications, Inc., 31 East 2nd Street, Mineola, NY 11501, 1973. 64p. Paper.
   A collection of puzzles, games, and stunts with matches.

8. Brooke, Maxey. *Coin Games and Puzzles*. Dover Publications, Inc., 31 East 2nd Street, Mineola, NY 11501, 1973. 96p. Paper.
   A collection of puzzles, games, and stunts with coins.

9. Dunn, Algela. *Mathematical Bafflers*. Dover Publications, Inc., 31 East 2nd Street, Mineola, NY 11501, 1980. 217p. Paper.
   A collection of challenging conundrums for the expert puzzlist. Well illustrated.

10. Dunn, Angela. *Second Book of Mathematical Bafflers*. Dover Publications, Inc., 31 East 2nd Street, Mineola, NY 11501, 1983. 192p. Paper.
    A collection of mathematrick-puzzles in probability, algebra, simple logic, insight, and equations. Illustrated solutions provided.

11. Emmet, E. R. *Puzzles for Pleasure*. Emerson Books, Inc., Madelyn Avenue, Verplanck, NY 10596, 1972. 256p. Hardback.
    A collection of puzzles whose solutions require careful logical thinking and reasoning. The puzzles, arranged in order of difficulty, provide a challenge for both the neophyte and the highly sophisticated thinker.

12. Emmet, E. R. *Mind Tickling Brain Teasers*. Emerson Books, Inc., Madelyn Avenue, Verplanck, NY 10596, 1978. 255p. 1978. Hardback.
    A collection of logic problems for the beginner. Provides exercise for the mind that develops the ability to think logically and reason effectively. As the book progresses, the degree of difficulty increases. No special knowledge of mathematics is required. Full explanations to solutions are provided.

13. Fujimura, Kobon. *The Tokyo Puzzles*. Gardner, Martin, editor. Charles Scribner's Sons, Vreeland Avenue, Totowa, NJ 07512, 1979. 184p. Paper.
    The first collection of puzzles in English by Japan's leading puzzlist. Puzzles that will probe mathematical skills and test patience, imagination, and common sense in the search for witty solutions.

14. Gardner, Martin. *Aha! Gotcha: Paradoxes to Puzzle and Delight*. W. H. Freeman and Company, 4419 West 1980 South, Salt Lake City, Utah 84104, 1982. 164p. Paper and hardback.
    A humorous and engaging collection of mathematical paradoxes. Spans six separate areas of mathematics—logic, numbers, geometry, probability, statistics, and time. Deals with three major kinds of paradoxes: the assertion that seems clearly false but is actually true; the assertion that seems clearly true but is actually false; and the line of reasoning that seems impeccable, but leads to logical contradiction. Should be of interest to better ability math students.

15. Gilbert, Jack. *Numbers, Shortcuts, and Pastimes*. TAB Books, Inc., P.O. Box 40, Blue Ridge Summit, Penn. 17214, 1976. 294p. Paper and hardback.
    An educational funbook of numbers and math games. Topics covered include tips for making complex numbers mentally manageable, tricks and shortcuts needed to perform in-your-head figuring, the art of estimating, checking, number curiosities, pattern finding in numbers, magic squares, parlor tricks, games, and puzzles.

16. Heafford, Phillip. *The Math Entertainer*. Random House, Inc., 400 Hahn Road, Westminister, Maryland 21157, 1983. 176p. Hardback.
A variety of materials for those who enjoy recreational mathematics. Provides for a better grasp of mathematics and mathematical reasoning. Complete explanations are provided.

17. Hunter, J. A. and Madachy, Joseph S. *Mathematical Diversions*. Dover Publications, Inc., 31 East 2nd Street, Mineola, NY 11501, 1975. 192p. Paper.
A collection of tricks and teasers that include topologic principals, alphametics, coin and change problems, relative ages, and time and distance problems. Well illustrated with drawings and diagrams.

18. Hunter, J. A. *Challenging Mathematics Teasers*. Dover Publications, Inc., 31 East 2nd Street, Mineola, NY 11501, 1980. 96p. Paper.
Includes story teasers and alphametics. Appendix offers special tips on solutions.

19. Johnson, Donovan A. *Games for Learning Mathematics*. J. Weston Walch, Publisher, P.O. Box 658, Portland, Maine 04104, 1972. 160p. Paper.
A book of mathematical games that include card games, bingo, graphing, games, sport games, relays, vocabulary games, and elementary arithmetic games. Emphasis is on basic math principles. Provides complete directions on how to play each game and how to find or make necessary game materials.

20. Kordemsky, Boris A. *Moscow Puzzles: Three Hundred Fifty-Nine Mathematical Recreations*. Gardner, Martin, editor. Charles Scribner's Sons, Vreeland Avenue, Totowa, NY 07512, 1982. 309p. Paper.
A Russian publication translated into English that makes use of units familiar to students. Includes geometry with matches, domino puzzles, dice puzzles, properties of nine, tricks, and magic squares. Ancient to modern vintage.

21. Mira, Julio A. *Mathematical Teasers*. Barnes and Noble Books, 10 E. 53rd Street, New York, NY 10032, 1970. 270p. Paper.
A collection of unusual and challenging mathematical problems, puzzles, riddles, and tricks. Range in difficulty is from items that are very easy to those that will challenge the gifted student. Illustrations and cartoons enhance the book.

22. Ouchl, Hajime. *Japanese Optical and Geometrical Art*. Dover Publications, Inc., 31 East 2nd Street, Mineola, NY 11501, 1977. 170p. Paper.
The book consists of variations in visual symmetry based on the circle, square, or alphabet. There are 746 original creations. All designs may be copied or reproduced.

23. Schuh, Fred. *The Master Book of Mathematical Puzzles and Recreations*. Dover Publications, Inc., 31 East 2nd Street, Mineola, NY 11501, 1969. 430p. Paper.
A collection of mathematical puzzles, stunts, and reactions. Well illustrated with drawings and diagrams.

24. Sherard, Wade H., III. *Mathmagic in the Classroom*. J. Weston Walch, Publisher, P.O. Box 658, Portland, Maine 04104, 1983. 140p. Paper.
A collection of math tricks to teach and challenge students that are based entirely on math and require no special skills. Common objects such as playing cards, dice, dominoes, coins, or matches are used to perform the tricks.

25. Shiro, Michael. *Another Thirty-Three Arithmetic Skill Development Games*. Pitman Learning, Inc., 19 Davis Drive, Belmont, California 94002, 1978. 87p. Paper.
A collection of games that teachers can use to drill students on basic arithmetic skills. Materials used for the games, such as tongue depressors, egg cartons, blank cards, pencil and paper, and cubes, are inexpensive and readily available.

26. Summers, George J. *Test Your Logic — Fifty Puzzles in Deductive Reasoning*. Dover Publications, Inc., 31 East 2nd Street, Mineola, NY 11501, 1972. 110p. Paper.
A collection of 50 logic puzzles ranging from simple to those tricky and complex enough to test the expert. No mathematics beyond algebra.

27. Woodward, Ernest. *The Math Detective*. J. Weston Walch, Publisher, P.O. Box 658, Portland, Maine 04104, 1984. 151p. Paper.
Over 400 mini-mysteries in mathematics. By following the math clues supplied students can pick "number suspects" out of lineups and solve the cases. The topics include whole numbers, fractions, decimals, percents, integers, and geometry. Range is from easy to difficult. Limited reproduction permission granted.